The Playbook for Leading Change

Leaders continually receive multiple messages on how to lead successful organizational change: "Create buy-in. Model the way. Connect strategies to the organization's vision. Garner input. Engage others in decisions. Co-design strategies." The confusion created by these multiple messages has contributed to a high failure rate in change initiatives, as organizations struggle with watered-down approaches that offer generic solutions instead of tailored, practical guidance. This book is a compendium of simple, easy-to-implement change strategies that work—all in one source.

When working with organizations such as American Express, Mayo Clinic, Eaton, Honeywell, Target, AT&T, US Bancorp, Kraft Foods, 3M, Johnson & Johnson, Nabisco, PepsiCo, the *New York Times*, and many community agencies, the authors have witnessed firsthand how leaders struggle with conflicting messages from various "flavor-of-the-month" models. The complexity of today's organizational environments—especially post-pandemic—has only magnified this challenge. Leaders seek clarity amid the noise and need strategies that are adaptable to their unique environments. This book provides simple, concrete strategies that, with a little help from AI, can be customized for immediate action—so leaders can breathe a sigh of relief with more confidence. When these strategies are implemented in manageable "baby steps," the probability of success improves significantly.

This book presents hard evidence in a non-academic fashion by showing why these strategies work and how to engage them most effectively. It helps leaders move beyond "gut instinct," which sometimes works but often fails, and instead adopt evidence-based approaches that can be applied with confidence. With organizational environments becoming increasingly complex, the need for clear, reliable, and practical solutions to change challenges is more compelling than ever.

Essentially, the authors provide a precise and quick read that will lead to tactical strategies for leading organizational change. They have taken the best-of-the-best practices from their three contexts (as leaders, consultants, and professors) and merged them into a single, straightforward book—it offers one-stop shopping for those who need practical guidance on navigating change. This book demystifies the process, equipping leaders with tools and insights that cut through the confusion and enable them to lead change initiatives with greater success.

The Playbook for Leading Change

Proven Strategies for Success

Mike Valentine and Mitchell Kusy

With Special Contributor Gilles Benoit
(on "AI-Enhanced Change")

Routledge
Taylor & Francis Group

A PRODUCTIVITY PRESS BOOK

Designed cover image: Shutterstock

First published 2026
by Routledge
605 Third Avenue, New York, NY 10158

and by Routledge
4 Park Square, Milton Park, Abingdon, Oxon, OX14 4RN

Routledge is an imprint of the Taylor & Francis Group, an informa business

© 2026 Mike Valentine, Mitchell Kusy, and Gilles Benoit

The right of Mike Valentine, Mitchell Kusy, and Gilles Benoit, to be identified as authors of this work has been asserted by them in accordance with sections 77 and 78 of the Copyright, Designs and Patents Act 1988.

ISBN: 978-1-041-03235-9 (hbk)
ISBN: 978-1-041-03233-5 (pbk)
ISBN: 978-1-003-62292-5 (ebk)

DOI: 10.4324/9781003622925

Typeset in Garamond
by Apex CoVantage, LLC

Contents

About the Authors

Dr. Mike Valentine is an experienced executive, consultant, and leadership coach with over 30 years of experience across multiple industries. Dr. Mike Valentine received his PhD in Leadership and Change from Antioch University. He has held senior roles at top companies, including the New York Times, Publishers Circulation Fulfillment, RJR Nabisco, PepsiCo, and Johnson & Johnson. He is the founder of Valentine Coaching and currently serves as a clinical associate professor at New York University's School of Professional Studies. Mike works with both for-profit and non-profit organizations, as well as international non-governmental organizations (NGOs), helping them tackle complex challenges and lead change. His coaching focuses on leadership development, team effectiveness, and talent growth. Mike's current research explores workplace dignity, participatory problem-solving, and how coaching can support leaders through change.

Dr. Mitchell (Mitch) Kusy is an organizational psychologist and professor in the PhD Program in Leadership & Change at Antioch University. Dr Mitch Kusy holds a doctorate in Organization Development from the University of Minnesota. He's also a Fulbright Scholar in organization development and has served as a visiting professor at the University of Auckland in New Zealand and the Kyiv-Mohyla Business School in Ukraine. Mitch has led leadership and organization development efforts at major organizations like American Express and Health Partners. He has been recognized as Minnesota's Organization Development Practitioner of the Year and has worked with top companies, including 3M, Mayo Clinic, the New York Times, Target Corporation, United Healthcare, Kraft Foods, Kaiser Permanente,

Rollerblade, United Way, and US Bank. He works with leaders and teams to improve leadership practices, build stronger cultures, and plan strategically. His latest research focused on how to erode toxic work cultures, which inspired his popular book, *Why I Don't Work Here Anymore*. Mitch is also the author of six business books that have been translated into six languages and are used around the world.

Contributing Author

Dr. Gilles Benoit is a senior scientist at *3M* with more than 70 patents. His work includes groundbreaking innovations—from helping develop optical fibers used in the first non-invasive lung cancer surgery to developing display technologies for global brands like *Apple, Samsung,* and *Microsoft*. He holds a PhD in materials science and engineering from *MIT* and has a strong track record of solving complex, global problems with advanced technology. Gilles brings *AI and Machine Learning* into practical use and has worked with a team of over 120 data scientists, delivering major process improvements with real financial results. A key voice in separating AI hype from real-world value, Gilles uses pilot projects to show what actually works. In his work, he explains why many AI tools fall short and introduces a powerful new approach called *Deep Causal Learning (DCL)*. In his writing, including *The Playbook for Leading Change*, he helps leaders make smarter, more precise decisions. Gilles is committed to helping organizations adopt AI in ways that drive real, lasting change—building a culture that's truly ready for the future.

1

Avoid the "Spread-It-Like Peanut Butter" Approach

1.1 CHAPTER PREVIEW

Ever tried spreading peanut butter on toast? You know how it goes. Every inch gets the same layer, whether it needs it or not. That's the way some organizations approach change: a one-size-fits-all method that doesn't consider the unique textures of the situation. But change isn't toast and a blanket approach rarely works. This book takes a different approach to driving change. It's not about spreading efforts thin like peanut butter. Instead, we focus on five core change principles and three instruments for change that help make change more successful. We also show how to apply these ideas in different situations, using clear methods and tips useful in real-world change efforts. Drawing from our decades of experience leading and consulting on engaging change across Fortune 500 companies, non-profits, healthcare, education, government, and beyond, we demonstrate how our five core change principles interacting with three instruments for change provide an effective path for successfully leading change initiatives.

In this book, you'll hear Mike's insights on change, not just from his work as a leader and consultant but also from his personal experience as a runner. His journey reflects what many leaders go through during times of change. Mitch shares real cases about when change works and when it doesn't with individuals, teams, and organizations. His perspective brings both empathy and reassurance for those leading change. Gilles, as a leader in artificial intelligence (AI) and scientist at 3M Corporation, brings a fresh take by showing how AI can shorten timelines, ease rollout, and improve the chances of success. His ideas offer practical ways to use technology to support change efforts and enhance what we cover in this book.

DOI: 10.4324/9781003622925-1

At the end of this chapter, we present a brief starter course on how to use AI to identify and customize tips, tools, and practices relevant to your own change situation. And within each chapter, we also include prompts and examples to help you get started in using AI to further draw on the knowledge and evidence from change experts and research. Think of each chapter as a combination of the wisdom we offer, the research we share, and the valuable capabilities AI brings.

1.2 WHY THIS BOOK?

1.2.1 We Help You Achieve Three Goals

We created this book with three goals in mind:

- **Beat the odds for change success**. Too many change efforts fail. We help you succeed. Even in unfamiliar change territory, we help you understand what's needed, why, and how.
- **Cut through the "noise" of change with confidence**. Change can be messy. Let's bring some clarity to the chaos and give you the confidence to tackle it. Here, confidence is built on helping leaders separate the forest from the trees.
- **Keep it practical with strong evidence**. No heavy theories—just real, research-backed strategies that we distill into everyday practices you can actually use.

When we've shared these kinds of tips with our client leaders and teams, the response has been reinforcing, as leaders often asked us, "When are you going to put all of these tips in a book?!" Well, we heard you and here it is! Practical tools. Evidence-based wisdom. AI-driven insights. While change is tough, the right tools can make all the difference. We offer you opportunities to use AI with helpful tips to personalize, speed up, and strengthen your approach to driving change. Let's get started by describing these four goals in detail.

1.2.2 Beat the Odds for Change Success

The odds aren't in a leader's favor. Consider strong evidence of a 60% to 70% failure rate of change initiatives.[1,2] There are many factors associated with these dismal results. In our leadership and consulting practices, we have discovered over several decades that leaders have heard multiple messages that confound change success. "Create buy-in. Model the way. Connect strategies to the organization's vision. Garner input. Engage others in decisions. Co-design strategies." And many more. Independently, these messages make a lot of sense. However, collectively, they can drown out the call for a cohesive plan of action. This has contributed to a high failure rate in change initiatives, as organizations struggle with a "spread-it-like-peanut-butter" approach that offers complex, generic solutions that rarely work. Instead, we propose tailored, practical guidance in a compendium of concrete, implementable change strategies that have a very high rate of success, based on strong evidence we present. Even within each identified challenge or opportunity, there are incremental steps leaders can take; this isn't an all-or-nothing proposition. We select practical, bite-sized actions that align with a team's or organization's current capabilities and realities.

1.2.3 Cut through the "Noise" of Change With Confidence

In leading and consulting with teams across a diverse mix of settings, we have witnessed firsthand how leaders struggle with conflicting messages from various "flavor-of-the-month" models. The complexity of today's organizational environment, especially post-pandemic, has only magnified this challenge. Leaders seek clarity amid the noise and need strategies that are adaptable to their unique environments. As consultants and leaders, we've seen firsthand the relief leaders feel with simple, concrete, and immediate strategies that promise both short-term wins and long-term success.

1.2.4 Keep It Practical With Strong Evidence

Another key reason for writing this book is simple: strong evidence matters. This book breaks things down in a practical, no-nonsense way, showing why these strategies work and how to use them effectively. Instead of relying on gut instinct (which fails more often than not), leaders can make confident, informed decisions based on evidence-driven methods. As workplaces get more complex, having clear, reliable, and actionable solutions for change is more important than ever.

1.3 THE PARADOX OF CHANGE

Change is happening all around us. It affects our work, our teams, and our organizations—sometimes in ways we witness or experience, and sometimes in ways we don't. If you're a leader, consultant, management coach, project manager, or human resources (HR) professional, you know that leading change is hard. Even with years of research, best-selling books, and good intentions, many change efforts still don't succeed. Tapping into the high rate of change failure we have noted previously, we acknowledge that the failure rate depends on the context of the study. For example, some researchers have demonstrated a 60% to 70% failure rate; others have 50% to 75%.[3,4] The exact number doesn't matter as much as the reality behind it. So, a better question is, "Why does change fail so often?" To help address this question, we have found that sometimes leaders don't realize how complex change really is. Other times, they may fail to link their big vision to real execution. Maybe they forget to involve the people who need to bring the change to life. In some cases, they include people too late. And often, they miss the chance to connect change efforts with larger business goals. Sometimes leaders focus so heavily on the change itself that they neglect the transition people must go through to make it work. These are just some of the many issues that fueled our book.

Each chapter tackles a major challenge in change leadership, offering practical ways to improve success and make change stick. Picture this scenario demonstrating how change initiatives can stall and fail. It's a small manufacturing company on the brink of a breakthrough. While we ask that you look beyond the setting, envision if any of these issues have surfaced for you, whether your venue is an educational institution, a community action agency, a hospital system, or a profit corporation. In this manufacturing setting, the leadership team unveiled a bold new process, brimming with confidence that this innovation will define the company's future. Months of meticulous planning, market research, and resource investment have led to this moment. Yet, as operations shift into high gear, the cracks begin to show. Misaligned workflows, silos between departments, and growing resistance from employees who once cheered the vision begin to unravel the plan. And these cracks in the armor happen in all kinds of settings. The leaders here are stunned. They had what seemed to be all the ingredients for success: a compelling strategy, adequate resources, and a detailed roadmap. But they missed the critical elements that truly sustain change—the readiness of their people, the power of relationships, and the processes that smooth the path from intention to impact. It wasn't a failure of ideas; it was a failure to anchor those ideas in the realities of the human experience. And isn't this the paradox of change? It's everywhere, unavoidable, and even predictable; yet it surprises us time and again. Why do organizations struggle to guide transformations that, on paper, seem destined to succeed? Could it be that our understanding of change is incomplete, immune to the nuances that turn intention into action and action into lasting impact? We'll explore this further with our specific templates for action, but first, a little primer in strategies for reading this book.

1.4 HOW TO READ THIS BOOK

This book is designed to be a practical read. It's one we hope you'll likely flip through again and again, marking pages with real, useful strategies for leading change. We've pulled together the best insights from our experiences as leaders, consultants, and professors into one straightforward guide. Think of it as your go-to resource for navigating change with confidence. No fluff, no jargon—just clear, effective, and practical tools to lead change successfully. Need further assistance? We also give you ready-to-use tips and prompts along the way to explore how AI can help you apply these tools within your own context of change.

To guide you in your reading of this book, we present an alternative to a cover-to-cover read. Please refer to Figure 1.1 as a resource that you can dip into when you need clarity, perspectives, or a new approach. As a leader, your time is valuable, so we present this option of focusing on the chapters that speak directly to your current challenges or most important opportunities. Reviewing the sample questions in the "bubbles" will help you identify the most relevant chapter that focuses on your primary challenge or opportunity.

1.5 FIVE CORE CHANGE PRINCIPLES

We introduce our five core change principles that combine top research, evidence-based practices, and our experiences in leading and supporting change:

Principle 1. Frame the Evidence for Change. Be clear on what needs to change and why.

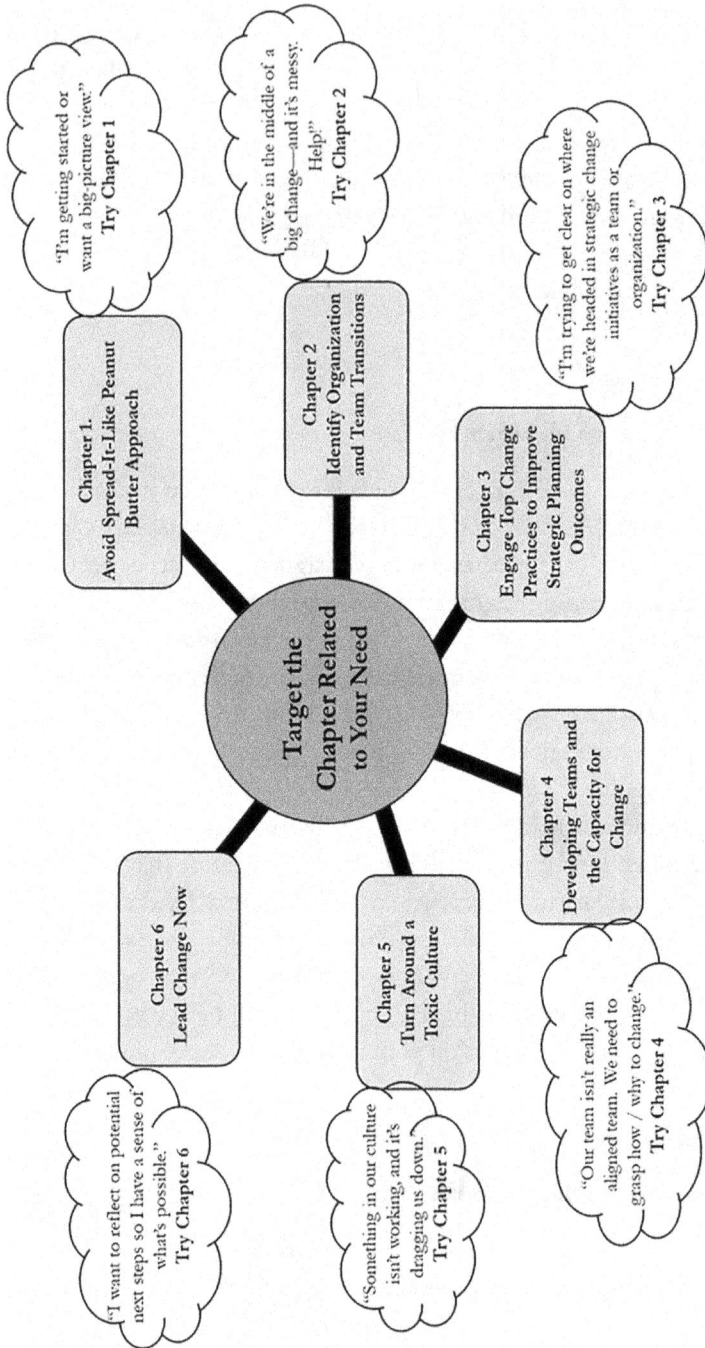

Target the Chapter Related to Your Need

Chapter 1.
Avoid Spread-It-Like Peanut Butter Approach

"I'm getting started or want a big-picture view."
Try Chapter 1

Chapter 2
Identify Organization and Team Transitions

"We're in the middle of a big change—and it's messy. Help!"
Try Chapter 2

Chapter 3
Engage Top Change Practices to Improve Strategic Planning Outcomes

"I'm trying to get clear on where we're headed in strategic change initiatives as a team or organization."
Try Chapter 3

Chapter 4
Developing Teams and the Capacity for Change

"Our team isn't really an aligned team. We need to grasp how / why to change."
Try Chapter 4

Chapter 5
Turn Around a Toxic Culture

"Something in our culture isn't working, and it's dragging us down."
Try Chapter 5

Chapter 6
Lead Change Now

"I want to reflect on potential next steps so I have a sense of what's possible."
Try Chapter 6

FIGURE 1.1

Presentation of an alternative to reading this book cover to cover. Feel free to navigate to the sections where your biggest challenge or opportunity lies.

Principles 2. Assess With Engagement. Design ways to assess wisely. Look at past and present insights to guide decisions with appropriate inclusion of others.

Principle 3. Embrace Systems Thinking. Envision the bigger picture and the interconnectedness of all the moving parts.

Principle 4. Target Results and Outcomes. Build on what makes a meaningful difference: first with results and then with outcomes.

Principle 5. Sustain What Works. Assess what is working and what is not. Keep the momentum going to sustain the initiative.

Although we are suggesting this specific order of the five core change principles when starting from scratch, it's not the only way to approach change. Just like how you may read this book chapter by chapter or skip around depending on your needs, the same flexibility applies to these principles. We like to think of these principles as part of a cycle, where things not only move forward but also loop back and sometimes even take unexpected turns. Figure 1.2 shows the general flow from principle 1 through to principle 5, with perimeter arrows representing the typical, linear progression. However, the figure also shows that we may need to revisit a principle that was previously believed to be accomplished (e.g., "looping back" movement from Principle 4 to Principle 2), as well as skip over some principles already accomplished (e.g., "progressive" movement from Principle 1 to Principle 5 skipping over of Principles 2, 3, and 4). This isn't just smart change leadership; it's simply how change happens in practice. If you are already in the midst of your change journey, consider engaging the principles as follows:

- Start with the next principle if the previous one has been achieved.
- Stop if you are in the midst of a principle and discover it has been accomplished.
- Revert to earlier principles if critical previous work has not been accomplished.

This approach allows for flexibility and adapts to the situation with movement forward and back as identified in Figure 1.2.

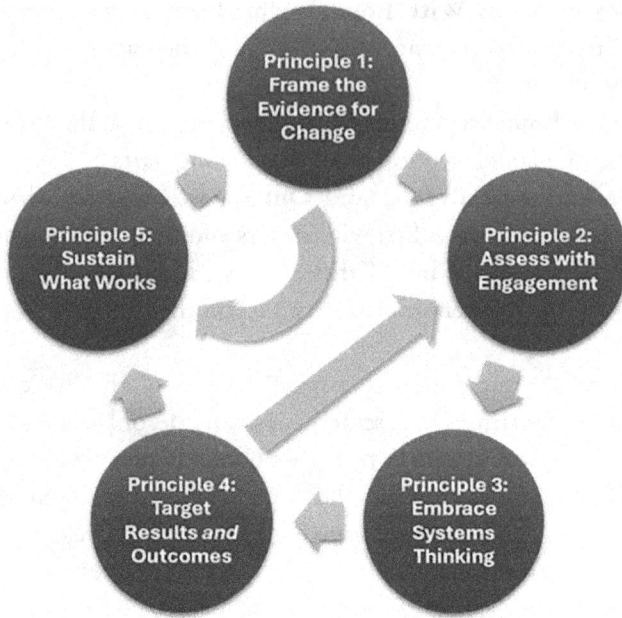

FIGURE 1.2

The five core principles, with the "usual" progression indicated by the perimeter arrows moving from Principle 1 to Principle 5. Also indicated is how progression may not always be so linear. For example, it may "loop-back" from Principle 4 to Principle 2, or skip over some principles to move from Principle 1 to Principle 5.

1.5.1 Principle 1. Frame the Evidence for Change

Don't Rush Through This First Principle

You would think framing the evidence for change clearly would be based on common sense, right? Too often, it's rushed through or buried in a mountain of organizational jargon. Research by Smith et al.[5] demonstrated that a well-articulated change is the path to success. As change consultants, we hammer this point home constantly. Consider a recent project with an oncology practice in which Mitch worked to frame their culture shift in a way that actually made sense. In sharing some of the evidence for why change is needed, other critical issues surfaced:

- **Not being explicit on the kind of work culture we want.** To counter this, the team made the unwritten rules more explicit. No more guessing games about "how things are done around here." They embraced this mantra: "If you don't know, ask."

- **Ignoring areas of concern.** To address these, they identified a more respectful work environment in these areas:
  - **How we handle disagreements.** Feedback should be clear, honest, and respectful.
  - **What we can do to make meetings more effective.** Be present. That means no texting at meetings, no interrupting, and engaging in active listening.
  - **How we can support each other.** Help each other out; go beyond our own workloads. Radical, we know.

All these team insights occurred just by framing the evidence for change. The organization took time to address these critical areas of concern before proceeding with the change initiative.

A Lightbulb Went on for a Positive Culture Shift

When the team in this oncology practice engaged this culture shift through just a few brief meetings, the client had a lightbulb moment: "Wow, no one's ever laid it out this clearly before." (We took that as a compliment.) Of course, not everyone jumped on board immediately. Some team members weren't thrilled about the culture shift, pointing out that their manager wasn't exactly leading by example. Fair enough. So, we dug deeper. Focus groups confirmed their concerns, and we delivered some constructive feedback to the manager. Our advice to her? Try these two steps:

1. **Ask your team for advice.** What specific actions they'd like to see from you. It's easier to lead when you know what people actually need.
2. **Be human.** Admit where you struggle; ask for support. Leaders don't need to be superheroes.

1.5.2 Principle 2. Assess With Engagement

Explore What's Working and What's Not

At its core, assessment is just a professional way of saying, "Let's figure out what's going on before we dive headfirst into implementing change." It's the process of gathering, analyzing, and interpreting information to understand what's working, what's not, and how we can improve. When it comes to organizational change, assessments help you identify the road ahead, spot potential potholes, and avoid driving straight into chaos. Just because leadership has decided that change is needed doesn't mean everyone else is automatically on board. We've seen it time and again: leaders assess and determine that change is necessary, as well as assume that's enough. It's not!

Case Scenario to Assess With Engagement

Imagine two organizations merging. You might think, "Well, the deal is done. Why do we need an assessment?" Even after the big decision is made, you still need teams to help figure out how to make the transition smoother. Mitch once worked with two merged educational institutions, trying to improve how teams from each organization (which were now one) might collaborate. He asked the merged team to assess how team members helped or completely blocked each other's problem-solving. It didn't take long for the team members to realize how they were still aligned with their "original" team. The assessment wasn't just a one-off survey; instead, it incorporated two brief meetings that revealed where the friction was and the first steps to address it over the next month. The result? Fewer bottlenecks, better collaboration, and fewer passive-aggressive emails.

1.5.3 Principle 3. Embrace Systems Thinking

Leading organizational change isn't just about having a direction and operationalizing it; it's about understanding the intricate web of moving parts within and around your organization as related to the change initiative. Enter systems thinking: the ultimate tool for leaders who want to navigate complexity without losing their minds. Systems thinking helps leaders and teams see the big picture, spot connections, and anticipate those pesky ripple effects. It's about stepping back from the chaos and realizing that teams, processes, and external forces are part of a larger ecosystem. With this understanding, change moves forward with fewer surprises and less frustration. Table 1.1 shows three dynamic systems thinking methods. We explore these here and more in future chapters.

Pfeffer and Sutton[6] did some fascinating research across industries, including airlines, oil refineries, and NASA. They found that brilliant work never happens in a flawed system. Even if you hire a team of geniuses, they'll struggle in a dysfunctional setup. But put a solid system in place, and even "ordinary" people can achieve extraordinary results. Systems thinking in

TABLE 1.1

Three Systems Thinking Tips

---

1. **Consider multiple possibilities.** At first, don't fall in love with a single process or action. Consider a few options before committing.
2. **Watch for triggering events.** Pay attention to internal or external influences that could derail your change efforts (e.g., a new compensation structure, market shifts, governmental funding, or economic downturns). Some things you can control; others, not so much.
3. **Think about the whole.** The best change efforts benefit the whole system, even if some parts feel the pinch. A healthy system means all the parts can thrive long-term.

---

your organization is like a fish tank. The water (your environment) affects how the fish (your people) behave. If the water is clean and stable, the fish thrive. If it's murky and full of unknown substances, you understand what happens. Leaders who ignore the internal and external forces shaping their organizations are like aquarium owners who forget to change the water.

1.5.4 Principle 4. Target Results *and* Outcomes

Some Hard Data to Chew On

Successful organizational change starts with understanding the results you want; that's just the beginning. The real question is, "What impact do those results have?" Consider this example: A large community action agency wanted to reduce bullying in the workplace. After a series of change initiatives, a culture survey showed a 75% decrease in reported bullying. That's a great result. But what's the outcome? Consider these:

- 25% improved performance with team members proactively coaching others
- 30% reduction in employee grievances related to unprofessional behavior
- 5% increase in new clients because employees were more engaged.

Focusing on both results and outcomes ensures that change doesn't just look good on paper; it actually makes a meaningful difference in the organization.

A Significant Mistake

One of the biggest mistakes in leading change is treating outcomes as something that can be defined at the end. Instead, they need to be clear from the very beginning. Outcomes should be:

- **Connected to strategy**. They should align with the organization's broader goals, like a three-year plan or core values.
- **Revisited and adjusted**. Change doesn't happen in a vacuum. What made sense at the start might need tweaking along the way.
- **Designed for momentum**. "Wins" along the journey help keep people motivated, just like making stops on a long road trip.

1.5.5 Principle 5. Sustain What Works

For many professionals, the word "evidence" brings to mind academic research—something that feels distant from real-world organizations. It sounds time-consuming, complex, and impractical. But we're here to change that! Yes, we have PhDs, but we're also hands-on professionals. Mitch is an organizational psychologist, professor, and consultant with years of experience. Mike has led Fortune 500 teams in operations and HR, alongside his work as a professor. Gilles is an MIT-trained researcher and engineering practitioner. We bring in evidence from our experiences, practice areas, and research, which are all needed to evaluate and sustain outcomes. This book isn't about abstract theories associated with evaluation and sustainability. We help leaders understand that evaluation isn't the final stage of change; it's actually at the beginning stage. Good evaluation starts with understanding the outcomes to be achieved and how to evaluate these outcomes.

1.5.6 A Structured Approach With Flexibility

In all the chapters of this book, we'll explore how to keep change going and measure success. But for now, remember this: evaluation starts on day one. Don't wait until the end to check if your strategy worked; build measurement into your plan from the start. This way, you'll stay on track and avoid surprises later. A solid change strategy that includes evaluation and sustainability doesn't happen by chance. Rather, it is a planned iterative effort to evaluate right from the very beginning and focus efforts on sustaining what works. As shown in Figure 1.2 even with a structured process for the five principles, adjustments may be needed along the way; the three instruments for change provide the kind of support needed. With clear goals, a solid plan, and the flexibility to adapt, you'll greatly increase your chances of successful change. Stay tuned for more!

1.6 THREE KEY FRAMEWORKS: INSTRUMENTS FOR CHANGE

One of the many experiences we have had helping organizations and teams lead change is that leaders sometimes bypass three important dimensions of change—what we refer to as the *Instruments for Change*. There are three: self, team, and organization. We frame these around three core questions:

- **Self as the Instrument for Change**. How can each person's commitment fuel success?
- **Team as the Instrument for Change**. What's the team's role in making the change happen?
- **Organization as the Instrument for Change**. How well is the change aligned with the system that needs to carry it?

The three instruments interact with the five principles; they do not stand alone. This template of the instruments for change interacting with the principles is pretty easy to understand when you review the core questions we have just provided. In this book, we present the interactive effects of the instruments with the principles. Choices made within one principle can shape challenges and opportunities within any of the instruments *and* within any of the principles to follow. It's also normal for conflicts to come up during a change process. People will view things differently. Sometimes politics, personal agendas, bias, or resistance can get in the way. How will your organization handle this? How will leaders make sure the change effort stays focused and doesn't fall off track? This is where strong leadership, critical thinking, and decisions based on real evidence make all the difference. Done well, this model of combining principles and the instrument for change becomes more than just a tool; it becomes the "secret sauce" to making change work.

To give you a flavor for the kinds of templates and actions we will provide in each chapter, we present one dynamic example here related to one of the instruments for change (self). Essentially, we demonstrate how to frame the change around self as the instrument for change. Specifically, the evidence for change is supporting the importance of self, beginning with trust as a key driver. We refer to the research of Frei and Morris,[7] who identified a term called the "trust wobble," which is their term for the ways trust in others is unintentionally eroded. It comes in three flavors:

- **Empathy wobble.** People aren't sure you actually care about them. (Are you nodding at meetings while secretly checking emails?)
- **Logic wobble.** People don't fully trust your reasoning. (Do others believe you know what you're talking about?)
- **Authenticity wobble.** You're not showing up as your real self. (Do colleagues see the same authentic person your friends and family do?)

To fix your trust wobble, consider these tips.

- **If you're an empathy wobbler.** Shift your focus from your own needs and pay more attention to the people struggling with the change. By helping others through the tough parts, you'll improve the whole team's ability to adapt and succeed with the change.
- **If you're a logic wobbler.** Stick to what you know for sure and build on it step by step. Don't feel the need to bluff. When you present clearly and logically, people will trust you more as a leader, making it easier to guide change successfully.
- **If you're an authenticity wobbler.** Stop worrying about what people *want* to hear. Be honest; say what really needs to be said. Even if it leads to some tough conversations, people will trust you more as a change leader, making it easier to move the organization forward.

In all three types of trust wobbles, the key factor is *you*, the leader, as the one driving change, as well as the impact you have on others. We've found three powerful ways to use this idea. First, when you openly share your own trust wobble, it sets a strong example for others. Second, it helps break the common belief that some people don't have trust issues; everyone may at some point. Third, it creates a more conducive space where others feel safe to explore and talk about their own trust wobbles and how this can impact change.

1.7 AI, YOUR GO-TO ORGANIZATIONAL CHANGE ASSISTANT

Who wouldn't appreciate having a personal assistant? Well, guess what? AI is here to be just that, backing you up as you implement the tips, tools, and practices we discuss in this book. Depending on the processes already in place, this task may seem daunting at first, but technology is your friend here. Need to generate questions for exploration, design surveys, or craft dynamic scenarios? AI has it covered. Plus, it can collect, analyze, and synthesize data quickly and systematically and present it back to you and your team in an objective and familiar fashion. It's like having a digital ally to handle the nitty-gritty, so you can concentrate on making those big moves toward success. As importantly, it can identify gaps in your thinking or actions, potentially revealing unforeseen discrepancies or challenging your assumptions. This gives you an opportunity to refine your strategy for change before you turn to implementation. And like any good tool, it works best when you know how to use it. While AI comes in many shapes and flavors, we'll focus primarily in this book on Generative AI (sometimes referred to as GenAI) as it is readily available to any leader. To help you get started, Gilles provided some ready-to-use prompts and examples in each chapter. Here are some general guidelines to keep in mind as you start crafting your own prompts:

- **Begin with explicit instructions.** Clearly state your objective at the outset. Define exactly what you want AI to accomplish. If you have background information or supporting documents, separate them from your main question; use clear markers like triple quotation marks (""""") or attach files as needed. We will demonstrate this process in the following chapters.
- **Use precise and unambiguous language.** Choose words that are specific and descriptive. Avoid slang, vague expressions, or industry jargon that may not be universally understood. The more precise your language, the more accurate and relevant the AI's response will be.
- **Outline your prompt.** Clearly outline your prompt. Specify the role you want AI to assume (e.g., "act as a business consultant"), the preferred tone (e.g., "formal," "concise," or "friendly"), and the format for the answer (e.g., bullet points, tables, or narrative). Include any relevant constraints, such as word limits or required sections.

- **Iterate and refine.** Don't settle for the first response. Submit your prompt multiple times and review the variety of answers. Use these iterations to identify what works best, then refine your prompt for clarity and effectiveness. This process will help you consistently achieve higher-quality outputs.
- **Leverage AI for prompt improvement.** Use AI itself to help you improve your prompts. Ask for feedback on clarity, specificity, or alignment with your goals. This iterative collaboration can help you spot ambiguities, optimize phrasing, and ensure your prompts consistently yield the most relevant and accurate responses. You can also ask what additional information would be helpful.
- **Prioritize data privacy.** Before including any sensitive, confidential, or proprietary information, review the data privacy policies of the AI tool you're using (e.g., ChatGPT, DeepSeek, Gemini, or Perplexity). When in doubt, consult your organization's legal or compliance team to ensure that you're handling information responsibly.

In each chapter, we provide examples of prompts related to relevant challenges and opportunities, which you can modify and customize for your specific context and needs.

1.8 ON TO THE CHAPTERS THAT DELVE INTO SPECIFIC CHANGE INITIATIVES

Effective practice in leading change sometimes begins with disrupting entrenched behaviors and challenging the status quo. At other times, it may begin with an opportunity. Either of these requires time and patience to allow new behaviors and habits to take root. And it demands constant pressure: steadfast commitment to resist the natural urge to backslide into familiar patterns. Each of the following chapters is designed to cut through fluff and provide actionable strategies. We illustrate best practices for implementation using concrete examples taken from our years of experience and research evidence. In the final chapter, we propose a framework to guide you in assessing the degree of certainty and agreement among stakeholders regarding your specific situations and the strategies on the table. By aligning these two critical elements, prioritization naturally emerges so you can start navigating change with precision and assurance right from the beginning, fostering both immediate progress and sustainable success. While each chapter can stand alone, we again encourage you to explore the entire book. Together, the chapters weave a cohesive narrative and reveal themes that will deepen your understanding of how to lead change effectively. As you move forward, let this book be your guide—a roadmap to navigating the complexities of change with clarity, confidence, and purpose.

As change leaders, we suggest you ask yourself and your team members several questions. Are we ready to embrace the disruption or new opportunity required for meaningful change? Are we prepared to invest the time needed to break old habits and form new ones? Are we willing to apply consistent pressure to push forward, even when the path gets difficult? Only through honest reflection on these questions can a serious and impactful practice emerge. To assist you, each chapter concludes with a table of key questions and practical tools related to the five core principles of change and the three instruments for change. To give you a preview of potential questions and related practices, please refer to Table 1.2.

TABLE 1.2

Self-Assessment Questions Associated with Learning Opportunities Related to Each Chapter

Book Chapter	Ask Yourself/Your Team	What You'll Learn
Chapter 2. Identify Organization and Team Transitions	How is our team navigating a change where the old ways no longer work? How are we seeking new ways that aren't fully established?	• How organizations and teams navigate transitions in response to three primary drivers of change: structural, process, and technology shifts • How leaders navigate through the three phases of transition: letting go, the neutral zone, and new beginnings—using real-world examples • The importance of addressing resistance to change by acknowledging emotions, fostering open communication, and crafting a compelling narrative that supports individuals in adapting and ultimately thriving through change

(Continued)

TABLE 1.2 *(Continued)*

Self-Assessment Questions Associated with Learning Opportunities Related to Each Chapter

Book Chapter	Ask Yourself/Your Team	What You'll Learn
Chapter 3. Engage Top Change Practices to Improve Strategic Planning Outcomes	How can we strengthen our team's strategy by actively involving the right people? How do we shift from just focusing on getting strategy done quickly to building long-term, sustainable successes?	• The importance of embedding top change practices into the three key phases of strategic planning: initiating, developing, and implementing • How to transform strategic planning from a routine exercise into an inclusive, actionable, and sustainable process • Common pitfalls that can derail strategic planning • Effective decision-making models • The critical roles of diverse teams across all phases, with practical strategies to ensure that strategic plans become robust tools that drive real organizational outcomes
Chapter 4. Develop Teams and the Capacity for Change	What practical team strategies might we design to improve our team's capacity for change? How might we foster collaboration and achieve stronger outcomes?	• How team development is fundamental to building organizational capacity for change • How high-functioning teams drive innovation, adaptability, and engagement relative to low-capacity teams through real-world transformation scenarios • How investment in team growth—especially through inclusive framing and collaboration—unlocks the full potential of teams as agents of lasting, positive change
Chapter 5. Address Toxic Work Cultures: Use for Any Work Culture Shift	What steps have we taken to build a respectful, high-performing workplace? How have we used a clear process to find problems, put solutions in place, and help individuals, teams, and the whole organization improve?	• How leaders can transform toxic workplace cultures into respectful, high-performing environments by applying five key principles of change • Evidence-based strategies that guide leaders in identifying organizational systems that promote toxic behaviors, implementing practical solutions, and sustaining positive cultural shifts • What respectful work cultures impact individual, team, and organizational performance

TABLE 1.2 *(Continued)*

Self-Assessment Questions Associated with Learning Opportunities Related to Each Chapter

Book Chapter	Ask Yourself/Your Team	What You'll Learn
Chapter 6. Lead Change Now. What Are Your Next Steps?	How can we use clear, practical steps to turn our big goals into a focused action plan? How might we engage the principles of change, especially when the team isn't fully aligned or there's uncertainty?	• A practical, step-by-step guide to turning organizational change concepts into actionable plans • How evidence-based frameworks like the Stacey Matrix and Cynefin Framework can be used effectively to drive short-term and long-term change success • How to prioritize change initiatives and foster team alignment by leveraging both structured dialogue and AI-powered tools • How to confidently implement and sustain transformative change

NOTES

1 Errida, A., & Lotfi, B. (2021). The determinants of organizational change management success: Literature review and case study. *International Journal of Engineering Business Management, 13*(21). https://doi.org/10.1177/18479790211016273

2 Jones, J., Firth, J., Hannibal, C., & Ogunseyin, M. (2018). Factors contributing to organizational change success or failure: A qualitative meta-analysis of 200 reflective case studies. In R. Hamlin, A. Ellinger, & J. Jones (Eds.), *Evidence-based initiatives for organizational change and development* (pp. 155–178). IGI Global.

3 Tollman, P., Keenan, P., Mingardon, S., Dosik, D., Rizvi, S., & Hurder, S. (2017). *Getting smart about change management*. BCG Perspectives.

4 Spencer, J., & Watkins, M. (2019, November 26). *Why organizational change fails*. ERE Recruiting Innovation Summit.

5 Smith, R., King, D., Sidhu, R., & Skelsey, D. (Eds.). (2014). *The effective change manager's handbook*. Kogan Page Publishers.

6 Pfefer, J., & Sutton, R. (2006). *Hard facts, dangerous half-truths, and total nonsense: Profiting from evidence-based management*. Harvard Business Review Press.

7 Frei, F., & Morriss, A. (2000, May–June). Begin with trust. *Harvard Business Review,* 112–121.

2

Identify Organization and Team Transitions

2.1 CHAPTER PREVIEW

Change rarely arrives in isolation. In fact, most organizational change is propelled by one or more of three primary drivers: structural, process, and technological. Structural drivers include reorganizations, mergers, or changes in leadership that redefine reporting lines and decision-making authority. Process drivers emerge when organizations introduce standardized procedures, compliance mandates, or new operational workflows. Technology-driven change disrupts familiar routines through the rollout of new digital platforms, systems, or tools. Often, these three drivers don't appear alone. In complex events like acquisitions, all three forces may converge, deeply amplifying uncertainty and rapidly altering the landscape of what people once considered stable.

These shifts challenge individual and team identities, organizational expectations, and the rhythm of change. And while the change itself may be swift, the transition of letting go, adjusting, and moving forward is where people struggle most. This is the space leaders must learn to navigate with empathy, insight, and strategy.

This chapter integrates five core change principles to help leaders support transitions:

1. **Frame the evidence for change**. Navigating uncertainty begins with clarity. How leaders build on evidence to frame the human experience of transition, especially in response to structural, process, or technology shifts, can shape how people interpret, absorb, and respond to what's changing.

DOI: 10.4324/9781003622925-2

2. **Assess with engagement**. Transitions gain momentum when people feel included. Leaders who actively engage those affected build shared ownership and trust by inviting reflection, listening deeply, and co-creating the path forward.
3. **Embrace systems thinking**. Transitions don't happen in isolation. Every adjustment in role, workflow, or mindset has ripple effects. Leaders who think systemically can anticipate pressure points, interdependencies, and unintended consequences.
4. **Target results *and* outcomes**. True transition is measured not only by completed tasks but also by how people adapt, realign, and grow. Outcomes should reflect both progress and well-being and not be measured by implementation milestones.
5. **Sustain what works**. Transitions take time. Sustaining momentum requires leaders to recognize what's working, reinforce progress, and invest in continued learning and support.

2.2 A VERY PERSONAL TRANSITION: MIKE'S STORY

To bring the interplay between change and transition into focus, consider Mike's personal transition experience. Mike wasn't just someone who went for an occasional jog; he was a runner. The kind who built life around early morning miles, tracked weekly progress like gospel, and taped race bibs to the wall not as décor, but as proof of perseverance. Running wasn't a hobby; it was his rhythm. It provided an anchor through career shifts, personal loss, and everyday stress. It was his identity. Then, everything changed. One medical appointment. One diagnosis. One irreversible truth: no more running. Ever.

The words were clinical, calm, and absolute. High-impact activity was no longer safe. One day, he was logging ten miles before sunrise. Next, he was staring at a doctor who had just stripped away the foundation of his life. Mike left with medical instructions and a body that suddenly felt unfamiliar. But the real shock wasn't physical; it was the silence that followed. No more morning runs. No laces to tie. No watch buzzing with reminders. Just absence. That was the change. But the deeper challenge was the transition.

His body had pumped the brakes, but his mind hadn't caught up. His heart still raced at 6 a.m., and muscles twitched with muscle memory. He grieved not just the motion but also the loss of self. He tried yoga and took walks, but everything felt like a placeholder. He was no longer who he had been and not yet anything else. This was the in-between frame: slow, uncomfortable, invisible. It's where the real work of change begins—where one sits with uncertainty and asks, *If I am not this, then who am I now?*

Then, something shifted. A friend invited him on a hike. Later, he took up cycling, first cautiously, then with curiosity. Slowly, presence replaced pace. Breath replaced finish lines. A new rhythm took shape. Mike didn't replace running. He rebuilt himself. And that is the heart of transition.

Change is the event: swift, observable, and sometimes disruptive. But transition is the process: the internal, human experience of adjusting, reimagining, and becoming. It moves in phases such as: letting go, lingering in the in-between, and eventually stepping into something new. Leaders often confuse the two. A restructuring, a new process, and a technology launch—these are changes. But what determines their success is how people move through the transition that follows. And that part is messy, emotional, and deeply personal. Consider these snapshots of various transitions:

- **Sarah**, suddenly reporting to a new leader in a restructured healthcare organization, is left adrift without a sense of belonging.
- **Yasmin,** a recently appointed Director of Programs at a regional organization focused on food insecurity, is leading a major transition to a centralized digital case management system.
- **Janelle,** an adult literacy instructor at a small community-based organization, experiences a shift in the organization's instructional model, from teacher-led lessons to a learner-driven coaching-style approach.
- **Mateo,** a trusted voice in the warehouse whom everyone relies on when they don't understand something, becomes a change agent when he starts helping others troubleshoot a new system.
- **Daniel,** newly promoted to operations director, is leading his team through a broad strategic transformation.

As we will illustrate in this chapter, each of them, in their own way, is running through the same stages of transition Mike did. They are not just adapting to change; they're living the transition.

2.3 PRINCIPLE 1. FRAME THE EVIDENCE FOR CHANGE

2.3.1 A Failed Transition

In our experiences working with organizations anticipating change or going through change, we often find that their leaders either undervalue how employees will experience the change effort or don't appreciate the stages of transition when they emerge. In either case, the impact on the overall change effort can be costly in terms of time lost, poor engagement, and a stalled effort.

Consider the following case of organizational change associated with a merger. After a merger, a mid-sized healthcare organization undergoes a major reorganization. Functional departments are collapsed into cross-functional service lines to streamline care and reduce redundancy. Sarah, a long-tenured billing manager, suddenly finds herself reporting to a new leader from outside the revenue cycle. Her team is blended with two new departments—scheduling and intake—functions she's never managed in her career. The announcement came quickly, with little explanation beyond a broad strategic alignment message. Uncertainty spread. Sarah began receiving daily questions from her team: *Will our jobs change? Do we have to reapply? Who's in charge of what?* Sarah, normally a steady voice in the organization, found herself disoriented. She didn't resist the change, but she couldn't lead it either. Without a clear framing of the "why," the "how," or the "what now," the team drifted. Morale dipped. Clarity eroded. And with it, the ability to adapt to the changing environment faded.

2.3.2 Understanding Transitions

William Bridges, a world expert in organizational and people transitions, reminds us that ignoring the transition part of organizational change can have dire consequences.[1] While the change effort in an organization is situational, such as introducing a new coaching process, implementing a new leadership structure, or adopting a new workflow, the transition is the human process of adapting to that change. For example, transition is the term we use to describe the internal process people go through to make peace with the old and embrace the new. Imagine standing in your office on a Monday morning. You've just received an email announcing a major restructuring. Your title is the same, for now, but your team has changed, your manager is someone with whom you've never worked, and the processes you've mastered over the years are being rewritten. On the outside, you keep your composure. But inside, you're navigating a brewing storm.

You might feel unsettled, not because you doubt the logic of the change, but because the ground beneath your professional identity has shifted. There's a subtle fear: *Will I still belong here? Will I be valued in this new setup?* Even a sense of loss, of routine, of confidence, of control. For others, it might manifest as frustration, a sense of being left out of the conversation, or confusion about how to move forward when the rules seem to be changing in real time.

These emotions aren't random. They're influenced by how the change is framed in the first place, by how much agency people feel they have in responding to this change, and by whether leaders acknowledge not just what's happening but also what it *means* for the people living through it. Past experiences with change, the level of trust in leadership, and the degree of clarity (or lack of it) surrounding the future will shape how people respond. In those first uncertain moments, they don't need canned, scripted speech; they need honesty. They don't need perfection; they need leaders to listen and respond with authenticity. What they feel in the moment is not just the change itself; it's about whether they believe anyone understands or acknowledges what it will cost them to adapt.

Framing the change transition effectively means understanding that transitions unfold in three overlapping stages: the ending, the neutral zone, and new beginnings. Each phase presents observable behaviors and challenges that leaders can recognize and address. Figure 2.1 provides a visual depiction of the three phases of transition.[2]

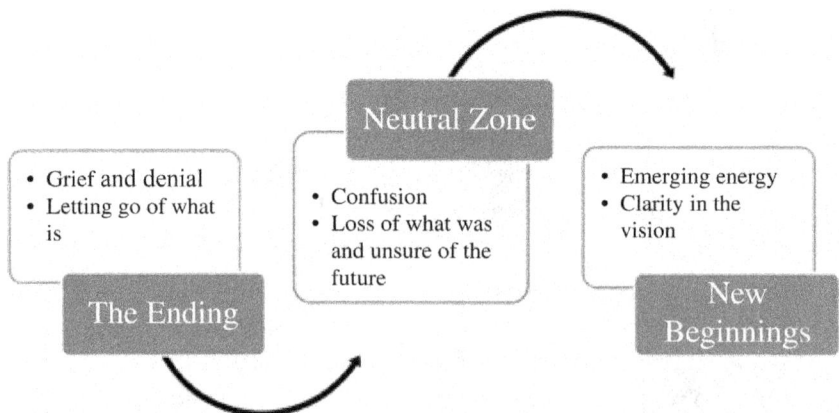

FIGURE 2.1
The stages of change transition.

The Ending: Letting Go of What Was

This stage begins the moment a change is announced. People may be asked to release roles, routines, relationships, or mindsets that once defined their work. Leaders might see signs of grief, denial, or nostalgia for what has been. For example, Mike will often hear employees struggling with new change stating that "This place used to feel like family, now we're just a number," an indication of holding on to a perceived feeling of safety. Another common reaction is when employees say, "We used to know exactly whom to go to for answers; now everything feels confusing," which reflects a longing for the clarity and stability of past routines. Resistance is often present in this stage, not as defiance, but as a natural response to loss and uncertainty. Even if the future is promising, people need space to mourn what's ending and alleviate the ambiguity of moving forward, as much as possible. In the previous example, Sarah found herself missing the clarity of her old reporting lines, not because she resisted progress, but because her sense of competence was tied to a structure that no longer existed.

The Neutral Zone

This is the messy middle, where the old ways no longer work, and the new ones aren't fully established. It's not only the most emotionally complex time, but it can also be the most creative phase. This phase is characterized by behaviors that display fatigue or impatience. We also find that conflict is most prominent in this phase of transition. For example, questioning leadership or the direction of the change is more likely to surface in this phase. Resistance often emerges here as people test whether the change is real, safe, and sustainable. The neutral zone can feel like standing in fog. The destination isn't yet observable. For leaders, it's tempting to rush through this discomfort. But it's in this zone that new identities are forged, trust is tested, and long-term success is built or lost. Leaders who slow down and provide clarity, reassurance, and consistent communication create space for creativity, collaboration, and problem-solving to thrive.

It is also in the Neutral Zone where work location can shape people's experience of transition most strongly. Individuals who are physically in the office may find reassurance in spontaneous conversations, informal feedback, and alignment among peers, helping them navigate uncertainty. Remote employees, on the other hand, often feel the fog more acutely unless leaders are intentional about communication and inclusion. Without deliberate efforts to create virtual touchpoints, remote staff may feel isolated in this phase, increasing the risk of disengagement or resistance. Leaders who recognize these differences and balance support across both groups are more likely to help employees move forward constructively.

New Beginnings

This phase is easily the most rewarding. In this phase, the vision for the change comes into focus, and individuals begin to take ownership over driving to the finish line. In the early stages of this phase, keeping the momentum takes intention on the part of the organization, as missteps here can lead to slipping back into the neutral zone. Typical behaviors that emerge in the new beginnings phase may include renewed engagement and alignment with the organization's priorities. New habits and norms emerge, and opportunities to reinforce trust provide leaders with the potential for new energy and confidence. But "new beginnings" require more than just time. They need deliberate reinforcement and recognition. Sarah's team, for instance, began to regain momentum only when their leader clarified new roles and created space for collaborative planning. When people experienced how their contributions mattered in the new structure, they began to take ownership.

2.3.3 Transition Considerations: The Three Cs

Change can feel like trying to reorganize your garage while your kids are still riding their bikes through it. It's messy, noisy, and easy to get discouraged. That's why a little structure can go a long way. Mike uses a concept he refers to as the "three Cs" to guide employees through the transition, not just the change. Simply stated, the Cs are:

- **Clarify** the context
- **Confront** the challenges
- **Craft** the story.

Clarify the Context

Before diving into a change, take a breath and look around at the environment. What's the organization's track record when it comes to change efforts? If past initiatives have left people exhausted, skeptical, or rolling their eyes every time they hear the word "transformation," you'll need to approach with extra care. Ask yourself this question: is this a light process tweak or a full-blown organizational identity shift? Also, consider how the organization has historically handled the people part of change. If the usual approach has been "announce it and hope for the best," then now's your chance to raise the bar. Taking into account the entire change environment, or what Mike refers to as the context, is key to shaping activities and communication that will ultimately enable support. Gilles suggests leveraging AI to analyze your context for potential gaps in awareness and to identify examples of organizations that have successfully navigated similar waters:

> *Role: Act as a business consultant. Context: our organization is going through a major change described in the attached document. Question: What are examples of similar organizations having successfully gone through this type of change? What are common hidden spots and best practices associated with this type of change that our organization should be aware of?*

Confront the Challenges

Imagine that you could picture the ripple effects of change. Change doesn't just impact processes; it shakes up confidence, habits, team dynamics, and sometimes people's sense of purpose. It's like changing the rules of a game mid-play: some folks adapt quickly, others freeze, and a few might storm off the field entirely. At the individual level, some people may quietly wonder, *Am I still good at my job?* or *Do I even fit here anymore?* Others may struggle with decision fatigue or feel like they're being asked to reinvent themselves overnight.

Teams might experience confusion about roles, friction between early adopters and skeptics, or a lack of direction when the old playbook no longer applies. And across the organization, unspoken resistance might brew under the surface if the culture isn't aligned with the change, or worse, if leaders are pushing for transformation while still rewarding old behaviors.

If you can anticipate these challenges, you'll be better equipped to smooth them out, or at least bring snacks for the ride. Use AI for scenario planning to help you envision what future states might look like and how the organization might respond. For example, follow the previous prompt with: *Now imagine that a couple of months in, friction between early adopters and skeptics starts to emerge. What could happen if the organization does not respond? How could the organization respond to keep momentum going?*

Craft a Transition Story

As many believe it to be true based on practice, people don't rally behind a new initiative because of a well-designed PowerPoint deck. They rally behind a story. They need a narrative that helps make sense of what's happening, why it matters, and where one fits in. Think of this as the "movie trailer" or "elevator speech" for your change: what's ending, what's at stake, and what the future could look like if we all lean in? The story should start by honoring what's ending and why. No need for dramatic monologues, just a simple acknowledgment that what's changing once had value, and it's okay to feel some loss. Then, explain that the path may be messy at times, and all the answers to challenges that emerge along the way may not be clear immediately. Resist the urge to sugarcoat or speak in buzzwords. People don't need jargon; they need truth. Finally, paint a vision of the future that's both hopeful and grounded. Make sure it has emotional weight, something people can connect to beyond just hitting targets or cutting costs. People want to feel like they're part of something meaningful, not just a line on an org chart. Essentially, then, to craft a transition story, you need:

- **A brief "trailer."** What's ending, what's at stake, and a glimpse of the future?
- **A path.** The truth about how to get there, as messy as this may be.
- **A vision of what's on the horizon.** Grounded in what people can connect with.

Once again, AI can help you here. Simply ask: *Based on the information provided, craft a short transition story that people can rally around about what's ending, what's at stake, and a glimpse of what the future may look like.*

In Table 2.1, we have identified how to engage the 3-C's based on our three instruments for change—individual, team, and organization. Notice how each cell provides a way to set the stage for transition planning.

Instructions for use:

1. Discuss the elements with the team or key stakeholders to understand where there may be opportunities to shift the negative to positive statements.
2. Identify strategies that can mitigate any risk presented by shifting the negative to positive statements.

TABLE 2.1

Transition Planning Cues of the Three Cs and Three Instruments of Change for Effective Transition Planning

Transition Planning Checklist		
Clarify the Context		
Individual	**Team**	**Organizational**
Acknowledge that many individuals have prior experiences with change that are negative.	Understand that the team may have experienced a change in the past that was not handled well.	Identify that the organization's overall track record with change is mixed or negative.
Confront the Challenges		
Individual	**Team**	**Organizational**
Share that individuals may be at risk of disengagement, burnout, or feeling left behind.	Recognize that team dynamics are likely to shift due to new roles, responsibilities, or members.	Understand that change fatigue may exist across the organization.
Craft a Transition Story		
Individual	**Team**	**Organizational**
Address the emotional needs of individual stakeholders engaged in the change.	Provide teams with tools to share and shape the transition story with their talent.	Identify consistent, compelling messages about the change that is being reinforced at all levels.

3. Expand your thinking by asking AI for additional ideas. Building on the previous prompts, try the following: *Context: Here are statements about our organization going through a major change: """insert here""". Question: What strategies should the organization consider using to reinforce positive statements and to turn negative statements into positive ones?*

Clarifying, confronting, and crafting in this way will help guide the transition. Leaders do this by helping people let go of what was, navigating the fog of uncertainty, and eventually supporting others to step into something new with purpose and clarity. Remember, transitions aren't linear. Some days will feel like breakthroughs. Others will feel like you're herding cats in a windstorm. That's normal. The point isn't to control every emotion or response;

it's to lead with empathy, communicate with intention, and keep checking in as the journey unfolds.

2.3.4 Framing Resistance During a Transition

To fully understand transitions means to acknowledge what happens when transitions get stuck or when the psychological needs of each stage are unmet. Resistance is often a symptom, not the root cause. It's a signal flare that someone, whether an individual, a team, or an entire department, is struggling to navigate their internal shift alongside the external one.

Although the psychology of resistance during change is complex and influenced by a range of personal and organizational factors, in its simplest form, resistance often stems from a perceived threat to personal security, whether that means job security, competence, status, or identity. Resistance doesn't always manifest as an outright verbal "no." Sometimes, resistance is much quieter. It shows up in passive disengagement, delayed deliverables, or the endless postponement of "just one more meeting" before a decision is made.

Think about a change you've experienced that required new behaviors or unfamiliar skills. The first question that often arises is, *Can I do this?* This isn't just about capability; it's about confidence, credibility, and, at times, survival. The mind scans the horizon for threats, not because people are unwilling to adapt, but because they're wired to seek safety. Resistance, then, is often less about opposition and more about protection. Leaders who frame resistance solely as defiance or negativity miss the opportunity to understand it as valuable evidence. It's emotional feedback. When surfaced and explored, resistance can serve as a diagnostic tool, a pulse check, on what people are afraid of losing, what they don't yet understand, or what support they still need. Rather than trying to "overcome" resistance, effective leaders learn to decode it. They ask, *What is this resistance telling me about the experience of this change? What fear or need might be unspoken? How can I create more clarity, agency, or reassurance for those affected?* In many cases, resistance is the beginning of engagement. When someone resists, it means they still care. The real danger is not resistance. It's silence.

To help leaders assess resistance when it becomes evident, try some simple activities that invite dialogue from others. The first is called the "Iceberg" activity. This activity can take as little as 10 to 15 minutes and does not need any materials. To conduct this activity:

1. Draw a simple iceberg on a flip chart or describe it aloud: "Imagine resistance is like an iceberg. What we see on the surface (like missed deadlines or pushback) is only part of the story."
2. Ask the group:
   - "What are some surface-level behaviors we've seen during this change?"
   - "What might be beneath the surface—fears, assumptions, or unmet needs—that are driving those behaviors?"
3. Invite the group to brainstorm and write both surface behaviors and underlying causes.
4. Identify a few top themes of what's under the surface. Discuss, "How might we respond differently if we understood these themes of what's under the surface a bit more?"

Another simple activity is one we have used in any number of situations called the "Start, Stop, and Support" roundtable. Like the iceberg activity, it does not require any materials per se, but Post-It Notes™ are helpful if you have them. In this activity, the leader frames it with this prompt: "To move through this change more effectively, I'd like to hear from you. What should we *stop*, *start*, or *support* during this transition?"

1. Ask team members to reflect silently for a minute, then go around and collect ideas:
   - **Stop.** What's not working or adding stress?
   - **Start.** What would help build clarity or momentum?
   - **Support.** What do you need from others?
2. Summarize themes and invite a brief discussion on what actions can be taken.
3. Monitor these actions in the future, discuss their success, and revise to address obstacles.

These activities work because they create a safe space for people to share concerns indirectly, lowering defensiveness and making it easier to surface major causes of resistance. They shift the conversation from reaction to observation in order to understand underlying motivations, which allows leaders to address the real drivers of resistance rather than just the symptoms.

Recently, Mike spoke with a leader whose team was struggling with changing priorities. When this leader expressed uncertainty about how to address this, Mike asked if she had considered how her team was experiencing the transition from the old priorities to the new priorities. After reflecting on her own transition challenges associated with the shift, she realized her reservations might mirror her team's concerns and decided to simply ask them. The message here is a simple one. We often see change as the problem of others, when in many cases, the struggles we experience as leaders are similar. With greater self-awareness, leaders can have a significant impact on addressing the transition struggles others experience.

2.3.5 Tailoring Transition Support to the Type of Change

While the emotional landscape of transition shares some universal truths, such as uncertainty, loss, and resistance, the specific challenges people face often depend on the type of change underway. A restructuring doesn't feel the same as redesigning processes, and neither evokes the same response as a major technology shift. Just as a good coach adapts his strategy to each athlete's needs, effective change leaders tailor their approach based on the driver of change. Let's look at the three most common drivers: structural, process, and technology. Then, we will explore the distinct transition challenges these bring, along with strategies leaders can use to support people through each.

Structural Change

Structural changes, such as reorganizations, mergers, or leadership shifts, often create deep identity disruption. People may lose their roles, teams, or sense of belonging. Reporting lines shift, decision-making processes become unclear, and relationships that once grounded people in their work may disappear overnight. Even when jobs are retained, people may silently wonder, *Do I still matter here?* There's also a status recalibration that happens. Someone who had an informal influence in the old structure may struggle to find their footing in the new one, leading to frustration or withdrawal.

Structural Change Transition Strategies

Think of structural change like rebuilding a house. People not only need to know the floor plan, but they also need to feel like there's still room for them inside. Leaders can use these strategies for structural change to help provide a plan for those navigating the transition.

- **Clarify the new structure early**. Even if it's not perfect, people need something to hold on to.
- **Acknowledge what's ending**. This is especially important to acknowledge the value of what people built under the old structure.
- **Surface unspoken losses.** Some of these involve influence, identity, and team cohesion; invite conversations about them.
- **Rebuild trust quickly.** This is easily accomplished through engaged presence, open dialogue, and accessible leadership.
- **Reinforce roles and relationships**. This helps people reconnect in the new configuration.

These strategies address both the practical and emotional sides of structural change, giving people clarity while also honoring their sense of identity and belonging. By doing so, leaders reduce uncertainty, preserve trust, and help teams reorient more quickly in the new structure.

Process Change

Process changes, such as the introduction of standardization or compliance protocols, often collide with habits, autonomy, and pride. People may feel like their expertise is being replaced by checklists or workflows designed without their input. There may also be fearful of being micromanaged or a sense that quality will be sacrificed in the name of efficiency. Teams may experience "change fatigue" if they're asked to abandon familiar ways of working too frequently, or if they don't understand the *why* behind the shift. Leaders can use the following strategies to support transition during process changes:

- **Co-create the process where possible.** People support what they help build.
- **Celebrate learning, not perfection.** Encourage experimentation and iteration.[3]
- **Give voice to concerns**. Focus on all concerns, especially those from staff closest to the work.
- **Reinforce meaning.** Connect the new process to improved outcomes for clients, patients, or stakeholders, not just metrics.

Think of process changes like introducing a new route on a commute. If people helped map it and knew it might get them there faster or with less stress, they would be far more willing to give it a try.

Technology Change

Technology rollouts, like launching a new digital platform, often trigger anxiety about competence, especially among those who don't see themselves as "tech savvy." Even those excited about the tool may worry about a loss of control or connection. What's often overlooked is that technology shifts are rarely just technical; they almost always reshape workflows, communication patterns, and power dynamics. Artificial intelligence is a prime example! When training is overly focused on the "how" and neglects the "why," adoption suffers. Strategies that can help shift the mindset during change driven by technology are as follows:

Technology Change Transition Strategies

- **Start with purpose.** Don't just explain *what* the system does; clarify *why* it matters and how it will help.
- **Provide multiple learning pathways.** Not everyone learns by clicking through a training module.
- **Create peer support structures.** Consider engaging tech champions or drop-in help sessions.
- **Acknowledge fear.** Yes, openly. Let people know it's okay not to be confident right away.
- **Celebrate milestones along the way.** Adoption takes time to reinforce the behaviors you want to see over weeks and months. That doesn't mean you can't celebrate. What it does mean is to celebrate milestones along the way—what we often refer to as "baby steps."

Think of technology change not as upgrading software, but as asking people to speak a new language. Help them learn. Speak it with them, patiently and consistently. Change efforts may be neatly categorized on a whiteboard or project tracker, but the transitions people experience rarely follow tidy lines. Leaders must tune into the type of change and adapt their support accordingly. Structural change requires attention to identity. When roles shift, teams are reorganized; when reporting lines change, people often wonder, "Who am I in this new structure? Do I still matter?" Process changes demand empathy for habits and pride. Leaders need to recognize that people may feel frustrated or even resistant to process change, not just because of the change itself, but because it disrupts routines they're used to and already "bought into." People often take pride in how they do their work, especially if they've done it well for a long time. Showing empathy means understanding that these habits are tied to a sense of competence and contribution. Finally, technological change calls for reassurance, patience, and partnership. Above all, people don't just want to know what's changing. They want to know that they'll be acknowledged, supported, and valued on the other side of change. And that's the real work of leading transitions.

Are you dealing with a different change driver or multiple drivers at once? Ask AI for assistance in crafting custom strategies that are relevant to your organization's specific needs. For example:

> Role: Act as a merger & acquisition expert. Context: Our organization is acquiring a startup company whose AI technology can benefit our product offerings. This major change requires structural change, process changes and technology change all at once. Question: What are strategies the organization should consider adopting to support its people with this very disruptive transition? Format: summarize these strategies in a table form.

Table 2.2 shows a few examples of strategies AI may recommend.

TABLE 2.2

AI-Recommended Strategies for Transition Support

Strategy Area	Key Actions to Support People during Disruptive Transition
Leadership Alignment	Ensure that leaders present a united front, reinforce commitment to the change, and provide access to leadership for staff questions.
Talent Retention	Identify and retain key talent; offer career development and clear communication about job security and growth opportunities.
Training and Development	Provide targeted training on new technologies, processes, and roles; facilitate peer learning and knowledge sharing between legacy and startup teams.

2.4 PRINCIPLE 2. ASSESS WITH ENGAGEMENT

2.4.1 Reading the Room, Not Just the Dashboard

Yasmin, recently appointed Director of Programs at a regional non-profit focused on food insecurity, was leading a major change: transitioning from a patchwork of spreadsheets and paper forms to a centralized digital case management system. On paper, it made perfect sense, with more accurate data, less duplication, and better service to clients. The vendor was mission-aligned, training sessions had been held, and the board was fully supportive. But about six weeks in, the energy started to shift. Volunteers were overwhelmed, community partners were missing updates, and staff began quietly reverting to the old ways of doing things.

Rather than pushing ahead with misplaced optimism, Yasmin paused. She hosted a few listening circles—nothing formal, just open conversations in the company courtyard, where staff could share their thoughts without fear of judgment. She also sent out a short, anonymous check-in survey and asked site coordinators to walk her through how their teams were actually using the new system. What she heard wasn't surprising, but it was revealing. Staff were brought into the *why*, but not the *how*. The training hadn't included part-time volunteers, some staff felt too embarrassed to ask follow-up questions, and the rollout pace didn't reflect the day-to-day realities of serving hundreds of families each week.

So Yasmin adjusted. She slowed the rollout, brought frontline voices into the planning, and shifted from formal training to short, peer-led tutorials. The tone changed. What started as quiet resistance gave way to cautious curiosity and, eventually, real adoption. By choosing to engage with the people at the heart of the mission, Yasmin turned a potential stall into a shared step forward.

2.4.2 Assessing Transition Readiness

Yasmin's experience highlights a commonly overlooked aspect in change transition leadership: the assumption that once a change is launched, people are automatically ready to move with it. The reality is somewhat different. Successful transitions require leaders to assess team members' starting points. And that's not just about communicating the change message. It's about tuning into three key essential transition elements: belief, preparedness, and capacity.

We want to share a supporting model with you, called the Theory of Planned Behavior (TPB).[4] The name isn't important, but the model gets to the heart of something every leader needs to understand: how people decide whether or not to even begin their transition through change in the first place. TPB was originally developed to predict the likelihood that an individual would change behavior. Its predictive design makes it somewhat unique and applicable for understanding transition behavior. TPB has been used across all kinds of contexts, and its basic premise is incredibly simple: people are more likely to take action, in this case, start a transition, when three things align:

1. **They believe the action is valuable.** This is what the model calls *attitude*. It really comes down to "what's in it for me."
2. **They feel confident they can actually do it.** The model refers to this as *perceived behavioral control*. Do I feel I will be able to do what a new thing is being asked of me?
3. **They sense support or approval from those around them.** The model calls this *subjective norms*. An easy way to think about this is this: are those I trust most on board with taking action?

Sound familiar? That's exactly what we experience during times of change. If people don't believe in the change, feel overwhelmed by it, or think no one else is really on board, they're going to hesitate or quietly opt out. That's why the following three areas are so important to assess, which we identify here and describe in the next three book sections:

- Belief
- Preparedness
- Capacity

Assessing Belief in the Change

Belief is where readiness starts. If people don't believe the change is necessary, valuable, or aligned with what matters to them or their team, you'll get compliance at best and resistance or indifference at worst. And here's the tricky part: belief doesn't always show up in big, bold statements. Often, it shows in what people *don't* say, in the energy they bring (or don't), and in overlooked signs that they either have bought in or are quietly opting out. Leaders should listen for signs of support or hesitation in belief. For example, listen for phrases of alignment like:

- *This is going to help us serve clients better.*
- *I can see how this fixes what we've struggled with.*
- *It's about time we made this change.*

If you hear comments like the following, it's important that these are not ignored:

- *We've tried this before.*
- *This is just another leadership fad.*
- *I'm not sure what problem this is really solving.*

These are indications of issues with belief. Sometimes, the most telling sign that individuals are questioning the "why" is silence. If no one's asking questions, pushing back, or trying to connect the change to their work, it may be because they haven't bought in, or they're waiting it out, or watching from the sidelines.

Assessing Preparedness

Even if people believe in the change, this doesn't necessarily mean they feel ready for it. Preparedness is the situation where belief turns into action or stalls out. Assuming people are on board with the "why" doesn't mean they know how to follow through. Preparedness reflects whether individuals feel they have the knowledge, tools, skills, and clarity needed to step into the change successfully. For example, it's not about how much training you've delivered; it's about how confident people feel about what to do next. Leaders can look for clear signs of hesitation. For example, if people are nodding "yes" in meetings but holding back when it's time to apply something new, that's a red flag. Delays, half-starts, or repeated questions about next steps may signal that they're not sure how to proceed. Watch for signs that teams are defaulting to legacy systems, old workflows, or familiar patterns, even when new ones have been introduced. This often isn't about defiance; it's about uncertainty. This is especially prominent with the introduction of new technology. We have repeatedly seen that, once introduced, individuals (including leaders) resist using the new system and, at the first sign of difficulty, will go back to their comfort zone. Prepared individuals are more likely to step forward, lead pilots, or champion the transition. If you're holding back, ask yourself: is it a lack of motivation or a lack of readiness? The language individuals use can be an indication of a lack of preparedness. Leaders can listen for any version of the following:

- *I'm still not exactly sure what this means for my role.*
- *We're waiting to see how others handle it before jumping in.*
- *We've had the training, but I'm not confident we're ready yet.*
- *We're figuring it out as we go.*

These statements often reflect a gap between understanding and execution. They're not signs of resistance; they're invitations to provide clearer support.

Assessing Capacity

Capacity is often the silent saboteur of change. You may believe strongly that this change is needed and even have the right skills lined up, but if people simply don't have the time, energy, or space to act, nothing moves. Capacity goes beyond simply headcount or task assignments; it's about whether people have *mental space*, *emotional resilience*, and *leadership support* to take on something new. Notice the connection between preparedness and support: the subtle cues people receive that indicate what's truly a priority and is accepted by others in their environment. When the signals individuals receive from leadership and peers don't reinforce the change, capacity drops fast. There are clear signs that leaders can look for that indicate capacity issues. Consider the following:

- **Overloaded teams.** Constant urgency is often a sign that there's no buffer for absorbing change, even when the change is welcome.
- **Signs of burnout or withdrawal.** Increasing absenteeism, turnover, or people who are "quietly disengaging" can be a signal that people are maxed out. Watch for emotional fatigue just as much as productivity loss.
- **Task conflict behavior.** If teams are consistently choosing "business as usual" work over change-related tasks, it can be a sign of resistance or conflict. When this is observed consistently, those teams are making survival decisions based on current bandwidth.
- **Minimal participation from mid-level managers.** If managers are not showing up to change-related sessions, contributing to planning, or reinforcing key messages, they may not have the capacity or may be modeling the belief that the change is optional.

Leaders can also look at how individuals describe their priorities. Here are some examples:

- *We don't have time for this right now.*
- *Something else will have to give.*
- *We're being asked to do more with less—again.*
- *Is leadership really behind this, or is it just another thing?*

Comments like these may sound like complaints, but they often reflect an honest assessment about reality. People aren't saying they're unwilling to change; they're saying they don't see how it fits with everything else on their plate.

Assessment Tool

Capacity doesn't always show up on a dashboard, but it may show up in the quality of conversations, the energy in the room, and the consistency of execution. If you're experiencing slippage, disengagement, or unexpected pushback, ask yourself: is this really resistance? Or are people just stretched too thin to give this their best shot? Table 2.3 is a simple way for leaders to make an assessment of transition readiness. Like any assessment, it is not absolute but should be considered holistically.

TABLE 2.3

A Simple Assessment Tool for Transition Readiness

	Agreement		
Belief	**Low**	**Somewhat**	**High**
1. People understand *why* the change is happening.			
2. People believe the change is aligned with our goals.			
3. There is a sense of shared commitment to the change across the team.			
Preparedness			
1. People have the training needed to succeed.			
2. Expectations during the transition are clear.			
3. People feel confident applying new behaviors, tools, or processes.			
Capacity			
1. People have enough time to focus on the change.			
2. Workloads are being adjusted to accommodate the transition.			
3. Leaders are saying that this change is a priority.			

1. To interpret the results, review the list and identify any questions where there is a low level of agreement with the statement.
2. Discuss each area with a group of stakeholders (your team or peers) to determine where there is a low level of agreement (these represent areas for improvement).

3. For areas that are deemed weak, explore ways to strengthen them with a group. Ask your team, *What would it take for us to improve the level of shared commitment across the team?* You may also consult AI for tips and practices to tackle each weak area.

4. Remember that weaknesses in any of these areas can become problematic to a transition and cause the transition to stall. It is important to address any areas that raise concerns or are identified as weaknesses. Which area needs the most attention right now to support a successful transition? Belief, preparedness, or capacity?

Assessing readiness is not merely a formality; it's a leadership act that shows people the transition is about *them*, not just the plan. And when belief, preparedness, or capacity comes up short, that's not a failure. It's feedback. It's a sign to pause, adjust, and re-engage with purpose. If belief is low, start by shifting the message from strategy-speak to real-world relevance. Help people connect the change to their actual pain points and goals. A reworded "why" that reflects their experience will go further than a perfectly polished slide deck. If preparedness is the gap, build confidence through clarity. Don't wait for a "go-live" approach; use simulations or small-scale pilots to let people *practice the change* before it becomes real. Early experience turns uncertainty into forward motion. And if capacity is the issue, show you're serious about making space. Ask teams, "What can we stop doing to make this possible?" Nothing earns trust faster than a leader who protects people's time during change. Readiness is a critical element of the transition process. If individuals aren't "ready" to start the transition through change, they will remain "stuck" in what is already in place. Forcing movement will likely produce resistance. When assessments suggest weakness in any element, dialogue and reframing will become a priority. Once movement emerges, leaders can pursue additional strategies to sustain momentum. These will be featured a bit later in this chapter.

2.5 PRINCIPLE 3. EMBRACE SYSTEMS THINKING

Organizational transitions don't unfold in a straight line, and they certainly don't happen at the same pace for everyone. When we zoom out and apply a systems thinking framework, we can see that within any organization, patterns of behavior emerge during a transition. These patterns aren't random.

They often reflect underlying adoption archetypes: predictable roles people play in response to change. Understanding these roles is key to making a transition stick across the system. However, systems thinking goes further than identifying individual roles. It invites us to consider how structures, relationships, and feedback loops influence behavior. For example, behaviors that appear as resistance may, in fact, be rational responses to pressures in the system, overloaded workflows, unclear communication channels, or unaddressed equity concerns. Consider a non-profit undergoing a shift to a digital case management system. In our opening case, the director, Yasmin, noticed that while some teams adapted quickly, others were lagging behind. Rather than treat this as a matter of individual will or skill, she mapped how information, training, and support were flowing (or not) across the organization. She found that certain hubs were overwhelmed, informal leaders were left out of planning conversations, and feedback wasn't making its way back to the central team. By adjusting the rollout to match the pace and needs of different nodes in the system and by reinforcing positive feedback loops, she helped the organization regain alignment. In systems thinking, the goal is not to enforce uniformity but to create the conditions for coherence. Transitions stick when we address not just who is resisting but also *why the system is producing this resistance*, and how we can adjust the environment to enable sustainable movement forward.

This idea isn't just intuitive; it's well supported by research. For example, in the writing of Rogers et al., the authors noted that change tends to spread through five categories: innovators, early adopters, early majority, late majority, and laggards.[5] Although this study identified five categories, the point is that in most organizations, about 15% to 20% are the first to adopt change and act as catalysts. For simplicity, we call this group the early adopters. Another two-thirds wait to see proof, clarity, or peer acceptance before jumping in. For this middle group, we will use the label, middle movers. And the final 15% to 20%, or late adopters, tend to resist until the change is all but settled, often requiring more time and trust to engage. Mostashari and Moore[6] further highlight that the biggest breakdown in change efforts happens not between early and late adopters, but between early adopters and the middle movers. Bridging this "chasm" requires intentional strategies that address the very different motivations and risk tolerance of each group. Layered throughout all of this are the organizational influencers—those trusted individuals, formal or informal, whose support can quietly rally others or subtly derail momentum. McKinsey research suggests that these influencers can be four times more impactful than formal leaders when it comes to sustaining change.[7] In systems thinking terms, these are leverage points: small nodes with large ripple effects.

It doesn't really matter how you label these groups. In every transition, you'll find a small group of early adopters, a much larger group of those "on the fence" or the middle movers, and another small group of late adopters. You'll also find a smaller group of organizational influencers, people whose support (or skepticism) has an outsized impact. When leaders understand how these archetypes interact, they can shift from pushing change to orchestrating momentum across the system.

2.5.1 Early Adopters

Early adopters are the ones who lean in quickly. They don't need much convincing; they "get it," and they're often energized by the opportunity to lead something new. In systems terms, they serve as initial nodes of influence, where energy, ideas, and confidence can begin to take hold. But their enthusiasm can't carry the whole system. If leaders rely too heavily on early adopters without engaging others, the change effort may get siloed or dismissed as "their thing." Leaders can leverage this group by involving them in sharing positive stories about the change and pairing them with other groups that are slower to adopt.

2.5.2 Middle Movers

This group waits. Not because they're resistant, but because they're cautious. They want to see how things go. They're usually open-minded, but they need clarity, proof, and peer validation before they engage fully. In systems terms, they are the largest group and the potential leverage point for organizational transition. When middle movers begin to shift, the broader organization follows. Focusing on your communication success stories and feedback loops can accelerate alignment across the system. Feedback can be particularly important to this group. Feedback loops are the reinforcing cycles of information and response that shape behavior across a system. We will examine feedback loops in more detail in Chapter 4, but in its simplest form, a feedback loop occurs when an action or change produces a result, and that result then informs future actions. These loops can be reinforcing (amplifying momentum) or balancing (slowing change to restore stability). For example, if middle movers pilot a new process and report improved efficiency, their results can be shared, prompting others to try the same process and creating a reinforcing loop of adoption. A feedback loop might result when a few middle movers experiment with a new process and see small wins. Their success is shared informally in team meetings or highlighted in communications from leadership. Others begin to notice, not just the process but also the social proof. As more people try to change and succeed, the story builds, credibility grows, and adoption accelerates. The system feeds itself in a positive direction.

2.5.3 Late Adopters

Late adopters are often labeled as resistant, but systems thinkers ask *why*. Sometimes they're skeptical for good reasons. They may have seen change efforts fail, or they may be tightly tied to existing ways of working that feel threatened. In some cases, they are boundary keepers in the system, holding important knowledge, routines, or relationships that others depend on. If dismissed too quickly, their pushback can trigger tension or slow the system down. But when engaged with respect, they can offer critical insight and unexpected support.

2.5.4 Orchestrating Archetypes Through Transition

Leaders don't need to drag everyone to the finish line. They need to orchestrate the conditions that allow different groups to move, each in their own way. That means energizing three archetypes: early adopters, supporting the middle movers, and respectfully engaging the skeptics. When leaders meet people where they are in the system, momentum builds—not from pressure, but from alignment. Table 2.4 provides simple strategies for each archetype integrated into the Bridges stages of transition featured earlier in the chapter.[8]

2.5.5 Examples of Strategies in Practice

Finding ways to encourage contributions from each group is key to engagement and their support. Meeting each archetype where they are in the transition will help them move through the transition. For example, try these approaches.

TABLE 2.4

Transition Archetype Strategies for Each Stage of Change Transition According to Bridges

Archetype	Ending, Losing, Letting Go	Neutral Zone	New Beginnings
Early Adopters	• Acknowledge what they're excited to leave behind. • Encourage them to coach others through loss.	• Engage them as champions for new processes. • Invite feedback on what's working and what's not.	• Let them tell success stories. • Recognize them publicly to signal momentum.
Middle Movers	• Normalize hesitation: "It's okay not to be sure yet." • Share how others are navigating the shift.	• Provide hands-on examples and clarity on roles. • Offer space for structured feedback.	• Reinforce small wins. • Ask for their ideas to sustain the new way.
Late Adopters	• Acknowledge the value of the old way of doing things and involve them in identifying what's worth carrying forward. • Acknowledge what's being lost.	• Give structured opportunities to observe others succeeding. • Break changes into small, low-risk steps.	• Let them validate improvements. • Ask them to help train or mentor others.

Early Adopter + Neutral Zone. *Can you help us pilot this new workflow with your team? Your feedback will shape the final rollout.*

Middle Mover + Ending Stage. *It's normal to feel uncertain. What's one thing that would help you feel more confident about this change?*

Late Adopter + New Beginning. *Now that things have settled, we'd love your perspective. How could we make this even better going forward?*

Follow Gilles' instructions to generate your own strategies and narratives: first attach Table 2.4 as a PDF file and then modify the following prompt for your needs:

Context: Our non-profit organization is adopting a new digital case management system. Role: Act as an organizational change consultant. Question: Customize the strategies in the attached transition archetype table to be more relevant and specific to our organization's situation; or Question: Replace the strategies in the attached transition archetype table with narratives a manager could use to address the situations in each cell. Format: Keep the original table format.

By combining archetypes with transition stages, leaders move from one-size-fits-all messaging to targeted, empathetic support. Instead of trying to "convert" everyone at once, they can guide people through change in a way that honors timing, roles, and emotional readiness, one thoughtful step at a time.

2.6 PRINCIPLE 4. TARGET RESULTS *AND* OUTCOMES

In times of change, it's tempting for leaders to zero in on the most visible indicators: metrics identified, milestones checked, and tasks completed. These are *results*, and while important, they only tell part of the story. Outcomes, on the other hand, reflect the real impact of change: shifts in behavior, improvements in culture, gains in trust, or increases in adaptability. For leaders driving organizational transitions, the key is to look beyond surface-level accomplishments and ask, *What has truly changed? What is different in how people work, think, or relate?* Note how this plays out in the example of a leader in a small not-for-profit organization.

In our previous scenario, Janelle taught adult literacy at a small not-for-profit organization tucked into a strip mall next to a laundromat. Her learners ranged from recent immigrants to adults rebuilding after years of underemployment. The organization had recently undergone a shift in its instructional model: from teacher-led lessons to a more learner-driven, coaching-style approach. The new model promised better long-term outcomes, but in the early days, it felt awkward and clunky. Teachers weren't sure how to "let go" of controlling the agenda, and learners seemed unsure of their new active role in defining it. Janelle admitted privately, *I feel like I'm doing less, but not in a good way.* At a Friday check-in, the director of the center handed everyone a stack of sticky notes and said, "Write down any moment this week when you saw someone, teacher or learner, step into the new way of working. One moment. One note."

Janelle stared at her pad. Then she remembered: during Wednesday's session, a student had helped a classmate troubleshoot a reading passage without waiting for Janelle's cue. It was small, but it was different. She wrote it down. So did the others. Within minutes, the wall behind them was covered in Post-It Notes™, tiny signs of change that, individually, might have gone unnoticed. Collectively, they were evidence: the shift was happening. The next week, the director started every team huddle by reading one sticky note aloud. They called it "evidence of emergence." It didn't track perfectly to a grant deliverable or a dashboard metric, but it signaled that the transition was taking root person by person, moment by moment.

2.6.1 Recognizing Shifts: Designing Ways to Celebrate Movement

Successful transitions don't always come with dramatic before-and-after snapshots. More often, they unfold in subtle behavioral shifts, renewed confidence, and growing alignment. Leaders who only look for bottom-line results may miss the powerful early indicators that signal the transition is taking root. In the ending stage, positive signs include people openly acknowledging what's changing, letting go of old roles or routines, and even expressing gratitude for what's being left behind. When a team moves from frustration to acceptance—or simply stops saying "this will never work"—it's a sign that emotional closure is underway.

As teams enter the neutral zone, encouraging indicators include experimentation, tentative collaboration, and growing curiosity. You might notice people asking better questions, adapting their approach without prompting or starting to help each other troubleshoot new processes. These moments may seem small, but they are signals of learning in motion.

In the new beginnings stage, signs of momentum become more observable: shared language that reflects the change, increased initiative, and a willingness to improve the new approach rather than simply comply with it. When people begin saying things like, "This actually fits how we want to work," or when habits form without reminders, the transition has moved from effort to embodiment. When leaders tune into these quieter signals, they gain insight into not just *whether* the change is happening but also *how well* people are adapting and aligning. Transition progress lives in these in-between spaces; recognizing them helps build the confidence and commitment needed to sustain momentum. Once you start to interpret the signs, it might indicate that positive shifts are underway, and highlighting these wins becomes increasingly important to drive the transition. Recognizing these moments doesn't require confetti, balloons, or corporate retreats. It requires attentiveness. A team that starts asking better questions, a reluctant adopter volunteering to pilot something, and people speaking more freely at meetings are transition outcomes worth celebrating because they reflect movement, not just measurement. Here are some activities and rituals that can fuel effective "wins" and transitions. The first one is based on the research of Amabile and Kramer, who demonstrated the power of what they call the "Progress Principle."[9] In their research, they found that providing feedback on progress toward a goal is powerful. Unfortunately, some leaders wait until the goal is achieved, missing an opportunity to celebrate milestones along the way. We adapt some components of this research here.

- **Start with a "One Win, One Learning" Round**
  At the beginning or end of a meeting, ask each team member to share one small win they observed (their own or a colleague's) and one thing they've learned during the change process.
- **Share Progress Pebbles on Post-It Notes**
  Create a physical or digital "progress wall" where people can post short notes recognizing moments of growth, effort, or mindset shifts (e.g., "Sam led a meeting using the new process model!"). Read a few aloud at the next team meeting.
- **"Transition Champion of the Week"**
  Nominate someone weekly who demonstrated adaptation or supported a teammate's transition. Track indicators like confidence, collaboration, or problem-solving, not just milestones.
- **"How's the Team Feeling?" Pulse Check**
  Use a regular three-minute team poll or quick show of hands (e.g., "How confident do we feel about the new process today?"). Track trends over time—visually if possible (e.g., a mood thermometer).
- **Reflective Check-Ins**
  Every few weeks, ask team members:
  - What feels easier now than it did a month ago?
  - When have you felt most collaborative or supported recently?
  - What part of the change are you feeling more confident about?
- **Transition Tracker Board**
  On a whiteboard or digital platform, create three columns: Confidence, Collaboration, and Problem-Solving. Team members can add Post-It Notes™ or comments under each when they notice related progress.

By shining a light on transitions even before final changes emerge, leaders help people see that change is already in motion, even if the scoreboard hasn't moved yet.

2.6.2 Reinforcing Support: Building Momentum for the Transition

Momentum is not a lucky break; it's something leaders actively cultivate. Once early movement is occurring, the job becomes reinforcing it through targeted support, encouragement, and visibility. This is when teams begin to believe that change is not just an obligation; it's working.

Key practices to build momentum:

- **Acknowledge effort.** Don't wait for perfection. A genuine thank-you for navigating uncertainty can go a long way.
- **Layer support intentionally.** Match coaching, resources, and check-ins to where people are in their transition journey.
- **Create "positive peer pressure."** Share success stories from early adopters to build aspiration and normalize new behaviors.
- **Adjust as needed.** Reinforcement also means listening to what's still unclear, what's getting stuck, and how we can course-correct with humility and speed.

The more that people experience that their efforts are noticed and supported, the more likely they are to embrace the change. Reinforcing support doesn't just keep the train moving; it helps people choose to stay on board.

2.7 PRINCIPLE 5. SUSTAIN WHAT WORKS

2.7.1 The Unexpected Change Agent

In our next transition story, Mateo wasn't on the official change team. He didn't have a title, a whiteboard, or a mandate. What he *did* have was a long history with the organization, a trusted voice in the warehouse, known for his dry humor, no-nonsense work ethic, and the unofficial role of "the person everyone asks when they don't understand something." When a major new logistics system was introduced, most managers focused their attention on formal communication and top-down performance metrics. But quietly, Mateo was doing something else. He started helping others troubleshoot the new system during breaks, translating jargon into plain English, and even cracking jokes to defuse the tension. "Change ain't bad," he told a colleague one afternoon, "it's just got a learning curve and a weird user interface."

What no dashboard could show, but everyone felt, was that Mateo's support made the transition stick. More people engaged with the system, issues were surfaced earlier, and adoption rates quietly improved. When a supervisor finally asked Mateo what made the change work, he shrugged and said, "I listened when people got stuck and tried to keep it from becoming a bigger deal than it was." Mateo wasn't a formal leader, but he was the kind of change agent every successful transition needs, and too often, organizations forget to invest in.

Leverage Informal Change Agents to Reinforce and Sustain Progress

Transitions don't sustain themselves; people do. And among them, a few key individuals can make or break long-term success. These are your change agents. They aren't always the most senior leaders, the loudest voices, or those with formal roles. More often, they are trusted peers, natural influencers, or cultural translators like Mateo, individuals others seek for advice and whose behavior they emulate. Change agents help bridge the gap between strategy and day-to-day reality. They're often early adopters who bring a unique combination of credibility, trust, and contextual fluency. In transitions, their role isn't just to "sell" the change but to decode it, model it, and normalize it. They help others see what's possible, navigate uncertainty, and crucially build momentum when leadership's presence is less present.

Organizations that intentionally identify and support change agents increase their chances of successful adoption. Research by Keller and Meaney of McKinsey & Co. found that organizations tapping into informal influencers (not just those in formal hierarchies) were over twice as likely to succeed in their transformation efforts.[10] Informal influencers are trusted, respected colleagues without official authority but with strong peer networks and the ability to shape opinions through everyday interactions. These change agents are essential in transitions because they help create local meaning. They interpret the "why" of change in a way that feels real and relevant to their peers. In doing so, they reduce resistance, reinforce mindset shifts, and often become the carriers of cultural transformation. Their impact is especially strong when change begins to wane as fatigue sets in or leadership attention shifts. This is where sustaining change often lives or dies. Supporting change agents is about equipping them to lead from where they are:

- Giving them early insight into the change strategy
- Creating safe spaces for them to voice skepticism or feedback with no negative repercussions
- Acknowledging their influence publicly, even informally
- Connecting them across silos to build a peer coalition of influencers

Ultimately, transitions succeed because a network of people carries the change forward when no one is watching. By investing in these informal leaders, organizations create a distributed support system that can carry the transition well beyond launch.

Feedback and Adaptive Learning. Don't Just Measure, Learn

Measuring performance is essential, but sustainability comes from the right kind of measurement. During transitions, traditional key performance indicators might lag behind human progress. Instead, leaders need a rhythm of feedback and adaptive learning. Adaptive learning is a continuous process of reflecting on outcomes, assessing what's working or not, and making timely adjustments based on evolving conditions. This approach encourages experimentation, supports agility, and helps organizations stay aligned as they navigate complexity and change. This means:

- **Make feedback easy and routine.** Short surveys, pulse checks, or "Start-Stop-Continue" team reflections help surface real-time insights.
- **Use learning loops.** A learning loop goes beyond just correction, which is the typical function of a feedback loop. It integrates reflection, insight, and adaptation over time. It asks not just *What should we change?* But *What are we learning about ourselves, our assumptions, and our environment?* Ask: *What's working? What's unclear? What do we need to revise?*
- **Focus on tracking behaviors, not just the results.** Are people asking new kinds of questions? Collaborating more openly? Using new tools or language? These signals matter.
- **Model vulnerability.** When leaders adapt based on feedback, they show that learning is part of the culture, not just compliance.

The most sustainable transitions are those where learning becomes continuous and self-correcting. Not everything will work the first time, and that's okay. Sustainability is less about perfect execution and more about thoughtful evolution.

Understanding the Dynamics of Resistance to Leverage Change

One of the most misunderstood dynamics in change leadership is resistance. Leaders are often trained to minimize it, push through it, or label it as noncompliance. In this framing, resistance becomes a problem to solve. But what if that view is incomplete? What if resistance is not a barrier to change but a vital source of energy and insight, one that, if engaged skillfully, can actually help sustain the transition over time?

This is the paradox: resistance often appears when people care the most. It may mask uncertainty, grief, pride, or fear, but beneath it lies deep investment. Leaders who learn to leverage resistance as data, dialogue, and direction unlock a richer view of the transition landscape. They begin to see where alignment is weak, where values are in tension, and where the old ways still hold meaning that needs to be honored or transformed. This kind of change leadership is rare. It takes patience, curiosity, and a willingness to slow down to listen deeply, especially when the signs of resistance are subtle or disguised as disengagement.

The following example illustrates how resistance doesn't always come in the form of open defiance. More often, it arrives in low-volume signals, offhand remarks, or a sudden drop in energy. If leaders are attuned, those signals can serve as turning points in how they understand and sustain change.

Daniel, newly promoted to operations director, had been leading his team through a broad strategic transformation for nearly three months. On paper, the initiative was on track, deadlines were being met, project dashboards looked clean, and no one had voiced outright objections. But something felt off. In meetings, discussions had grown thinner. Fewer people volunteered ideas. When Daniel asked for input, he was met with polite nods or vague agreement. A once-energetic team had grown quiet and formal. It wasn't until a Friday afternoon check-in with Marcus, one of his most experienced team leaders, that the underlying issue surfaced. As they reviewed a new reporting process tied to the transformation, he offered a faint smile and said, "We'll get it done—just not sure anyone's thrilled about it."

Daniel paused, taken aback. "What do you mean?" Marcus shrugged, not confrontational, just matter-of-fact. "It's . . . fine. It's just a lot of change. Some of the folks feel like things they were proud of are being pushed aside. But hey, it's what the company wants, right?" The comment lingered. It wasn't resistance in the loud, confrontational sense. It was a quiet resignation. And that was harder to detect and potentially more dangerous. Daniel didn't have a clear response. Not right away. But over the weekend, he revisited team feedback logs, listened to recordings of recent meetings, and began to see a pattern: quiet compliance masking quiet disengagement. Rather than pushing forward with a planned rollout session, he invited a cross-section of team members to a low-pressure "story session." His only prompt was: *Tell me about a time we've done great work you were proud of—what made it work?* What emerged was insight. His team hadn't rejected the future; they simply hadn't had a chance to grieve what they were being asked to leave behind. That conversation didn't make resistance disappear; it gave Daniel a clearer map of what needed to be honored and carried forward to sustain the change ahead.

2.7.2 A Practical Formula for Addressing Resistance

Mitch has successfully used a model for many years that takes the form of a formula, which is attributed to the work of David Gleicher and populated by the work of Beckhard and Harris: $D \times V \times F > R$.[11] This simple formula can help you and your team understand what's needed for successful change. It states:

D = Dissatisfaction with how things are now, multiplied by:
V = Vision of a better future, multiplied by:
F = First steps to get started, must be greater than
R = Resistance to change, or resistance takes over.

This formula is represented in the following way: $D \times V \times F > R$.

Let's dissect this a bit more. Because it's a multiplication formula, if any one of the three parts (D, V, or F) is missing or very weak (basically zero), then you won't get past the resistance to change because the product is 0. So, for change to happen, you need all three:

- **Dissatisfaction.** People must feel a strong reason to change (Dissatisfaction with the way things currently are).
- **Vision.** They need to know where they're headed (Vision of an intended future).
- **First Steps.** They need to see how to begin (First steps for individuals, teams, and even the organization).

Here's a recent experience Mitch has had with a client and how each part of the formula came to life in team discussions.

Dissatisfaction. Providing strong evidence is crucial here. Something like, "If we don't address this change now, here are some negative things that can happen in the future. And on the positive spin, if we do make these changes, our lives will be better in the following ways."

Vision. What does success look like for us as a team? "Let's discuss our perceptions of why we're doing this." This is often unclear or not shared enough. A strong vision should inspire and guide.

First Steps. People often ask, "What do I do first? What do we do first?" Believe it or not, this important step is largely ignored by many leaders. Break this down into self, team, and organizational steps so everyone knows where to start. That's when the light bulbs go on. Specifically, Mitch asks the team, "What are your personal first steps; the team's first steps?"

Resistance to Change. The first three factors (D, V, and F) impact R. So, to understand how to reduce resistance, it's about identifying actions to increase D, V, and F.

Try this with your team to make it a conversation with impact. Introduce the formula: D x V x F > R. Ask: Where are we strong? What's missing? Then ask: are there other things we need for change that are not part of the formula? People often suggest ideas like this. We need more "C" = Competent team members. Or we don't have enough "P" = Professional development opportunities. Or in our past change work, we didn't have enough "O" = Ongoing communication. And they're right! The goal is to make the formula real and useful for your situation. And here's one final tip: use this model not just as a tool but also as a conversation starter. It helps teams understand what drives effective transitions and what might be holding them back. And if people suggest some new variables, this is a great start to buy-in into the transition. Keep it simple, keep it clear, and make it your own.

2.7.3 Resistance Isn't the End. It's a Signal

Sustainable transitions require engagement, which often begins with discomfort. Leaders who interpret resistance solely as defiance may miss crucial insight into what matters most to people. In practice, resistance is rarely irrational. It often signals one or more of the following:

- A competing commitment or value worth protecting
- A sense of loss, identity threat, or uncertainty
- A belief that something essential is being overlooked

When leaders shift their perspective from "overcoming resistance" to *leveraging* it, they unlock new sources of insight, adaptation, and long-term ownership.

Frameworks for Positive Engagement With Resistance

Two models that Mike has used extensively while working with organizations going through change are Immunity to Change and Appreciative Inquiry. Each approach can be used to leverage resistance to enable positive support for organizational transition. Mike has used Immunity to Change to help uncover emotional barriers to move the transition forward. Immunity to Change can be used with individuals and teams. Appreciative Inquiry can help reframe resistance as aspiration. This approach is a great way to foster engagement and ownership in shaping the future state. Let's look at each approach and how it can influence positive shifts from resistance to support.

Immunity to Change

Robert Kegan and Lisa Lahey's Immunity to Change framework suggests that resistance often stems from hidden commitments that protect individuals from perceived threats.[12] Leaders can use structured reflection or coaching-style dialogue to uncover these beliefs and explore their origins. When individuals feel safe to surface underlying assumptions, change becomes less threatening and more achievable. Immunity to Change is easy to use in situations where resistance is present. Mike has used an easy activity to help shift the resistance mindset. Table 2.5 provides some simple instructions for leaders wishing to try the Immunity to Change approach.

TABLE 2.5

Instructions for Using Immunity to Change for Resistance

---

1. **Frame the purpose:**
   Let's explore what might be holding us back—beneath the surface—in supporting this change fully. This is about insight, not blame.
2. **Guide participants (individually or small groups) through four questions:**
   You can draw these on a whiteboard or hand out a worksheet.

Source of Resistance	Questions
• Commitment	What is the change goal or behavior you are genuinely committed to?
• Behaviors	What are you (or we) doing—or not doing—that works against this goal?
• Hidden Commitment	If we're being honest, what might we be more committed to than the change? What are we protecting?
• Big Assumptions	What belief might be fueling that hidden commitment? (e.g., "If we give up control, we'll lose quality.")

3. **Debrief with reflection: ask:**
   - *What did we learn about ourselves?*
   - *Which of these hidden commitments is most important to explore further?*
   - *What small experiment could we try to test one of our assumptions?*

Appreciative Inquiry

Appreciative Inquiry is a strengths-based approach to organizational change that focuses on what's working well, rather than on fixing problems. It follows a five-stage process:

1. **Define**. Clarify the focus of inquiry.
2. **Discover**. Identify strengths and peak experiences.
3. **Dream**. Envision what is possible by building on those strengths.
4. **Design**—Co-create structures and processes that support the vision.
5. **Destiny**. Implement and sustain the change through ongoing learning and adaptation.

Appreciative Inquiry reframes what is often labeled 'resistance' as an expression of positive intent and concern—signaling attachment to past strengths or unmet needs rather than refusal to change. In this sense, such reactions become sources of insight and energy for change. When someone resists a change, they may be defending a value (such as stability, fairness, or excellence) that feels threatened. Leaders can invite participants to share

TABLE 2.6

Instructions for Leaders Using Appreciative Inquiry to Address Transitions

---

1. **Gather a small team or cross-functional group (four to six people):**
   Optional: set up chairs in a circle or use breakout groups.
2. **Give this prompt:**
   Tell a story about a time when we went through a change—big or small—that worked well. What made it successful? What values or strengths were present?
3. **Facilitate round-robin sharing (three minutes per person):**
   Encourage others to listen deeply and jot down key themes.
4. **After the circle, reflect together:**
   • *What strengths did we hear repeated?*
   • *What do these stories tell us about what matters to us during change?*
   • *How might we bring those same strengths into the current transition?*
5. **Close with a co-creation invitation:**
   Based on what we heard, what's one way we could design this change, so it feels more aligned with our values?

---

stories of when change felt successful and affirm the strengths people want to protect.

Mike has leveraged Appreciative Inquiry with teams to promote engagement. In Table 2.6, Mike provides instructions to use Appreciative Inquiry to help identify strengths.

AI can facilitate the use of either approach within your own team by generating custom narratives specific to your situation. Adapt the following prompt for your needs:

> *Context: Our organization is adopting a new AI-powered inventory management system, and our operations director is sensing resistance from his team. Role: Act as a corporate psychologist. Question: Provide instructions and detailed narratives to guide our operations director in using the Immunity to Change (or Appreciative Inquiry) process with his team.*

Reframing Resistance for Long-Term Sustainability

In the final stages of transition, sustaining change depends less on mandates and more on shared meaning. By engaging resistance with curiosity and compassion, leaders model the very adaptability and psychological safety they seek to cultivate. In this light, resistance is not a roadblock. It's a relational mirror—reflecting what matters, what's missing, and what must be reconciled for change to truly take hold.

2.8 KEY TAKEAWAYS

2.8.1 The Three Instruments for Change

This chapter has explored why transitions are not the soft side of change; they are the *sustaining* side. Successful change demands more than a blueprint; it requires a roadmap for the human journey from what was to what's next. Transitions are intertwined with the three instruments for change. They are as follows:

1. **Self as the Instrument for Change:**
   - **Promoting individual engagement throughout the transition.** The more involved individuals are in crafting the future, the faster individuals will pass through the stages of transition.
   - **Recognizing the archetypes of transition.** These patterns of response, ranging from early adopters to late movers, allow leaders to calibrate their support, engagement strategies, and communication style and meet people where they are rather than where leaders wish them to be.
2. **Team as the Instrument for Change:**
   - **Gauging transition readiness and capacity.** Readiness is about whether teams feel prepared and capable of making the shift.
   - **Leveraging resistance as a form of engagement.** Resistance, approached with curiosity and empathy, often reveals deeper commitments, important tensions, and gaps in awareness that, once addressed, can strengthen the change effort and deepen trust within teams.
3. **Organization as the Instrument for Change:**
   - **Understanding the current environment.** Transitions begin in a context shaped by organizational history, past change efforts, and the stories people carry with them. Appreciating that context helps leaders anticipate what may accelerate or inhibit movement within organizations.
   - **Considering organizational challenges.** Transitions are shaped by people's emotional, cognitive, and social experiences, and surfacing these challenges early builds resilience.
   - **Crafting a compelling transition story.** Stories help align people not just to the *what* of the change but also to the *why* behind it.

2.8.2 The Five Principles of Change

To help you reflect on this chapter, we have compiled a list of self-assessment questions and tools mentioned in this chapter for the five change principles in Table 2.7.

Transitions are where real change happens. They are not a phase to rush through; they are the bridge that carries people from intention to implementation, from compliance to commitment. Leaders who attend to transitions with insight, empathy, and strategy bring their people with them.

TABLE 2.7

Self-Assessment Questions and Tools Related to Leading Transitions

Principles of Change	Self-Assessment Questions	A Highlight of Tools Introduced in this Book to Address these Self-Assessment Questions
Frame the Evidence for Change	Have we considered what will be required to move individuals through the three stages of transition?	• Stages of Transition • Transition planning checklist for the three "Cs": Context, Challenges, and Crafting the story
Assess With Engagement	Have we assessed the organization's readiness for change? Do we understand the organization's capacity for change?	• Theory of Planned Behavior (belief in the change, confidence they can make the change, and perception of support)
Embrace Systems Thinking	Have we considered how each transition archetype will influence the change transition?	• Transition archetype strategies checklist
Target Results *and* Outcomes	Do we have a plan to celebrate progress and shifts in mindset when they emerge? Are we tracking indicators of transition shifts?	• Progress Post-its • Success Story Spotlight • Reflective Check-Ins • Transition Tracker Board
Sustain What Works	Have we identified informal, influential change agents? Have we created strategies to leverage resistance to support transition?	• Immunity-to-Change Framework • Appreciative Inquiry

2.9 MOVING ONWARD: STILL LIVING IN TRANSITION

When we opened this chapter, we shared a personal story about a transition, one marked by slow, steady shifts that challenged Mike's habits, his identity, and his sense of balance. At that time, running was a defining part of who Mike was. Letting go of it felt like letting go of a part of himself.

Today, Mike still runs, but it's mostly on a treadmill. Yes, even that small detail hints at a subtle kind of resistance. A tether to something familiar. A way to stay close to the past while cautiously exploring the future. But the story didn't end there.

In the space where long-distance running once lived, Mike has created something more balanced. Cycling, hiking, strength training, and meditation have become part of a more intentional routine—one that supports not just endurance but also presence. This wasn't a planned reinvention. It emerged through openness, small choices, and a willingness to ask: *What does movement look like for who he is now, not who he used to be?* His transition continues. And that, Mike has learned, is the point. Transitions don't always come with final destinations. They unfold, evolve, and invite us to move— not always fast, but always forward.

In letting go of the certainty of his running identity, Mike has made space for possibilities he previously hadn't considered. And in that space, he has found new habits and new ways of being. This personal story is like the many stories we have heard from individuals resisting and embracing individual, team, and organizational transitions.

NOTES

1 Bridges, W. (2009). *Managing transitions: Making the most of change*. Da Capo Press.
2 Bridges, W. (2009). *Managing transitions: Making the most of change*. Da Capo Press.
3 Thomke, S. (2020). Building a culture of experimentation. *Harvard Business Review*, *98*(2), 40–47.
4 Ajzen, I. (2020). The theory of planned behavior: Frequently asked questions. *Human Behavior and Emerging Technologies*, *2*(4), 314–324.
5 Rogers, E. M., Singhal, A., & Quinlan, M. M. (2014). Diffusion of innovations. In *An integrated approach to communication theory and research* (pp. 432-448). Routledge.
6 Mostashari, F., & Moore, G. (2025). Crossing the chasm: How to expand adoption of value-based care. *NEJM Catalyst Innovations in Care Delivery*, *6*(4), CAT-24.
7 Keller, S., & Meaney, M. (2017). *Leading organizations: Ten timeless truths*. Bloomsbury Publishing.

8   Bridges, W., & Bridges, S. (2019). *Transitions: Making sense of life's changes.* Balance.

9   Amabile, T., & Kramer, S. (2011). *The progress principle: Using small wins to ignite joy, engagement, and creativity at work.* Harvard Business Review Press.

10 Keller, S., & Meaney, M. (2003). *Tapping the power of hidden influencers.* McKinsey Quarterly. https://www.mckinsey.com/featured-insights/leadership/tapping-the-power-of-hidden-influencers

11 Beckhard, R. (1989). *Organizational transitions: Managing complex change.* Addison-Wesley.

12 Kegan, R., & Lahey, L. L. (2001). *The real reason people won't change* (p. 75). Harvard Business Review.

3

Improve Strategic Planning with Top Change Practices

3.1 CHAPTER PREVIEW

One of the most visible and potentially sustainable actions an organization can take to drive change is strategic planning, which is like charting a course for a long journey. Strategic planning does not need to be a complex, top-down exercise; it can be any intentional process that shapes future aspirations toward change, whether at the scale of an entire organization or within a single team or initiative. Many organizations set out with grand intentions, but somewhere along the way, they lose their direction—or worse, never really follow it in the first place, or do not know how to sustain the initiative. The primary reason? Lack of top change practices to guide and improve the effort. This chapter incorporates benchmarks to rethink and improve the planning process, helping you move toward more effective and engaging methods. Our goal is to support you in working with key stakeholders to create not just a strategic roadmap, but one shaped by fresh design approaches, smarter decision-making, and sustainability. These approaches are also standalone methods you can easily use in other change initiatives. It's a win-win! With these tools, you'll reach your goals with greater clarity and success.

We'll walk through real-world cases of strategic planning, both triumphs and disasters, to uncover what works, what doesn't, and why. You'll learn how to build strong strategic planning teams, balance real-time and step-by-step planning, and bring diverse voices to the table in a way that actually makes a difference in the sustainability of your outcomes. We'll show you how to pinpoint the key decision-making models that can make or break strategic change. Tools like AI are often an overlooked resource. While AI won't magically provide methods to achieve a strategic direction, it can

DOI: 10.4324/9781003622925-3

sharpen your thinking, challenge biases, and make the process smoother and more successful. Of course, no technology can replace good, solid human judgment. Together, we'll break down the planning process into bite-sized, actionable steps, improving your strategic planning performance. Whether you're leading a global organization or a small team in a non-profit agency, these principles and practices can help you turn big ideas into real, tangible outcomes: a key goal of strategic change.

3.2 CRITICAL INCIDENT: A FLOP THAT LEFT AN INDELIBLE MARK

Here's a true story from early in Mitch's career—one that stuck with him as a classic example of how *not* to do strategic planning. Mitch was at a strategic planning session with high hopes. The CEO kicked things off with a pep talk: "You're here because we need your help shaping the future of our organization. We value your ideas, and we're counting on everyone here to contribute." Mitch thought, *This is it! Finally, a chance to shake things up and drive real change into the future.* But his excitement didn't last. It became painfully clear that the leadership had already made up their minds about what the strategy would be. The whole event was just for show. The "strategic plan" that emerged was a massive, three-inch-thick notebook—too bloated to be useful and completely detached from the ideas the stakeholders at the event shared during the session. Here's where it all went wrong:

- **The illusion of input.** Leaders asked for ideas from others but never intended to seriously consider these. If you're not going to take input seriously, at least be honest about it and tell people what you plan to do. Period.
- **No clarity on decisions or boundaries.** It's okay to say, "We can't use this idea," as long as you explain why. If you have no intention of using the feedback, tell your audience the rationale for the decision. With decisions of strategic importance, what *does* help is when leaders communicate the boundaries up front. For example, when considering strategic initiatives to improve employee engagement, salary increases might be off-limits. Once communicated, the consideration of other

alternatives is on the table and prevents getting bogged down in irrelevant discussions. Authentic leadership is about transparency.

- **No synthesis.** Input needs to be boiled down into actionable themes, not left as a chaotic mess of suggestions. Sound tedious? Today, you can leverage AI meeting assistants for automated transcription and note-taking, meeting summarization, and thematic analysis, as you'll discover later in this chapter. Here's a heads-up to a sample prompt:

    From the meeting transcript, create a concise summary that distills the discussion into clear, actionable themes. Remove repetition, eliminate irrelevant details, and organize the output into well-labeled sections. Each theme should include 1 to 2 suggested next steps.

- **A notebook, not an actionable plan.** A plan no one references is no plan at all. Out of sight, out of mind. And even when it does make an appearance, it's more of a museum piece than a working document; people aren't actively using it to guide their work.

This experience taught Mitch the importance of real-time, engaged, and authentic strategic planning—the kind we'll explore in this chapter. Strategic planning doesn't have to be a complex puzzle. By using our five simple change principles as your foundation, you can create a process that's both effective and inclusive. We'll dive into these principles and show you how to avoid common pitfalls so you can lead strategic change with purpose and clarity. All these failures not only highlight what not to do but also present opportunities for strategic planning "growth" upon which to improve. That's why this chapter is about rethinking and refining the viewpoints of designing and sustaining a strategic direction.

3.3 A BIRD'S EYE VIEW

Before we dive into how the five core change principles improve strategic planning, let's first take a step back and look at the overall process. Figure 3.1 identifies our three key phases of strategic planning (initiating the planning process, developing the plan, and implementing and sustaining the plan) and the four types of teams that engage these phases (the leadership team, the design team, the "max-mix" team, and the goals team). In this figure, you can see the interaction among the various phases and the engagement of each of the four teams.

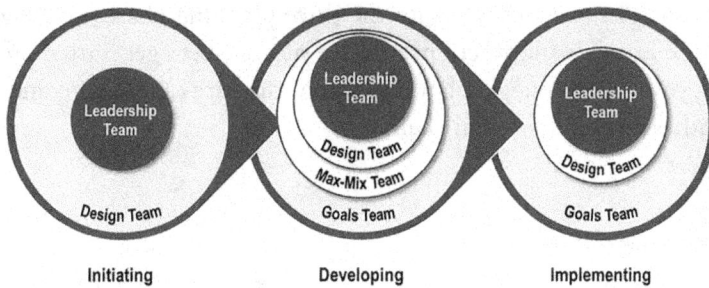

Initiating	Developing	Implementing

FIGURE 3.1
A flow diagram of embedded change teams within the strategic planning process.

In Table 3.1, we identify how each of these three phases of strategic planning aligns with the five core principles. Notice that the only two teams that interact with all five change principles are the leadership team and the design team. The other two teams—the max-mix team and the goals team—are engaged at selected points.

TABLE 3.1

A Matrix of How the Change Teams Align within Each Strategic Planning Phase

Phases of Strategic Planning ⟹	Initiating the Planning Process	Developing the Plan	Implementing and Sustaining the Plan
Interaction with the Principles of Change ⟹	*Principle 1. Frame the Evidence for Change*	*Principle 2. Assess with Engagement* *Principle 3. Embrace Systems Thinking*	*Principle 4. Target Results and Outcomes* *Principle 5. Sustain What Works*
Strategic Team Engaged ⬇			
Leadership Team	Establishes intentions for strategic change	Provides feedback and contributes as needed	Maintains accountability for the life of the strategic plan
Design Team	Designs the process	Creates the plan with max-mix and stakeholder teams	Consulted in implementation and sustainability
Max-Mix Team		Creates the plan with key stakeholder constituents	
Goals Team		Begins the initial work of goal development	Implements the new strategic plan and engages other stakeholders

In this chapter, we will dive into the three planning phases and highlight each of the team's work functions to drive success. Let's get started on transforming your next strategic plan into a tool that drives real outcomes—not just another bookend for your shelf.

3.4 PRINCIPLE 1. FRAME THE EVIDENCE FOR CHANGE

3.4.1 The Initiating Phase: Engaging the Leadership Team and the Design Team

Role of the Leadership Team

In most instances, a leadership team initiates the strategic planning process. We recommend that they put a stake in the ground by providing strong evidence for why strategic planning is needed. Please note that when we refer to the "leadership team," the meaning depends on the context. For example, if the strategic plan is for the whole organization, the leadership team might be the executive team. But if the planning is happening within a department, it could be that a group of managers is the leadership team. There are many possible setups. The important thing is that a core group of responsible influencers is the directional guide and linchpin throughout the planning process. At this point, this team is setting the stage for the "why" of establishing a strategic direction. The leadership team is key, but typically the heavy lifting is done by the design team.

Role of the Design Team

Design team members may generally be involved in all three phases of strategic planning: initiating the process, developing the plan, and implementing and sustaining the plan. They are the workhorses of the entire process. A great design team includes both formal leaders (those with roles and authority) and informal leaders (those with influence and trust). One non-profit Mitch worked with got it just right by including a mix of executives, community organizers, union-represented employees, and even a clerical supervisor on the design team. By bringing diverse voices in, you make smarter decisions.

3.4.2 A Key Design Team Task: Avoiding Typical Strategic Planning Failures

One of the first things with which we engage the design team is to help them understand why strategic planning sometimes does not work, and how to avoid these ineffective practices. This is really important because many leaders and stakeholders have this concern, even if they don't voice it out loud. This is your chance to bring this hidden worry into the open and talk about it honestly. Strategic planning has often been compared to a soggy paper map: outdated and unclear. No wonder it gets a bad rap! Studies have demonstrated that less than 50% of strategic priorities are effectively accomplished.[1] Other, more recent researchers found similar results, which discovered anywhere from 60% to 90% of strategic plans fail before initiatives are even launched.[2] Table 3.2 identifies some of the top reasons for strategic plan failures.

TABLE 3.2

Top Reasons Strategic Planning May Not Achieve Expectations and How to Turn These Unmet Expectations Around

Reason for Failure	How to Course-Correct
Lack of buy-in	Build buy-in through decision-making.
Murky vision and goals	Design clear, concrete, and behaviorally specific paths; align with connection to higher-order vision or values.
Communication fumbles	Don't drop the ball! Communicate before, during, and after—even when you have nothing to report. And celebrate small everyday wins.
Too many priorities	Pare it down. Focus on a handful of achievable goals; it's quality over quantity.
Sustainability flop	Assemble follow-up teams with accountability baked in—what we refer to as "goals" teams.
Technology aversion	Embrace AI tools to lighten the load and add regular automated reviews of your planning progress.
Underestimating the impact of change	Understand the complexities of change, particularly in light of the many dimensions of systems thinking.

In the next few sections of this chapter, we'll address these failures and how to avoid "strategic malaise," where employees are jaded because they've been through this journey before, and all they received was a "flavor of the month" fad that left them hungry for real direction and results. What's causing the buy-in blues? Fumbles before, during, and after. In particular, we have found that when the design team takes time to consider how decisions are made, it helps them better understand the planning process. It also makes it easier for them to explain to other key stakeholders why clear decision-making methods are important.

Decision-Making Models: For the Design Team and Beyond

As you read this section, we ask you to consider adapting these methods to other venues beyond strategic planning because these decision-making models can be used in any situation where clear, solid decisions are needed. In the context of strategic planning, we liken this to setting out on an expedition. You might have the map (your strategy), the destination (your goals), and even a capable team (your stakeholders), but without a well-calibrated compass for decision-making, you're likely to get lost in the fog of uncertainty. One pivotal question often overlooked in this journey is, *How will decisions be made along the way?* This question is the key to buy-in, whether you're charting a course with a small team, navigating the waters of a non-profit department, or steering the massive ship of a corporation. We have adapted a decades-old decision-making model from Vroom and Jago[3,4] and contemporized it for successful decision-making.[5] As indicated here, three perspectives are needed for effective decision-making.

- **Expertise**
  Ask yourself: Does the knowledge required to move the plan forward lie primarily with the leader(s), others on the team, or the entire team? *Translation:* If you're the captain and you're the only one who knows how to sail through a storm, it's your call. But if the crew holds vital insights about the reef ahead, better consult them.
- **Commitment**
  Consider: How critical is it that the group feels invested in the decision? *Translation:* A leader can mandate, "Full steam ahead!" But if the crew isn't rowing in unison, the ship's progress will be slow, if not stalled altogether.
- **Cost of Time**
  Reflect: What are the constraints of time and risk?

Translation: If the decision is urgent, you might need to act fast with limited input. But if there's room to breathe, it's worth taking the time to explore options and build consensus.

Making tough decisions can feel like solving a puzzle with missing pieces. When choices are tricky, it helps to step back and look at the bigger picture. One great tool for this is the Cynefin Framework, created by Dave Snowden.[6] Think of it as a decision-making method that helps leaders figure out what kind of situation they're dealing with and the best way to handle it.

It sorts decisions into five categories:

- **Clear**. The "no-brainer" zone. Use best practices and follow the usual steps.
- **Complicated**. The "call the experts" zone. Gather data, ask the pros, and analyze.
- **Complex**. The "let's experiment" zone. Try different things and learn as you go.
- **Chaotic**. The "act first, fix later" zone. When everything is on fire, put it out first!
- **Chip Away**. The "where do we even start?" zone. Break it into smaller parts and sort them into the other four categories.

Gilles has used this method when there are multiple options and people can't agree on the best one. It helps leaders select the right approach for each part of a decision instead of trying to force one-size-fits-all thinking. We'll cover this framework and walk you through a detailed scenario in the last chapter of this book.

It's critical that the design team shares the decision-making model they selected upfront as the strategic planning begins. Think of decision-making styles as tools in a toolbox, each suited for specific tasks. Sometimes you need a hammer; other times a screwdriver. The art of leadership lies in picking the right tool for the situation. Let's explore three approaches that help leaders navigate their way to action. And when these approaches are used, share these *before* the decision is made, not during or after. Table 3.3 provides a decision-making model we have used successfully not only in strategic planning initiatives but also in hundreds of other organizational change initiatives.

Let's explore these decision-making models in greater detail below.

TABLE 3.3

Top Decision-Making Models for Smooth Movement from Design to Action

Method	How This Method Should Be Used
Leaders decide without team member input.	Let people know if certain decisions have already been made and why.
Leaders decide with team member input.	Share with others that informed decisions will be made by: • Analyzing themes from the input. • Including multiple stakeholders in this analysis as appropriate and relevant. • Sharing an understanding that the decision may not accommodate all interests.

The group decides via consensus.	While a preferred method, consensus has contingencies:
	• It's not about agreement; it's about support.
	• Two primary benchmarks improve consensus:
	  – Provide time parameters.
	  – Identify default mechanisms.

The leader decides without the team members' input. Sometimes, the decision is already made before the strategic planning process begins, and that's okay (sometimes). But the key to success here is transparency. People need to know what's set in stone and why. Otherwise, it feels like being left out of the process. An example of this is a healthcare client who faced a non-negotiable merger. The focus in their strategic planning process shifted from debating the merger, which was not on the table, to brainstorming and then synthesizing how to make the merger work most effectively. These clear boundaries helped everyone channel their energy effectively. A tip to frame the "givens" clearly and early on goes something like this: "This is what's already decided, and here's why. And here's what we need help with."

Leaders decide with team members' input. The method of asking for input may seem pretty clear, but sometimes it is not, and perhaps even confusing. Here's an example of how a design team might frame input in the following way. While we may not be able to do what everyone wants, what we *will* be able to do is assess common areas of concern/opportunities. Some of the ways to make this work are:

- Collect input and group it into themes.
- Involve both leaders and team members in reviewing the themes.
- Explain why certain ideas were or weren't included.

This is often highly effective because it includes others in the process, which builds trust and bridges the gap between leadership and teams. It's important that everyone feels involved, even if you're the one making the final decisions. And don't forget to ask your favorite AI assistant for its input as well! It might provide an insightful and unbiased assessment of the situation the team is facing. Here is a fun example based on the "Six Thinking Hats" technique, developed by Edward de Bono:[7,8] *Context: """Insert a description here or attach it as a document""". Role: Act as an organizational psychologist. Question: Utilizing Edward de Bono's Six Thinking Hats technique, create distinct perspectives that six hypothetical team members might hold regarding the provided context.* This technique allows you to analyze situations from six distinct perspectives—logic, emotion, caution, optimism, creativity, and process—to foster more balanced and effective decision-making.

The group decides with consensus. Consensus is often the gold standard for collaboration; it's not about everyone agreeing, but about everyone supporting the decision. Some tips for achieving consensus include:

- **Define "consensus" upfront**. It's about support, not unanimous agreement. Additional tip: many people misconstrue consensus for unanimous agreement; it is not!
- **Set time limits for decisions**. For example, 30 minutes to pick top priorities or perhaps two weeks for people to gather virtually to discuss.
- **Have a backup plan.** This is your default mechanism if consensus isn't reached; it's like a tie-breaking vote, or the leader's decision, or those most passionate about the decision.
- **Ensure that the process to consensus is participatory.** It's important that all voices are heard and dominant perspectives don't overrun others and claim consensus when others have not had input. Remember, sometimes those who feel marginalized may just accept consensus because they don't feel that they will be "heard anyway." Round-robin strategies and silent generation of ideas can help here.

We recommend proceeding with caution. Default mechanisms are useful only when consensus is not achieved within the stated time parameters. For example, resorting to majority rule can create polarization, resulting in "winners" and "losers," similar to the aftermath of an election. But sometimes you must do this to move the decision forward. We have discovered that asking people if they can support the decision without later engaging in "passive-aggressive" behavior helps! Clients using these models report smoother decision-making, stronger engagement, and better outcomes. Whether you're merging companies, brainstorming solutions, or planning the next big strategic direction, the right approach is like a compass; it keeps you pointed in the right direction.

Teams as the Instruments for Change

As part of framing the evidence for change, team members want (and need) to know how strategic decisions will be made. This is at the heart of making teams instruments for change. The design team has the key responsibility here. The following are tips we have coached leaders to use effectively:

- **Share your decision model early**. Sharing the decision-making model at the start of the strategic planning process is not only a mark of authenticity but also crucial in building trust in both the process itself *and* in leadership, as everyone has a right to understand how decisions are made.
- **Define leadership decisions clearly**. When leaders make it crystal clear what decisions are for stakeholders to make, it can feel like a breath of fresh air and fosters a sense of empowerment. More importantly, outcomes are more successful because clear ownership and process free people to do their highest value work.
- **Set expectations on input**. Defining the decision-making process is like handing out a playbill before the show starts. People know how their time and energy will be valued and where they can make the biggest impact.

These tips demonstrate that the decision-making models we use in strategic planning are broadly applicable. Many of Mitch's clients have said, "We could have used these methods in our meetings in the past—and we will from now on!"

3.5 PRINCIPLE 2. ASSESS WITH ENGAGEMENT

3.5.1 Sleuth Work of the Design Team

There is no magic to the activities of the design team. We have discovered that each design team's process is unique; it depends on the context of the situation. Table 3.4 provides a sampling of activities the design team undertakes.

The design team is like the pit crew for your strategic planning race car. With the right mix of people, AI, and a clear game plan, they ensure that the process runs smoothly, efficiently, and with just enough flair to keep

TABLE 3.4

Sample Activities in Which a Design Team Engages

1. **Reinforces the purpose laid out by the leadership team**. Why are we doing this? In other words, what's the end game? With whom do we need to touch base to improve our work?
2. **Acts as an archivist**. Hunts down any existing plans or reports that can save everyone from reinventing the wheel. Incorporates past work; don't start from scratch if you don't have to.
3. **Spreads the knowledge**. Decides what to share with participants and when. Engages articles, research, or AI-generated summaries of opportunities and challenges.
4. **Imagines the scenarios**. Uses AI to whip up scenarios to engage during the planning event.
5. **Plans the event**. Designs the agenda, activities, and timelines to keep things moving.
6. **Selects the type of diverse talent needed**. Brings diverse voices to the table. These include different roles, backgrounds, levels, and perspectives.
7. **Chooses stakeholders for the strategic planning venue**. Identifies stakeholders using a mix of random draws, volunteers, or leader picks.
8. **Hypes it up (to an extent)**. Crafts announcements and reminders that won't get lost in the noise. They think of this as their event's marketing campaign. We suggest not over-promising. It's important to be authentic. It's much better to promise less and deliver more.
9. **Sets the rules**. Outlines how decisions will be made to avoid confusion.
10. **Defines success**. Asks, "How will we measure success?" Sets clear outcomes and metrics.
11. **Breaks it down**. For large groups, it considers multiple sessions and uses AI to stitch the results from these venues into one cohesive story.

everyone engaged. After all, a well-organized strategic planning event isn't just productive; it's a masterpiece process in motion.

3.5.2 Strategic Change with AI

When it comes to strategic change, AI isn't here to take over the show; think of it as your assistant with an impressive memory and a knack for spotting patterns. It won't give you all the answers, but it can definitely help you ask smarter questions. For example, AI works a bit like a librarian with a turbo-charged brain. It sifts through all resources you identify (e.g., books, journal articles, newspaper articles, and TV appearances) from public records to internal reports and fills in the blanks with logical next steps. But keep in mind, it's not a crystal ball. It's more like a brainstorming buddy who sometimes pulls out gems and other times needs a little context to avoid going off-track. One great way to put AI to work is scenario planning (another term for "What if?" questions). Imagine you are part of the design team, trying to avoid big pitfalls in launching the strategic planning event. You could ask AI something like this:

> *Context: We are a design team charged with planning a strategic planning event. Attached is our current plan. Role: Act as a strategic planning specialist. Question: What potential risks or issues could arise during our strategic planning event? Additionally, what response strategies would you recommend if these challenges arise? Style: Format the response as a table.*

Below are some examples of AI responses, shown in Table 3.5. AI can help you anticipate and get ready for any situation!

TABLE 3.5

Examples of AI Responses Using Scenario Planning

Potential Risk/Issue	Description/ Warning Signs	Recommended Response Strategy
Inadequate Contingency Planning	No backup plans for technical failures, facilitator cancellations, or emergencies	• Have backup equipment and flexible schedules. • Rehearse responses with your team before the event.
Poor Resource Allocation or Execution	Budget overruns, missed deadlines, or resource bottlenecks during event execution	• Use project management tools (Gantt charts, checklists) to track tasks and deadlines. • Regularly review progress, monitor resources, and reallocate them as needed.

The design team may start by collecting and summarizing both internal and external data as foundational information to support the planning event. At this stage, the leadership team gives the design team support and confidence to take over. Its main role now is to stay updated on the progress and make adjustments if necessary. Essentially, the design team is the major driving force here. Internally, the design team may dig through previous culture surveys, focus group reports, and exit interview data, for example. Externally, they may include industry surveys, market research reports, competitive analyses, press releases, social media content, and financial documents, for example. To help in the process, the design team may decide to leverage AI to uncover additional information and analysis tools. AI can provide activities or considerations that the design team may not have thought about. For example, AI may suggest options for how the team could sort through the data. Think of AI as your overachieving intern: it can crunch numbers, spot trends, and generate insightful reports with efficiency. Whether it's identifying industry disruptors or summarizing key insights for the Board, AI brings that extra edge to the design team's work, but it is not the end-all. It's one of many methods that we promote in this book to make your strategic planning concrete, interesting, and, well, come alive. Here's a sample prompt Gilles created for your design team might use to put AI to work (make sure to attach your supporting material, e.g., your company's annual report, your community's value statement):

> *Role: Act as a business analyst. Prompt: Summarize the main challenges our company faces in the attached document and suggest strategic solutions to enhance our competitiveness. Style: Aim to provide an impactful and brief overview for an upcoming strategic planning session with key stakeholders. Keep your language clear and concise. Constraints: Use data-driven insights from the attached document. If referring to data outside the attached document, cite the source it came from, such as a recent industry report. Keep the length of the report to 250 words or less.*

3.5.3 The Critical Incident Detective

If you want to get really specific about understanding your organization's or team's successes and failures inherent in strategic planning, try the Critical Incident Technique. Think of it like Sherlock Holmes for strategy; you dig into past successes and failures, looking for clues about what worked and what didn't. For example:

- "When did we totally nail it with our customers?"
- "What caused that project trainwreck three years ago?"

Critical Incident Technique is a tried-and-true method used to gather specific, significant examples of behavior, events, or processes that have had a meaningful impact on achieving (or failing to achieve) an objective.[9,10] We have given it a contemporary twist with clients to identify why customers were dissatisfied with a product or service. That led to clear, evidence-based steps to address the identified issues and improve outcomes.[11] Critical Incident Technique also has utility in coaching work with teams and individuals. It can be useful in identifying those events (incidents) that most influence a person's perception or biases about a situation. Mike has used the Critical Incident Technique as a basis to explore assumptions made about an event. AI can be your Watson here. It's amazing at digging through data, whether it's customer feedback, support issues, or even social media posts, to uncover patterns and generate hypotheses. Gilles has found the following prompt to be a great starting point:

> *Context: Attached is a document containing customer feedback, support issues, and social media posts about our lead product. Role: Act as an application engineer. Prompt: Analyze the provided context to identify common themes or reasons why our customers may be dissatisfied with our product. Summarize the key factors contributing to customer dissatisfaction and suggest possible areas for improvement and innovation.*

AI is like a sous chef in the kitchen of strategic planning. It chops the vegetables (prepares critical components for the plan), adds ingredients for the sauce (fine-tunes approaches), and lets you focus on the main course (makes smart decisions). Just remember, it's here to assist, not replace your team's creativity and judgment.

3.6 PRINCIPLE 3. EMBRACE SYSTEMS THINKING

3.6.1 Why Systems Thinking Matters in Strategic Planning

A study in community colleges demonstrated that systems thinking isn't just an academic exercise but actually boosts organizational performance.[12] And since strategic planning is all about improving performance, why not leverage this powerful tool? Let's explore three key systems thinking frameworks and how these can supercharge your strategic planning sessions.

Consider Multiple Possibilities

Picture this. You've invited 125 stakeholders to the strategic planning event. One of the ways to consider "multiple possibilities" is through the vehicle of brainstorming at the actual event and beyond. Brainstorming is a way to consider "multiple possibilities" throughout the process, at the actual event and beyond. Rather than asking people to brainstorm from their usual perspectives (a recipe for "same old same old"), try these twists:

- Think like someone from another industry; how would a tech startup solve this?
- Put yourself in different shoes; what would make their experience of your product or services even better through the views of a customer, a student, or a patient?
- Channel your inner colleague from another department; what's their secret ingredient for sustainability? What internal processes might they find inefficient or frustrating?
- Invite AI to the party, challenging your assumptions and objectively assessing your strengths and weaknesses without any ulterior motive.

Brainstorming doesn't have to be a tedious task. With some creativity, it can be a great way to spark fresh ideas. But here's an important tip: many teams stop after coming up with ideas. What really matters is taking the time to narrow that list down and focus on the most important next steps or key areas to explore further.

Pay Attention to Triggering Events

Triggering events are like the weather on your strategy journey. Some you can plan for; others you just have to adapt to. Sometimes it's about adjusting the plan; sometimes it's about being ready with weather protection. In your session, try this sequence:

1. Have participants silently list factors that could derail success, writing down everything that could go wrong.
2. Share these with a partner, who picks the most intriguing one.
3. Post these "top picks" on a flipchart and narrow them down as a group to the five biggest threats. Or, if in remote or hybrid work situation, use a digital whiteboard on your virtual collaboration platform.

For added fun, plug these into AI and see what comes out—because who doesn't love a wildcard? Then, identify proactive steps to handle these triggering events, ensuring you're ready for both the positives and the negatives. Try the following:

> *Role: Act as a systems thinking expert. Question: what are triggering events that could affect our strategic plan as potential headwinds or tailwinds that the team should be on the lookout for? How would the team respond? Format: Return a table of triggering events and recommended responses.*

Here are some examples of the many events AI came up with, as indicated in Table 3.6.

TABLE 3.6

Examples of AI Responses Around Triggering Events to Consider during Strategic Planning

Triggering Event	Recommended Response
Market downturn	Reassess forecasts, prioritize cost control, and identify new segments.
Entry of disruptive competitor	Conduct competitor analysis, accelerate innovation, and refine the value proposition to the consumer.
Key talent loss	Review succession plans, enhance retention programs, and recruit quickly.
Negative media or reputation event	Deploy crisis communications, engage and keep stakeholders informed, and remediate issue.
Supply chain disruption	Identify alternate suppliers, diversify sources, and adjust operations.

AI might churn out a mix of wild "plot twists" and realistic challenges. The advantage? You can compare what AI suggests with what your team brainstorms, blending the human creativity with technology's pattern-spotting powers. Another option? Have your strategic planning team use AI during the event. Let participants create their own "what if" scenarios, sparking discussion and fresh insights.

Be Cognizant of the Whole

Picture your organization as a big, happy family. Sometimes, what's good for the family as a whole might not be in the best interest of individual members. Here's an exercise to explore this dynamic within the strategic planning process:

- Ask participants to consider how short-term changes might affect them personally (because many want to know, "What's in it for me?").
- Share these insights with others during the strategic planning process—those who might have a vested interest. Identify the top two changes that could benefit the group overall.
- Discuss these as a larger group (within the event and/or beyond) to land on three or four short-term interests or actions that balance individual and collective needs.

Challenge Assumptions

Every strategy comes with hidden assumptions, like the fine print on a contract. If you don't check this regularly, it might come back to bite you. Use a systematic process to identify and prioritize risky assumptions, then validate or invalidate them. Think of it as decluttering your organizational closet; some things spark joy, and others need to go. One approach we have used is to ask the design team to identify all high-risk elements of the strategy. Attach the assumptions associated with the risk and then consider what information, if known, would validate or invalidate the assumption. The team could then begin to take action on addressing assumptions. For example, in one situation where an organization was rolling out a hybrid work policy as part of its talent strategy, a major assumption was uncovered: *Employees will see hybrid work as a benefit, leading to increased engagement.* It's easy to assume everyone wants the same thing, but sometimes they don't. To challenge this assumption, the design team broke this down in the following ways:

- What if some employees prefer fully remote work and see hybrid as a step backward?
- What if collaboration actually suffers because teams struggle with in-office coordination?
- What if hybrid policies create unintended inequities between employees with different home and commute situations?

To validate or invalidate these assumptions, they asked AI to gather performance trends from other organizations based on these assumptions before committing to a full-scale rollout. Table 3.7 shows a summary table of key trends and potential implications identified by AI.

TABLE 3.7

Examples of AI Responses about Key Trends and Implications Associated with Hybrid Work

Assumption/Concern	Key Trend	Implications
Employees see hybrid as a benefit.	Many do, but a significant minority prefer fully remote; engagement is on par among fully remote.	Hybrid may not satisfy all; offering choice is key.
Collaboration suffers in hybrid work.	Clear communication is critical; some report coordination challenges.	Invest in tools and protocols; monitor collaboration effectiveness.
Flexibility aids retention.	Flexibility is a top reason for staying; rigid policies risk turnover.	Consider offering both hybrid and fully remote options where possible.

By proactively testing assumptions, design teams can gain real-time insights, make informed decisions and mitigate risk. By embracing systems thinking, you're not just planning; you're orchestrating a symphony of ideas, ensuring everyone plays their part in harmony.

3.6.2 Uncovering Biases With Systems Thinking: Seeking Strategic Clarity

Biases are like those sneaky smudges on your glasses; you don't always notice them, but they can blur your vision and impact your decisions. The tricky part? Many cognitive biases operate invisibly, influencing your thinking without you even realizing it. That's why awareness is key to uncovering them. Luckily, systems thinking is here to polish your perspective. While there are many types of biases that can shape strategic planning, we'll focus on three common ones—how they can mess with your strategic thinking and how you can fight back with the power of engaged, real-time planning. Let's dive into three common biases known as recency, Occam's Razor, and inertia.

Recency Bias: The Champion of Poor Decisions

Recency bias is the situation in which we pick the "best" idea simply because it's fresh in our minds. Here's an example of how systems thinking can save the day. In your design team (or other strategic planning teams, which we will get to shortly), a team member should ask the team to pause and note something like, "Wait, what about this other idea?" Or someone else might bravely declare, "Yeah, but my experience with that wasn't so great." Real-time collaboration in the design team brings in fresh perspectives, grounding the group in a broader, more balanced reality.

Tip. Defuse tension. If someone is clinging to the newest idea like it's their phone charger, gently remind them, "Let's wait a bit until this idea is fully charged."

Occam's Razor Bias: The Shortcut That's Not Always Sharp

Occam's Razor is rooted in the 14th-century principle attributed to philosopher William of Ockham (the modern version is spelled "Occam"). This bias tells us that the simplest explanation is often preferred. While this principle has value in science and philosophy, in decision-making it can morph into a cognitive bias. Leaders may default to the easiest or most intuitive solution without adequately testing alternatives, especially under time pressure. Here's a way systems thinking can help. Run a pros-and-cons analysis on multiple options. Brainstorm the pros and cons. Select the top ones in each category that people from different departments and functions gravitate to. Now analyze. By weighing the pros and cons, you're less likely to fall for the "easy answer" trap.

Tip. Encourage the group to consider moving beyond the most obvious solution by getting out of their own "skin." Engage AI. Here's how you might do so:

Context: I have a list of ideas and assumptions about a particular problem. Here are the details:

1. *[Briefly describe the problem or situation.]*
2. *[List Idea/Assumption 1]*
3. *[List Idea/Assumption 2]*
4. *[List Idea/Assumption 3]*
5. *[Include any additional relevant context or information].*

Role: Act as a business professor. Prompt: Apply Occam's Razor principle to help me identify the simplest explanation with the fewest assumptions. Provide reasoning behind the selected answer.

Inertia Bias: The Comfort Zone Conundrum

Inertia bias is sticking with what we know because it's familiar; this is like always sitting in the same spot at every meeting. It's comfortable, but it keeps you from exploring better options by talking with someone new next to you. The following tip is an easy exit from inertia bias.

Tip. If someone is clinging to their comfort zone, you can joke, "Let's try something new; change is scary, but so was trying sushi for the first time, and now look at us!"

Organization as the Instrument for Change

When we talk about cognitive biases, it's important to consider the organization's perspective. There are two key reasons biases have such a strong impact at the organizational level. First, these biases can spread quickly across the whole organization. Like wildfire, once they take hold, they can gain momentum and start shaping the way things are done. The second reason is that one of the best ways to tackle these biases is to address them right away in real-time during the strategic planning process. In Table 3.8, you'll find a summary of the key cognitive biases that can throw a wrench in any strategic initiative.

TABLE 3.8

Here's a Summary of the Cognitive Biases That Can Derail Your Strategic Planning Initiative

Cognitive Bias	What Helps Erode Its Power
Recency	Diverse perspectives in real-time discussions
Occam's Razor	Pros-and-cons analysis to explore all options
Inertia	A gentle push out of one's or a team's comfort zone

3.6.3 The "Max-Mix Team" Process: Systems Thinking in Action

When you're trying to get a whole room full of stakeholders (everyone who has a vested interest in the success of this initiative) involved in strategic planning, you've got to think ahead. You will soon see that "grassroots" engagement does not mean a haphazard invitation to all. That's where the design team comes in. They've got two big jobs: first, to create the process, and second, to make sure engagement is given a front-row seat in the process.

Enter the star of the show: "max-mix teams." A "max-mix" team is not an overstuffed psychological term. In fact, we did not create the term. It actually comes from the work of Kathie Dannemiller as engaged by Robert Jacobs.[13] While the term used by these consultants was "max-mix group," in the extensive engagement of this process with hundreds of organizations, Mitch has found the term "team" more relevant, as you will soon discover. The max-mix teams represent a "maximum mixture" of the whole system of stakeholders in the room—essentially, every table (in-person or virtual) at the event is like a mini-version of the whole group. For this application, we are interpreting the "room" as a physical one in space. However, we have adapted this model to virtual rooms and engaged the same methods with equal success. At each table, you'll have organizational representation. For example, one key leader, a support staff member, a manager, a couple of supervisors, and a couple of union-represented employees. Voilà! A maximum mixture of perspectives. Think of these groups as engaging the best of systems thinking.

Don't leave this max-mix representation to chance. The design team needs to play matchmaker before the event even starts, and that is why we place this important work in the "initiating the process" phase of strategic planning. This is not musical chairs, where people grab a seat and hope for the best. It's a strategic seating chart, designed to ensure that every table has the right mix of people. What is "right?" Something that promotes a diversity of perspectives, experiences, longevity, and levels, just to name a few key factors. Why is handpicking so important? Because if you leave it up to chance, you're more likely to end up with groups that are underrepresented or overrepresented. Why is this bad? It presents lopsided approaches to strategic change.

Here's where a little tech magic can make your life easier. AI tools can help create activities tailored to group sizes, time constraints, and even quirky situations (like two departments that can't seem to get along). AI can also help shuffle participants into "max-mix" teams. Ensuring no two members from the same department, mixing different levels of hierarchy, and factoring in past dynamics.

Here's a fun example you can develop and adapt for your own needs:

Context: Here's a list of people and their personalities: Marcus is overly talkative, Lena rarely speaks up, Diego interrupts, David likes to lead, Eugene participates in good ways, Sherry has been adamant that this is a waste of time, Nora is supportive of this, Malik has voiced his lack of enthusiasm for this, Isabel is neutral, Jean is overly talkative. Role: Act as an event planner. Prompt: Create two groups of five with a good blend of personalities in each group.

AI handles the juggling, so you can focus on the big picture. The max-mix process is all about creating the rich blend of voices, so the strategic planning process is rich and inclusive. One secret to a successful event is in the well-planned seating. Figure 3.2 provides an illustration of this max-mix team representation.

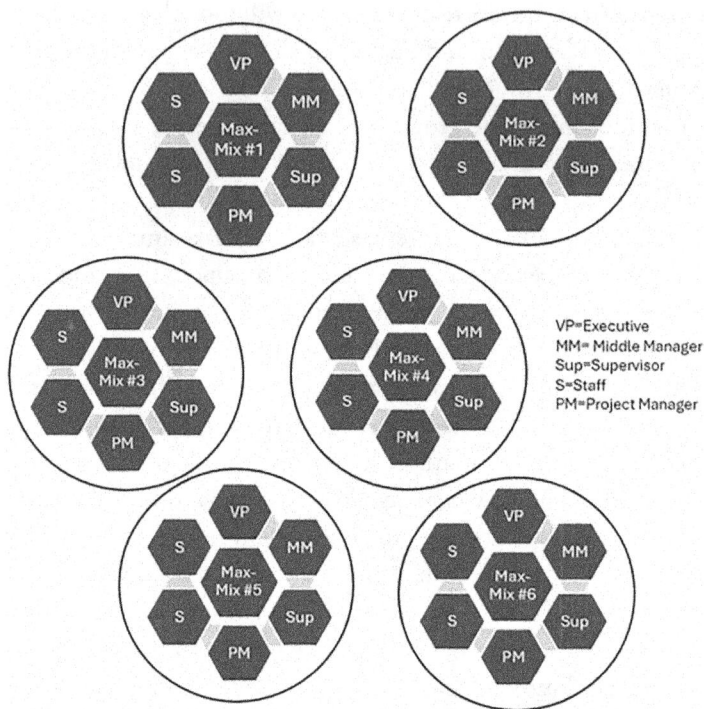

VP = Executive
MM = Middle Manager
Sup = Supervisor
S = Staff
PM = Project Manager

FIGURE 3.2
Stakeholder representation of max-mix teams in the strategic planning venue.

Let's look at a recent event Mitch helped stage at a medium-sized manufacturing company. Their design team decided to bring stakeholders together for strategic planning. Picture this: round tables, no one at the head, and a lively hum of conversations flowing around the room. Each table had a "mini-facilitator" (someone from the organization who previously attended a one-hour training session in basic facilitation guidelines). To keep the dialogue moving and ensure that everyone had a speaking part, these mini-facilitators didn't just stand by; they contributed to the action, too. If you're hosting your event online, platforms like Zoom or Teams can work just as well, but the principle is the same: create max-mix teams and make sure every voice is heard, not necessarily equally but at least with an opportunity to contribute. Here's another casting tip: don't throw two sparring personalities into the same group unless you want fireworks. Further, if someone has a habit of dominating the script, the mini-facilitator can keep the spotlight off any one person. And whatever you do, avoid creating tables full of leaders or people from the same department; this is about blending the cast to create fresh dynamics.

Why does all this matter? Because when you bring together individual voices that don't usually sing in harmony, magic happens. Self is key here as the instrument for change. After these events, we often hear comments like:

- "Wow, I never looked at it that way before."
- "Hearing from someone I never interact with opened my eyes."
- "If I'd known this perspective earlier, I wouldn't have been such a roadblock."

These are just some of the countless examples of how mixing up the cast leads to richer conversations, greater understanding, and stronger commitment to change. Other benefits include broadened team perspectives. We often think of long-term groups that work together regularly as stable. While this is one type of team, there's also the ad hoc team: those temporary teams that pop up within a larger group for specific tasks. Like our max-mix teams! It's important to recognize these dynamic teams and help them perform at their best, even in short bursts of collaboration. Here's one tip for the mini-facilitators of these max-mix teams. Before the event starts, pull them aside for a quick pep talk. At the event, the mini-facilitators at each max-mix team should remind everyone that this is not a solo act. If they're prone to stealing the show, offer these two additional tips:

- **The "Rule of Three."** Wait for three other people to speak before you jump back in. It's like playing conversational hopscotch; give others a chance to land before you leap.
- **The Matchstick Rule.** When you speak, imagine holding a lit match. Keep it short enough that you don't burn your fingers. And no, you can't cheat with those long fireplace matches!

In this way, you are acknowledging the important role of the team as the instrument for change. With these tools in hand, your planning event can be less like a boardroom debate and more like an inspiring performance that gets everyone excited for the next act—strategies that are clear, outcome-driven, and sustainable. This is where AI can really help! A great question to ask might be the following. *Role: Act as a leadership coach. Question: what are some top tips and strategies for getting team members who are new to each other to engage quickly? Style: Format your answer in a table.*

3.6.4 Making Strategic Planning Inclusive without Overcomplicating It

Engagement is about inclusivity, not exclusivity. Historically, strategic planning initiatives have been exclusive; typically, the higher one was on the organizational "ladder," the greater the probability that they would be invited to the strategic planning table to the exclusion of others who may have been important to include. While we certainly understand that everyone may not be invited to the strategic planning venue, there are important ways that inclusivity can be improved. Here are some examples from our own consulting practices that we present in Table 3.9.

We'll explore these three areas in the next few sections.

TABLE 3.9

How to Improve Inclusivity in Strategic Planning

1. Instead of thinking "large," simply consider a bit "larger."
2. Take some "baby steps."
3. Strategic planning doesn't stop when the meeting ends.

Consider a Bit Larger

If your team is used to inviting 50 people, why not stretch a little and aim for 75? So, large doesn't necessarily mean "most" or "all." Yet, bigger isn't always better in planning. When we address this with our clients, we share with them the following graph of challenge × productivity in Figure 3.3. Pushing the number to, say, 100 participants could cause a decrease in productivity at the event because the challenge is too great. You want to find that "sweet spot," which may be with 75 participants.

FIGURE 3.3
The challenge × productivity matrix.

On the side of inclusivity, Mitch has often shared with clients that it doesn't mean flipping the whole system upside down overnight. Start small. Invite a few voices from different corners of the organization who weren't previously at the table. Don't let strategic planning feel like an exclusive club. Invite people from different levels and departments. Different perspectives can bring surprising and meaningful insights. Find activities and approaches that provide multiple ways for participants to actively participate. We particularly appreciate activities that generate ideas and then build on those ideas using all voices. We have used Liberating Structures[14] successfully to identify activities to promote inclusivity. The process of *Liberating Structures* is a curated set of over 30 simple, yet powerful, facilitation techniques designed to foster deeper engagement, creativity, and collaboration. Unlike traditional meeting formats that often rely on top-down communication or open discussions dominated by a few voices, these structures, or activities, create intentional formats where everyone, regardless of role, title, or personality, can contribute meaningfully. Each structure has a clear purpose and set of steps that can be easily adapted by any leader to different settings, from team planning sessions to large-scale organizational change initiatives. By decentralizing control and encouraging diverse input, Liberating Structures help unlock a group's full potential and surface ideas and insights that might otherwise go unheard.

Finally, remember, you can keep the engagement going even after the planning session wraps up. Share the results, gather feedback, and keep people in the loop. Inclusivity is more of a marathon than a sprint. Sustaining it over time builds trust and buy-in.

Take "Baby Steps" to Find Your Sweet Spot

Strategic planning is a balancing act. Too little effort, and you're stuck in neutral; too much, and you're spinning your wheels. Think of productivity as a seesaw: push just far enough to find that perfect balance point. For example, if your team is torn between a one-day or two-day event, why not try a 1.5-day event? Some clients find starting the evening before, then wrapping up with a full day, keeps things in digestible "chunks" (and avoids those awkward "two-days-away-from-work" objections). The idea is simple: stretch slightly beyond your comfort zone but stop short of too great a challenge. Taking "baby steps" is your ticket to progress without sacrificing productivity and engaging that "sweet spot."

Strategic Planning Doesn't Stop When the Meeting Ends

Strategic planning doesn't stop when the event ends. Think of the planning venue as the launchpad, not the whole rocket. After the event, you've got time to bring in additional stakeholders, refine ideas, and share results across the organization. This perspective can ease design team worries about "leaving people out." Let your team know that those not in the room will have opportunities to contribute later; strategic planning is a marathon, not a sprint. It's also an excellent message to share with the broader organization: if you're not in the venue, don't worry. We'll invite you at some point to be part of the journey. And then share precisely how others may be included. This is part of the sustainability phase of strategic planning, which we cover later in this chapter.

3.6.5 Field Logistics: Prepping the Strategic Planning Venue

Planning Takes Time. Accept It and Plan Accordingly

If your strategic planning event lasts 2.5 days, expect the design team to spend roughly the same amount of time getting everything ready. Yes, it sounds like a lot of effort, but "planning the planning process" can make the difference between success and failure. If your team wraps up all the planning in one day, congratulations: you've found the unicorn of design teams. The key here? When planning the process, leave as little as possible to chance. Try to dot every "i" and cross every "t" regarding the process. For example, double-check that no one spelled someone's name wrong on their badge or name tent, and correct titles are used, for example. Strategic planning is all about preparation.

Flipcharts, Laptops, and Clearing the Clutter

In a physical event, discussions usually get recorded in two ways: on flipchart paper and digitally via a laptop. Why both? Well, think of flipcharts as the "sticky notes of strategy." Writing things down on paper engages participants and prevents anyone from asking, "Wait, what did Bob say 10 minutes ago?" Auditory learners track the conversation, while visual learners follow the written notes. Everyone wins. But there's a catch: flipcharts can pile up fast. Before you know it, your walls look like an abstract painting of strategic ideas, and the clutter becomes a distraction. That's where laptop recording comes into play. After each activity within the venue, have someone who is not part of the group conversations type up the key points from the flipcharts and print them out. Hand these fresh pages to participants, clear the flipchart clutter, and move on. It's like tidying up a kitchen between courses; you keep the space functional, and everyone appreciates the clean slate. The bonus? No more wrestling with mountains of flipchart paper that won't stay put or pages sticking together! It's a win-win for efficiency, effectiveness, *and* sanity. With everything captured and distributed in real time, participants can focus on the discussions at hand rather than being distracted by the cluttered walls. In a virtual event, leverage tools such as digital whiteboards to capture and visually organize ideas, automated meeting notes to transcribe conversations in real time, and AI meeting assistants to regularly summarize content and feedback into the next conversation.

The Design Team's Checklist: Turning Chaos into a Well-Orchestrated Ensemble

Here's a running list of top logistics items that we have discovered enter every design team's drawing board in Table 3.10.

TABLE 3.10

Top Logistics for the Design Team to Consider

1. **Who's in the Room?** Treat your planning session like a casting call. Who *needs* to be there? Full board, a few, or none? Decide if invites are handpicked, open, or random. Choose wisely; your cast drives the show.
2. **Max-Mix Teams: A Blend of Talent**. Mix roles, areas, and levels for richer conversations. Aim for teams of four to seven. Pre-assign groups for synergy. Need help? AI can sort participants into the perfect mix.
3. **Mini-Facilitators: Conversation Guides**. Small groups can wander; mini-facilitators keep things on track. Decide if they need training and prep them with a quick crash course if needed.
4. **Who's Running the Show?** Facilitator: internal or external? Insiders know the people; outsiders bring fresh perspectives. Either way, choose someone who can keep the energy high and the flow smooth.
5. **Prework: A Must-Have Map**. Don't let people walk in cold. Assign light prework: videos, articles, or AI-curated content. It preps minds and surfaces hidden insights before the session begins.
6. **Executive Summary: One Page, All the Gold**. Afterward, capture the best ideas in a crisp one-pager for stakeholders. AI tools can help surface key insights quickly and clearly.
7. **Decision Rules**. Set rules up front. Does the board decide? Is consensus needed? If not, what's plan B? Majority vote, leader call, or board override? Will you share just the vote or explain why people felt strongly?
8. **Event Coordination: Logistics Matter**. Behind a great session is great prep. Checklist:
   - Supplies: Flipcharts, bold markers, Post-It Notes™, laptops, printer
   - Seating: Round tables, pre-assigned name tents
   - Audiovisuals: Microphones (at max-mix tables?), projector, recording setup
   - Refreshments: Coffee, tea, snacks, and lots of water
   - Output: Typed-up notes after each activity; distribute immediately in real time
   - Roles: Assigned mini-facilitators to max-mix teams
9. **Set the Stage but Stay Loose.** The design team acts like a choreographer: plan the flow, set the scene, and leave opportunities for brilliance. With good prep and flexibility, people leave feeling energized, not drained.

The Max-Mix Process Is "Real-Time" Engagement

Imagine running a relay race, but instead of passing the baton to the next person, everyone is running and strategizing together at the same time. That's the essence of real-time change. It's assessment and action happening simultaneously or at least in very close proximity to each other, like piloting a new design and testing along the way. Real-time change isn't your traditional, slow-motion strategic planning process. Here's the old, traditional way: the sequential *non*-real-time approach. It feels more like a long assembly line of stages:

1. *Input stage.* You start with a survey.
2. *Reflection stage.* The design team reviews the data.
3. *Confirmation stage.* Then, perhaps focus groups discuss the results.
4. *Hopefully, this works stage.* The design team writes up a plan.
5. *Let's operationalize stage.* They execute the plan.

By the time you reach the finish line, the momentum and often the enthusiasm may have fizzled out. Real-time engagement ditches the relay race for a group sprint. Instead of working in separate phases, everyone jumps in together to share concerns, brainstorm possibilities, and propose actions in one dynamic session. It's assessment and action "smashed" together into a seamless process. (Think peanut butter and jelly—it's just better when combined.) The magic of real-time change lies in its ability to create energy and buy-in. One of the biggest reasons strategic plans fail is a lack of commitment. Shared decision-making fixes that and doing it in real time supercharges the process. It's a quick back-and-forth that keeps everyone engaged. Let's take a closer look in this next section.

The Strategic Planning Funnel: From Brainstorming to Big Decisions

To ensure that a cohesive strategic plan emerges from the various max-mix teams, a process is needed to engage cross-team sharing and alignment of findings and ideas. We've found that an iterative process of max-mix team discussions, followed by large-group processing, back to max-mix teams, etc. is most effective. Something akin to this:

1. **Start broad. Max-Mix teams brainstorm.** Begin with divergent thinking: brainstorming wild and wonderful ideas. Everyone contributes, and no idea is too big or small (yet).
2. **Zoom in. A large group narrows down.** Shift to convergent thinking, where the focus narrows, and ideas start shaping into actionable plans.
3. **Repeat with modifications.** Cycle back to brainstorming as needed or narrowing down, both within the domain of the large group and max-mix teams. Each pass refines the focus, moving the group closer to its strategic goals.

Think of it like a funnel. At first, it's wide open, with ideas flowing freely. As you go through subsequent iterations, the funnel narrows, with each round bringing more clarity and precision. By the end, you've filtered out the fluff and are left with solid, actionable strategies. The max-mix process isn't a solo act; it's part of a larger orchestra. The smaller max-mix teams generate diverse ideas, while the large group discussions bring everyone together to refine and align on priorities. It's like alternating between jam sessions and full rehearsals to create a masterpiece. With each cycle of brainstorming and decision-making, the group gets closer to hitting the right note, which is the initial identification of the strategic goals. And as the funnel narrows, you can almost hear the harmony of a shared direction taking shape. By keeping things dynamic and collaborative, the real-time max-mix process ensures that strategic planning feels less like a chore and more like an energizing sprint toward success. The design team may decide to shift the converge and diverge activities between the max-mix groups and large group based on need. Figure 3.4 demonstrates this strategic planning funneling process.

Here's an example of this strategic planning funneling process. Picture this. You're navigating a merger with another organization. Everyone on board has

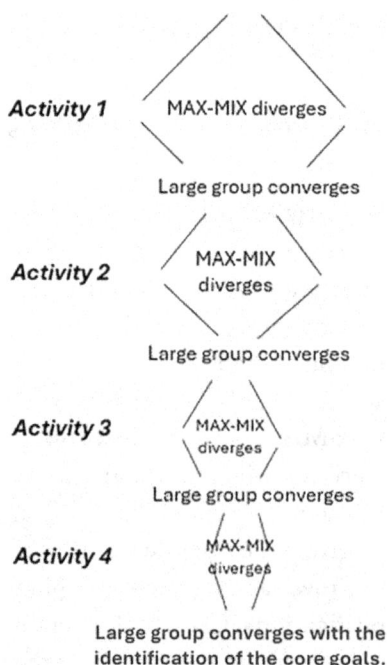

Activity 1 MAX-MIX diverges

Large group converges

Activity 2 MAX-MIX diverges

Large group converges

Activity 3 MAX-MIX diverges

Large group converges

Activity 4 MAX-MIX diverges

Large group converges with the identification of the core goals.

FIGURE 3.4
The strategic planning funnel in which actions are modified based on need.

heard whispers about the journey ahead: some thrilling, some a bit ominous, and some completely off the charts. The first order of business? Clearing the fog. In Activity #1, the assignment is for your "max-mix team" to gather all the rumors, assumptions, and expectations about why you're merging. This is your "diverge" moment: every idea gets tossed into the brainstorming soup. No judgment, no filters—just stir it up. Then converge in a moment in Activity #2 where the "top three reasons" are shared with the large group, where the magic of convergence begins. Together, the large group trims the excess (like editing a rough draft of a bestseller) until you have, say, 20 solid reasons. From there, they "diverge" to gather more perspectives and converge to find clarity, like a rhythmic dance between chaos and order. By the time this iterative "diverge-converge" process wraps up, you'll have identified the strategic goals for your plan. Depending on the activity, each step is either assessment (what are we dealing with?) or action (what are we doing about it?). As well, the converge/diverge process alternates—sometimes the max-mix teams diverge or converge. Likewise, for the large group. Over 2.5 days (or however long your agenda spans), this process transforms the initial chaos into a solid draft strategic plan based on these real-time methods. By the end, they won't just have a plan; they'll have ownership, clarity, and—dare we say it—a shared sense of excitement for the voyage ahead. Toward the end of this event journey, the goals team takes over. Enter the goals team.

3.6.6 The Goals Team

One of the most interesting discoveries we've seen in this strategic planning process is how quickly the max-mix teams become real teams. How do we know? Not just from watching them work well together, but from their reactions. After these teams help create the strategic goals, we tell the whole group, "Great job! Now that you've created the goals, we're disbanding the max-mix teams." And what happens? The room lets out a collective groan. They don't want to split up because they've clicked. That's how we know they've truly come together with a shared purpose and effective teamwork. Once we explain what's next, forming new "goals teams" focused on each specific strategic goal, they understand, although they are a bit disappointed because their experience has been so worthwhile.

Here's how we form those goals teams:

- We ask, "Which goal do you want to work on for the rest of the session?"
- And "Who's not here today that should join one of these teams later?"

These new teams are then responsible for refining the goals, coming up with tactics to achieve these, and figuring out how to measure success. It's a smooth handoff from idea generation to action planning.

3.6.7 Putting It All Together: Two Sample Venues

Now that we've laid the groundwork for weaving evidence-based change practices into our strategic planning, we'd like to show you what this looks like in action. Below are two sample formats, essentially detailed agendas, that serve as prototypes for how your planning event could be structured, as demonstrated in Table 3.11.

TABLE 3.11

A Sampling of a 1.5-Day Max-Mix and Large-Group Agenda That the Design Team Created for Purposes of Designing a Successful Merger

Day 1: Setting the Stage and Diving In	1. **Welcome and Warm-Up**. We kick things off with a hearty welcome, a quick overview of the day, and a rundown of the ground rules.
	2. **Let's Hear It: The Good, the Bad, and the Uncertain**. In small, max-mix teams, we'll brainstorm what's good about this merger and what's got folks sweating bullets. Think of this as airing the laundry—both clean and dirty. Each group narrows it down to the top three positives and top three concerns.
	3. **Large-Group Conversation**. All the max-mix teams come together. Everyone shares their top threes, and we work as a team to distill them down to the top five "goods" and top five "concerns" related to this merger.
	4. **Merger Boot Camp**. A crash course in mergers and acquisitions from some experts who've been around the block. They'll share success stories, lessons learned, and a few "what-not-to-do" tales. Think of this as a merger survival guide.
Break	5. **Meet AI: The New Consultant in the Room**. We put AI to work! On the basis of your earlier brainstorms, we'll feed AI some questions and see what it spits out. Let's say AI agrees with us about 40% of the time, but the other 60%? Brand-new stuff. Small groups will brainstorm their top three questions about this new data.
	6. **The Great Questions Spinoff**. Each max-mix team shares their top three questions, and as a team, we distill them down to the five juiciest, most burning questions.
	7. **Expert Opinions: The Plot Thickens**. We've invited some merger experts to tackle our top five questions. Expect a lively dialogue as we dig into the details.

TABLE 3.11 *(Continued)*

A Sampling of a 1.5-Day Max-Mix and Large-Group Agenda That the Design Team Created for Purposes of Designing a Successful Merger

Lunch	**8. Action Time: Work Culture Check**. Back to the max-mix teams to answer this biggie: what should our work culture do to make this merger shine? And what habits should we kick to the curb? Oh, and don't forget to factor in those pesky cognitive biases (recency bias, Occam's razor, and inertia bias), which we shared in the homework assignment. Bias—proof your answers before sharing!
Break—Stretch, Hydrate	**9. Work Culture Clash or Collaboration?** Each group shares their top actions, and we boil it down to the top five "supportive" and "unsupportive" cultural elements. Plus, a quick recap on how those cognitive biases showed up and what we did about them.
	10. Pro-Con Showdown. Let's analyze those top actions with a pro-con showdown. AI can even referee if needed. Groups will share their refined ideas.
Adjourn—Day 1 complete! Congratulations!	
Day 2: Putting It Together	**11. Strategic Goal Smackdown**. Big group time! Each max-mix team shares its top three responses to strategic goals. Together, we'll distill these into the holy grail of the top five strategic goals for a successfully merged culture.
	12. The Goals Team Comes into Play. Max-mix teams disband. Enter the goals teams. Each team tackles one of the top five strategic goals. Your mission is to come up with three concrete action steps that'll make this goal happen. Bonus points for creativity and practicality.
Break	**13. Show and Tell**. Each goals team presents their action steps to the larger team. We'll refine, discuss, and most importantly, celebrate all the progress.
	14. Drafting the Dream Plan. The design team wraps things up by sharing next steps. All the great ideas will be distilled into a cohesive draft plan, which will be shared through an interactive virtual platform. This is where everyone in the organization can chime in, ask questions, and give feedback. The goals teams will continue their work, with additional stakeholders joining them who were not part of the session today. Finally, engage in "small tests of change," also known as "pilot tests," due to the strong evidence supporting their effectiveness.[15] Instead of jumping headfirst into massive goals, we suggest piloting the goals in bite-sized pieces.
	15. Sustaining the Plan After This Event. This is where the rubber meets the road. The goals teams will work on their plans and be given quality time to do this. These goals teams will have key responsibility for creating the plan for how each goal will be achieved and how they will measure success.
Adjourn—You did it! Now Let's Turn the Plan Into Action!	

Table 3.12 provides another example of a different strategic planning event related to creating a new culture of respect that impacts personal well-being, team performance, and organizational productivity. Compare and contrast with the previous example in Table 3.11.

TABLE 3.12

A Second Example of a Strategic Planning Venue Related to Creating a New Culture of Respect That Impacts Personal Well-being, Team Performance, and Organizational Productivity

Day 1: Setting the Stage	
5:30 PM—Welcome and Overview	Keith and Iris will kick things off by celebrating past wins and setting the tone for the next 1.5 days. Think of it as a team huddle; we're here to plan a winning strategy for the next three years related to creating a new culture of respect that impacts personal well-being, team performance, and organizational productivity.

Key points about the process of strategic planning:	• Why traditional planning often flops.
	• How *we* are going to do it differently: with everyone involved and fully committed to the mission.
	• Three reasons this inclusive approach works:
	   1. People care more when they're involved.
	   2. Better ideas come from diverse minds.
	   3. Ownership makes the plan stick.

5:55 PM—Ground Rules. Let's keep this simple:	1. Brainstorm boldly, and don't sweat total agreement. We seek consensus: we're aiming for "I can live with it." 2. Phones off or on vibrate. If you need to get an emergency call, please leave the room. 3. Respect each other with active listening, as we discussed in one of our previous training sessions. 4. Share your thoughts (yes, even if you're not the most verbal person. All ideas are welcome!). 5. Got questions? Write them on Post-Its and stick them in our "parking lot."
6:15 PM—Artificial Intelligence Insights	We'll peek into the AI crystal ball to answer this: how do we integrate a culture of respect? Or maybe AI has a curveball for us to consider? Let's see what the data indicate.
6:20 PM—Max-Mix Teams in Action	Everyone will be engaged in max-mix teams to dig into the AI findings. Each group will brainstorm one big question to ask Keith or Iris. Flipcharts, quick consensus, and short answers: 15 minutes, tops.
7:00 PM—Open Forum.	It's an all-hands discussion. We won't aim for agreement here: just good ideas.

TABLE 3.12 *(Continued)*

A Second Example of a Strategic Planning Venue Related to Creating a New Culture of Respect That Impacts Personal Well-being, Team Performance, and Organizational Productivity

7:15 PM—Systems Thinking	A quick session on seeing the big picture. We'll focus on: • Exploring different possibilities of creating this new culture of respect. • Spotting early warning signs when it may go awry. • Understanding how all the pieces fit together, including with customers.
7:45 PM—Adjourn **Day 2: Diving Deep**	
9:00 AM—Mission Check-in	In groups, we'll discuss what our mission means today. This is a quick 10-minute conversation, followed by sharing insights with the larger group. No debates. Just observations.
9:30 AM—AI Meets the Marketplace.	AI has analyzed why respect is important in our industry. Let's hear what it has to say. Staff will share six short presentations (five minutes each) with the highlights.
10:15 AM—Break Time	Stretch, grab coffee, and recharge.
10:30 AM—Panel Discussion	The presenters will field questions on whether respect has a bottom-line impact; we'll encourage a lively back-and-forth. Think of it as your opportunity to be a wiser strategic planner.
11:30 AM—Stakeholder Analysis	Who are the people who care most about our success? Everyone will jot down ideas on Post-Its, organize them into themes in their groups, and identify the top three stakeholders. Then the larger group will decide on the final list.
12:15 PM—Lunch	
1:00 PM—Core Focus Areas	Time to brainstorm what we need to focus on for the next three years, in association with our core value of respect and dignity. In groups, we'll come up with ideas, refine them, and then let AI offer its opinion. The larger group will narrow it down to six big priorities related to how a culture of respect impacts our business.
2:30 PM—New Teams, New Goals	The max-mix teams have now disbanded. They are replaced by "goals teams." Each of the goals teams will begin working on one of the goals. In these new groups, participants will brainstorm strategies needed to achieve the goals for ten minutes. Then, they will determine via consensus a first cut at the strategies to share with the large group. To do this, they are to arrive at a consensus based on this matrix in Figure 3.5, in which the "baby steps" to change success start with high-impact, easier steps first quadrant (Q1). Executive coach Amy Jen Su has found that this is also an effective coaching strategy in conflict situations.[16]

THE MAX-MIX GROUPS FIRST CUT AT TOP ACTION STRATEGIES

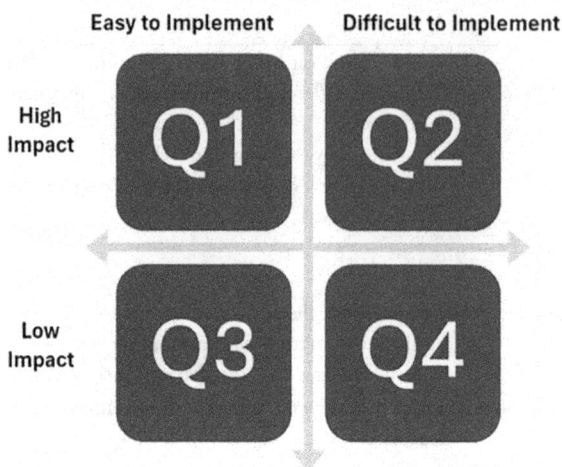

FIGURE 3.5
Matrix for arriving at top actions in Quadrant 1 (Q1) and Quadrant 2 (Q2).

This matrix provides a structured vehicle for developing final goals for action, based on these quadrants:

Quadrant 1 (Q1). These are your short-term goals: the low-hanging fruit that's easy to pluck.

Quadrant 2 (Q2). These are the long-term goals, the "bigger fish" that might require breaking into bite-sized tasks.

Quadrants 3 and 4 (Q3 and Q4). For these, we'll largely ignore them unless there's a compelling reason to shift gears.

We suggest wrapping up this process by forming new "goals teams," each focused on one of the priorities. These teams will brainstorm strategies to achieve their goals and share a first draft with the larger group. Adjourn with these goals and celebrate what has been accomplished!

With this agenda, we're setting the stage for not just a plan but also a shared vision. We often end this by dedicating 45 minutes to a large-group discussion to iron out the details and ensure potential alignment regarding our new culture of respect, questions remaining, and how we address these top questions in the next 30 days. The final consensus will be shared with the board for their review and approval. Back to the scenario at hand, Keith and team close the session, summarizing our progress and next steps.

3.6.8 The Team Process to Shatter Silos in Strategic Planning

One of the biggest game changers in this strategic planning process is to create a more united force for better ideas, buy-in, and strategic change. That's been the core approach in our strategic planning work with four teams: the leadership team, the design team, the max-mix teams, and the goals teams. We've all heard about silos, those invisible walls that separate teams or departments. The team process here is designed to knock those walls down in real time. Sure, max-mix teams might not have unlimited decision-making power, but they're given significant responsibility to further the strategic planning results within defined boundaries. Likewise, the design team is planning much of the planning event, and the goals teams are living out the plan.

This isn't just an exercise in teamwork; it's a powerful way to make the strategic plan stick. Max-mix teams start the process, and then the baton is passed to goals teams to carry it forward. These groups, managed by a core coordination team, are tailored by the organization, which can name them whatever it likes, whether it's "Vision Builders" or "Team Awesome." Be creative!

The beauty of these teams lies in their positive power. They generate synergy that doesn't just stay in the meeting room; it spills over into the organization. People begin to understand diverse perspectives, the "why" behind different ideas, and they become designers of turning disagreements into actionable decisions. Over time, they sharpen their skills in cooperation, conflict resolution, and negotiation. Need evidence that this works? A meta-analysis of 40 studies (20 of which used rigorous data analyses) found that silos are a massive roadblock to organizational success.[17] Why? Because they threaten internal cooperation and strategic alignment. The unexpected win from the phased process and team structure we've described here is that they don't just break down these barriers; they foster behaviors that translate into stronger collaboration back at the workplace. Leaders often report that this process ignites a sense of unity that they didn't know their teams were capable of.

3.7 PRINCIPLE 4. TARGET RESULTS *AND* OUTCOMES

3.7.1 The Goals Team Now Spins into Follow-Up Action

In the previous section, we shared with you how the goals team began its work toward the end of the strategic planning event. Once the event is over, the goals team shifts into high gear, and the real work begins, turning ideas into outcomes. The key here is moving from results to outcomes. An example of a result might be to improve patient service scores; an outcome might be to demonstrate how these scores were associated with decreased hospital admissions. Outcomes are the tangible impacts your organization wants to see in three stages: immediate, intermediate, and long-term. While the months depend upon what the goals teams determine are relevant, here's an example from one client:

1. **Immediate (0 to 3 months)**
2. **Intermediate (3+ to 12 months)**
3. **Long-term (more than 12 months)**

Next, we look at how to set up your organization for success, with teams that ensure these outcomes are measurable, achievable, and on track.

3.7.2 Building the Goals Team beyond the Event

We've helped organizations at this stage in one of two ways. Some organizations form a single goals team to work on the small number of goals that come out of the strategic planning event. Others create separate goals teams for each individual goal. In the latter case, the design team may step in to help manage and coordinate the process. Both approaches work well; it just depends on the organization's needs and structure. Although the goals team is first formed during the strategic planning event, the team composition isn't final. Those who weren't at the event may still need to be added. Here's an example of how to build the next version of the goals team:

- **Invited stakeholders** who have a history of bringing in key insights
- **Volunteers** who are excited to roll up their sleeves
- **Random selection** for a wild card (because every team needs this for enhanced ideas and creativity)

3.7.3 Team as the Instrument for Change

The goals team is the primary instrument for change here. One of the factors they wrestle with is how to identify outcomes in concrete and behaviorally specific ways. It's crucial to first identify the right criteria for what makes an outcome effective. Table 3.13 identifies how you nail outcomes down in concrete ways.

TABLE 3.13

How to Nail Down Your Outcomes in Concrete Ways

---

1. **Define key performance indicators (KPIs).** What's your scoreboard? It could be financial growth, customer satisfaction, internal efficiency, or employee development. Whatever it is, make sure everyone agrees on how success will be measured. Here's another way AI can be of assistance. Share the goals the team is working on and ask AI to perform an analysis of KPIs associated with each of the goals. Then make some mutually informed decisions.

2. **Turn KPIs into meaningful outcomes.** KPIs show results, but outcomes show impact. It's important to connect the two. For example, say your customer satisfaction scores (KPI results) go up. But if that doesn't lead to more people signing up for your service, the improvement didn't actually change the outcome that matters. Always ask: *What difference does this result make?* That's how you turn results into outcomes.

3. **Set target dates.** Deadlines help keep work on track, but it's important to stay flexible. Use short timeframes to test small changes and see what works. This helps you adjust quickly and avoid wasting time. Even with long-term goals, break them into shorter steps with clear target dates. It keeps progress moving and is easier to manage.

4. **Analyze the data.** Use a mix of tools: surveys, focus groups, interviews, or even AI. Both numbers (quantitative data) and stories/interviews/focus groups (qualitative data) matter. For example, tracking turnover rates is great, but don't forget to ask why people are leaving (exit interviews are a goldmine).

5. **Communicate, communicate, communicate.** Share progress early and often, even if it's just baby steps. Let other teams know what's happening and reach out for help if needed. Bonus tip: even if there's nothing new to report, say that. People appreciate not being left in the dark.

3.8 PRINCIPLE 5. SUSTAIN WHAT WORKS

3.8.1 The Goals Team Continues Its Momentum

So, you've got your strategic plan rolling. The goals are set, the goals team is in action, and measurable outcomes are identified. But how do you keep this well-oiled machine running without letting it fizzle out? The short answer: there's no one-size-fits-all solution. There is no single template that'll address all your planning and evaluation needs. The best way to sustain the planning initiative is for the goals team to select a project planning template that suits their needs. Figure 3.6 identifies top areas for consideration when finding project management templates for the goals team.

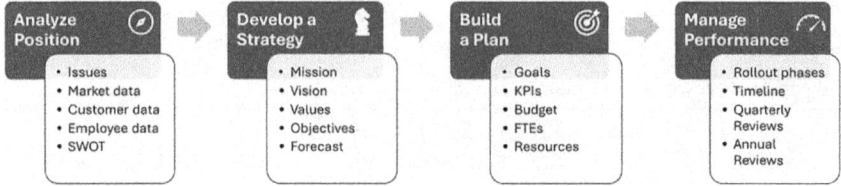

FIGURE 3.6
Top areas of consideration for identifying project management templates for the goals team.

Want to find templates for your goals team? Consider using AI as described below. For additional tips on relevant criteria, consult Table 3.14.

TABLE 3.14

Tips for Finding Additional Criteria for a Project Planning Template. Select These Based on Need

---

Goals identification. A clear list of what you're trying to achieve

Outcomes for each goal. What success looks like—specific, measurable outcomes tied to your goals.

Actions required. The step-by-step game plan to reach your outcomes.

Measurement process. A way to evaluate progress and know when you've hit the target.

Target dates. Deadlines for each phase—flexible but realistic.

Assigned responsibilities. Who owns each goal, outcome, action, and evaluation step?

Resources needed. Budget, people, tools (even AI), or anything else required for success.

Contingencies. Approvals or decisions are needed at any stage to keep things moving.

Stakeholder refresh. Periodically ask, "Do we have the right people involved?" If not, stop, pivot, and bring in the right expertise.

Celebrate successes. A dedicated space to plan how wins (big or small) will be acknowledged. It's often overlooked, but it's a critical morale boost.

Flexibility. It should adapt to your organization's goals, not the other way around.

Clarity. If it looks like a jigsaw puzzle, keep scrolling.

Usability. Can everyone easily update it? If not, it'll just gather digital dust.

Depending upon the context, the goals teams can ask AI something like:

Role: You are a strategic planner and consultant. Context: We are engaged in strategic planning for a large corporation XYZ and have identified four primary goals we want to achieve, which are """"insert here"""". Question: Suggest templates that will aid us in organizing and structuring our planning process effectively.

Constraints: Recommend templates or frameworks that can support our goals and encompass the following criteria: """insert here""". Format: Output the template as a table with a brief rationale below it.

Consistency is key. All teams should use the same template to make it easier to compare and share progress across the organization. Templates are just tools; they require the right process and people to be effective:

- **Facilitator selection.** Determine who will guide each team. Choose leaders who can balance structure and collaboration.
- **Decision-making process.** Define how the team will make decisions. It may be that the method is based on the goals. That's fine. Just make this clear.
- **Team engagement rules.** Establish guidelines for respect, participation, and collaboration.

These "soft skills" are actually the foundation of hard results and clear outcomes. They're what ensure that every meeting, discussion, and update stays productive and on track. And while particularly effective with the goals teams, these skills are also useful for any of the other strategic planning teams. For example, they can help clarify who is *Responsible, Accountable, Consulted*, and *Informed* (RACI) for each key goal or phase of the strategic planning process. This terminology, based on the RACI matrix—a standard responsibility assignment framework—helps clarify ownership and reduce confusion throughout the planning process. Let's ask AI to help us identify the roles of the different teams during each phase of the strategic planning in Table 3.15.

TABLE 3.15

Identification of Team Roles from an AI Point of View, Using the RACI Matrix in Each Phase of the Strategic Planning Process: Initiating, Developing, and Implementing

Team	Initiating	Developing	Implementing
Leadership Team	A	I	A
Design Team	R	A	C
Max-Mix Team		R	
Goals Team		C	R

R = Responsible (Does the work)
A = Accountable (Ultimately answerable for correct completion)
C = Consulted (Provides input, two-way communication)
I = Informed (Kept up to date, one-way communication)

This is just meant as a starting point, of course. You and your team should review and adjust these allocations based on your specific decision-making model and team structure.

3.8.2 Communicate and Iterate

Another critical piece of the puzzle is communication. Each "goals team" should send periodic executive summaries to leadership, the other teams, and potentially the entire organization. What makes a great executive summary? Here's what to include:

- **Introduction.** A quick recap of the team's follow-up work since the strategic planning event.
- **Goal.** Which ones they're tackling.
- **Outcomes and strategies.** Progress on outcomes, action plans, resources, and deadlines.
- **Recommendations.** Any additional insights or proposals.
- **Future activities.** What's next on the team's agenda?
- **Feedback opportunity.** Provide opportunities for input from leadership, other teams, or employees to refine the process.

When shared across the organization, these summaries keep everyone informed, involved, and invested in the strategic planning journey. With the right combination of a cohesive template, clear communication, and team engagement, the strategic planning process can thrive. Remember to revisit the template and process regularly, celebrate the wins, and remain flexible when adapting to challenges. AI offers an incredible advantage for streamlining and enhancing strategic planning communication. Here's how it can be effectively used, as indicated in Table 3.16.

TABLE 3.16

Ways to Engage AI to Streamline Strategic Planning Communication to the Organization

1. Drafting executive summaries.
The design team will gather input from all goals teams and use AI to draft an executive summary tailored to the organization's needs. The prompt could include a page limit and incorporate relevant figures or infographics to clarify processes and outcomes. The summary could be paired with a visually engaging presentation to share with all stakeholders, showcasing milestones, results, and lessons learned.

TABLE 3.16 *(Continued)*

Ways to Engage AI to Streamline Strategic Planning Communication to the Organization

2. The goals team as drivers of change. Sustaining a strategic plan's momentum requires teamwork at its core. The goals teams play a dual role:
  1. **Implementation.** They carry out actions tied to specific goals and track progress, not too frequently to be annoying and not too distantly to miss critical gaps and conflicts.
  2. **Communication.** They maintain an open line with other teams and leadership, ensuring alignment and transparency.

3.9 KEY TAKEAWAYS

3.9.1 The Three Instruments for Change

This chapter highlighted the transformative power of real-time strategic planning by emphasizing three interconnected systems of change:

1. **Self as the Instrument for Change:**
   - **Engage diverse stakeholders.** Use max-mix teams to gather diverse perspectives.
   - **Foster buy-in via decision-making.** Engage personal investment in the process.
2. **Team as the Instrument for Change:**
   - **Engage the leadership team**. Help them understand the importance of engaged decision-making.
   - **Establish a design team.** Lead the process with agility and collaboration, focusing on the journey as much as the destination.
   - **Involve max-mix teams**. Promote their diverse perspectives.
   - **Activate goals teams.** Drive sustainability by aligning actions with strategic goals.
3. **Organization as the Instrument for Change:**
   - **Integrate AI.** Leverage AI to expand capabilities, from creating summaries to streamlining processes.
   - **Promote whole-system change.** Emphasize how small, medium, or large organizations can benefit from systemwide improvements.

By balancing individual contributions, team efforts, and organizational strategies, this framework offers a robust pathway to achieving sustainable growth.

3.9.2 The Five Principles of Change

To help you reflect on this chapter, we have compiled a list of self-assessment questions and tools mentioned in this chapter for the five change principles identified in Table 3.17.

TABLE 3.17

Self-Assessment Questions and Tools Related to Strategic Planning

Principles of Change	Self-Assessment Questions	A Highlight of Tools Introduced in this Book to Address these Self-Assessment Questions
Frame the Evidence for Change	Have we determined how decisions will be made throughout the strategic planning initiative? Have we clarified the complexity of the challenges we face?	• **Decision-Making Model.** Helps determine whether decision-making should be leader-driven, consultative, or consensus by assessing expertise, commitment, and time. • **Cynefin Framework.** Categorizes challenges as clear, complicated, complex, or chaotic to guide the selection of the appropriate decision-making process.
Assess With Engagement	Are we turning input into actionable themes instead of just collecting ideas? Are we using techniques to gather different viewpoints?	• **Critical Incident Technique.** Uses data from significant events to identify which outcomes and success factors matter most. • **6 Thinking Hats Technique.** Helps assess the provided context, where each "hat" represents a distinct perspective within the team.
Embrace Systems Thinking	Are we considering how strategic priorities connect across the system? Have we dug into possible unintended consequences?	• **Cynefin "Chip Away" Method**. Breaks complex or ambiguous problems into smaller, manageable parts for better analysis and action. • **Max-Mix Team Process.** Ensures all stakeholder groups are represented, surfacing system-level connections and interdependencies.
Target Results *and* Outcomes	Do our goals balance short-term wins with the long-term vision? Are we checking if our measurement tools reflect both leading and lagging indicators?	• **AI Thematic Synthesis.** Boils down input into clear, actionable themes directly tied to mission and outcomes. • **AI Bias Analysis.** Challenges assumptions and ensures goal alignment with organizational mission.

TABLE 3.17 *(Continued)*

Self-Assessment Questions and Tools Related to Strategic Planning

Principles of Change	Self-Assessment Questions	A Highlight of Tools Introduced in this Book to Address these Self-Assessment Questions
Sustain What Works	Are we using tools to regularly review progress and adapt as needed? Have we assigned clear accountability for sustaining each initiative?	• **Project Planning Templates.** Supports ongoing tracking of goals, outcomes, responsibilities, and adapting plans in real time. • **RACI Matrix.** Clarifies who is Responsible, Accountable, Consulted, and Informed for each initiative—eliminating ambiguity and ensuring follow-through on actions.

NOTES

1 Badzik, V. (2021). Why strategic initiatives fail—Lessons from a practitioner. In *The public productivity and performance handbook* (pp. 106–115). Routledge.

2 Barnett, M. (2024, July 11). Failure to launch: Why 60%-90% of business strategies fail before they start. *Forbes*.

3 Vroom, V. H. (1973). A new look at managerial decision making. *Organizational Dynamics 1*(4).

4 Vroom, V. H., & Jago, A. G. (1974). Decision making as a social process: Normative and descriptive models of leader behavior. *Decision Sciences, 5*(4). https://doi.org/10.1111/j.1540-5915.1974.tb00651.x

5 Vignesh, M. (2020). Decision making using Vroom-Yetton-Jago model with a practical application. *International Journal for Research in Applied Science and Engineering Technology, 8*(10), 330–337.

6 Nachbagauer, A. (2021). Managing complexity in projects: Extending the Cynefin framework. *Project Leadership and Society, 2*, 100017.

7 Aithal, P. S., Kumar, P. M., & Shailashree, V. (2016). Factors & elemental analysis of six thinking hats technique using ABCD framework. *International Journal of Advanced Trends in Engineering and Technology (IJATET), 1*(1), 85–95.

8 Kivunja, C. (2015). Using De Bono's six thinking hats model to teach critical thinking and problem-solving skills essential for success in the 21st century economy. *Creative Education, 6*(3), 380–391.

9 Flanagan, J. C. (1954). The critical incident technique. *Psychological Bulletin, 51*(4), 327.

10 Schwartz, H. L., & Holloway, E. L. (2025). *Essentials of constructivist critical incident technique.* American Psychological Association.

11 Bott, G., & Tourish, D. (2016). The critical incident technique reappraised: Using critical incidents to illuminate organizational practices and build theory. *Qualitative Research in Organizations and Management: An International Journal, 11*(4), 276–300.

12 Davis, A. P., Dent, E. B., & Wharff, D. M. (2015). A conceptual model of systems thinking leadership in community colleges. *Systemic Practice and Action Research, 28,* 333–353.

13 Jacobs, R. (1997). *Real time strategic change: How to involve an entire organization in fast and far-reaching change.* Berrett-Koehler Publishers.

14 Lipmanowicz, H., & McCandless, K. (2013). *The surprising power of liberating structures: Simple rules to unleash a culture of innovation.* Seattle, WA: Liberating Structures Press.

15 Thomke, S. (2020). Building a culture of experimentation. *Harvard Business Review, 98*(2), 40–47.

16 Jen Su, A. (2025, Summer). Get over your fear of conflict. *Harvard Business Review Special Issue,* 28–29.

17 Bento, F., Tagliabue, M., & Lorenzo, F. (2020, July 24). Organizational siloes: A scoping review informed by a behavioral perspective on systems and networks. *Societies, 10*(56). https://doi.org/10.3390/soc10030056

4

Develop Teams and the Capacity for Change

4.1 CHAPTER PREVIEW

Organizational change often rises or falls on the shoulders of teams. In strategic planning featured in chapter 3, you read how teams were central to facilitating the strategic planning process and instrumental to successful implementation of strategic organizational change. Yet, despite their central role, teams are frequently underutilized as drivers of meaningful change. Their potential to innovate, adapt, and solve complex problems sometimes remains locked away, overlooked in favor of top-down strategies and siloed decision-making.

This chapter delves into the transformative power of teams during organizational change. Its central premise is clear: the more teams develop, the better equipped they are to navigate the complexities of change within an organization. It amplifies the voices of those often overlooked: the team members whose insights, creativity, and frontline expertise have the potential to drive meaningful progress but are too often excluded from the process. It illuminates the missed opportunities for innovation, the challenges that remain unresolved, and the frustration of individuals eager to contribute yet left without a seat at the table.

This chapter isn't just about what's been lost; it's about what's possible. It's about how team development can unlock the full potential of teams, fostering a culture of engagement, collaboration, and shared ownership. It's about the ripple effects that high-functioning team behaviors can have on organizational change outcomes and the lasting benefits of developing change readiness from the ground up.

DOI: 10.4324/9781003622925-4

We begin with an overview of what makes teams tick: the key behaviors and dynamics that define high-functioning teams. We then examine team development through the five change principles, providing actionable insights and participatory strategies for teams ready to step into their full potential as change agents. This isn't just a chapter about theory; it's a call to action. A call to listen, to include, and to empower. Because when teams participate fully, change doesn't just happen, it thrives.

4.2 A CRITICAL INCIDENT

4.2.1 The Case of HorizonTech: A Tale of Two Teams

The following scenarios are based on a hypothetical client company of ours, extracted from real events; we have changed names and contexts for purposes of anonymity and confidentiality. HorizonTech, a mid-sized tech company specializing in software solutions for healthcare systems, embarked on a bold organizational transformation. Facing increased competition and declining market share, the leadership team decided to shift from a traditional hierarchical structure to a more agile, team-based model that rewarded ambitious goals. The transformation aimed to encourage risk-taking, speed up decision-making, and empower employees to take ownership of innovation. Teams across the organization were invited to apply this model in ways that best fit their goals. Here, we're sharing how two teams—Team Alpha and Team Beta—put this new model into action.

Team Alpha: Efficiency over Engagement

Tasked with redesigning one of the company's flagship products, Team Alpha was led by a manager who believed that success came from a clear, compelling vision and a structured approach to execution. He valued efficiency and momentum, ensuring that meetings were productive and tightly focused. He encouraged participation but within defined parameters; team members were expected to contribute within their areas of expertise rather than engaging in broader discussions. Decision-making was streamlined to prevent delays, with the manager taking the lead to maintain progress and avoid unnecessary back-and-forth.

At first, the team appeared to be functioning well. Clear directives reduced ambiguity, and the rapid decision-making allowed the project to move forward without bureaucratic slowdowns. However, as challenges emerged, the limitations of this structured approach became evident. A veteran designer noticed recurring user complaints early in the process but found it difficult to surface these concerns meaningfully. While feedback was welcomed, there was little room for deep discussion or follow-up that might have challenged the project's momentum. As the redesign progressed, team members increasingly worked in isolation, assuming others would handle issues outside their immediate scope. The lack of open collaboration meant that small misalignments compounded over time. By the time critical gaps were recognized, course corrections were costly and disruptive. The product was ultimately delivered late and over budget, failing to meet expectations. While the team had operated with discipline and focus, the absence of a more adaptive and inclusive approach left members frustrated. Two key contributors left the organization shortly after the project's conclusion, citing a lack of engagement and professional growth.

Team Beta: Strength through Development and Collaboration

Meanwhile, Team Beta, from the same organization, took on a different kind of challenge: reimagining internal processes to align with the company's agile vision. Their leader believed that success depended not just on smart execution but also on cultivating a team capable of tackling complexity together. While efficiency was still valued, the leader prioritized building an environment where people felt comfortable sharing insights, questioning assumptions, and learning from each other. The team held structured but open-ended discussions, ensuring that multiple perspectives were considered before key decisions were made. Regular check-ins, reflective debriefs, and informal knowledge-sharing helped build trust and alignment. When an unexpected challenge arose, like integrating a new project management tool, the team didn't just react. Instead, they took the time to explore options collectively, balancing different viewpoints before settling on an approach that streamlined workflows without overwhelming staff. The result was a project that not just met expectations but actually exceeded expectations. The team's ability to collaborate and adapt led to additional improvements that enhanced the company's agility. More importantly, the experience strengthened the team's sense of ownership and engagement, fostering a culture where innovation and participation were seen as integral to success. As a result, morale remained high, and their solutions were enthusiastically adopted across the company.

4.2.2 The Lesson

Both teams operated within the same organization, under the same broader change mandate, and with access to similar resources. Yet, their outcomes couldn't have been more different.

- Team Alpha's focus on speed and efficiency, at the expense of early team development, left it ill-prepared to navigate challenges. The lack of deep collaboration undermined its potential for adaptation and innovation.
- Team Beta's emphasis on trust, collaboration, and shared accountability enabled it to thrive. The team developed the capacity to lead and sustain change, creating lasting improvements beyond the immediate project.

These scenarios highlight a critical insight. Effective teams are developed. A team's ability to implement, support, or lead organizational change depends on deliberate investment in collaboration, resilience, and innovation. Team development isn't an afterthought; it's the foundation of team and organizational success.

4.3 A BRIEF OVERVIEW OF TEAM DEVELOPMENT

4.3.1 Team Development and Participation during Change

Teams are the heartbeat of any organization. They drive strategy, deliver results, and shape culture. At their best, they function like a well-tuned engine, navigating complexity with precision and purpose. But when teams falter, that engine sputters. Progress stalls, coordination breaks down, and opportunities slip by. There's significant historical evidence that points the way to the importance of an effectively developed team. For example, as team expert J. Richard Hackman has noted, "When you have a team, the possibility exists that it will generate magic. But don't count on it."[1] More contemporary viewpoints have gone further and identified how pronounced team *ineffectiveness* is. Despite countless tools and frameworks, only about 20% of teams ever achieve sustained high performance.[2] Why do so many fall short, and what sets successful teams apart during change? After decades of leading and observing teams, one insight consistently stands out: a team's ability to lead or implement change is closely tied to its stage of development.[3,4] Like building a house, high-functioning teams need a solid foundation of trust, clarity, and coordination before they can effectively navigate uncertainty and drive transformation. Only with focused team development do any of these attributes emerge.

4.3.2 The Connection between Development and Support for Change

The more a team develops, the more capable it becomes of navigating complexity and driving meaningful, lasting change. Team development is not a linear journey; it requires continuous attention to the interpersonal and structural dynamics that enable high performance. Over the years, many models have emerged to help teams understand and improve how they work together. While they may differ in structure and language, most share a common foundation. Many team models describe stages of development and identify typical behaviors, challenges, and needs at each stage. These models remind us that trust, clarity, communication, and commitment are not one-time achievements but ongoing necessities for team success. One particularly practical team model is the Drexler/Sibbet Team Performance Model.[5] The model highlights seven stages of team development:

1. **Orientation**. Team members look for purpose.
2. **Trust building**. They look for shared identity.
3. **Goal clarification**. The team looks for direction.
4. **Commitment.** The team looks to align approaches.
5. **Implementation**. They establish roles.
6. **High performance**. The team finds an effective rhythm.
7. **Renewal**. The team looks for what is next.

The model illustrates the cyclical nature of team growth, showing that teams often loop back to earlier stages, such as clarifying goals or rebuilding trust, as they face new challenges or shifts in membership. This recursive approach makes it especially useful during periods of organizational change, when stability and clarity may be disrupted.

Today's leaders can accelerate team development using contemporary tools. AI-enhanced collaboration platforms, for example, now offer real-time insights into team dynamics. With just a few data points, these tools can suggest targeted strategies to enhance cohesion, clarify purpose, and support collaboration. Leaders might prompt these tools by asking: *Analyze recent team feedback and communication patterns to identify strengths, gaps, and actionable strategies to improve trust, clarity of goals, and collaboration.* During virtual meetings, AI can also support leaders in sustaining meaningful connections with their team. For example, AI assistants can:

- track participation levels to ensure all voices are heard
- flag shifts in tone that may indicate disengagement
- even recommend tailored prompts to re-engage quieter members.

Leaders can use these insights to balance airtime, check for clarity, and follow up with individuals who may need additional support. By pairing attentive human leadership with AI-driven nudges, leaders maintain stronger connections with their teams, even when working across distance and digital platforms. Rather than relying on guesswork or outdated assumptions, leaders can now guide their teams with precision, focusing their efforts where the team most needs support to grow and adapt. We'll provide further examples of how to leverage AI later in this chapter. Understanding team development helps leaders match support to need. Figure 4.1 is our team development model, which identifies three developmental stages of teams using labels common to several development models and showing the relationship between the stages of development and the capacity to support change.

In the foundation stage, teams focus on basics, establishing roles, engagement guidelines, and coordination, but may struggle with conflict or change. As teams become more effective, they seek alignment, communicate with greater focus, and move toward a shared purpose. In the high-performing stage, teams learn to innovate and lead change, becoming adaptive and more resilient. The following section demonstrates how to make this come alive with real activities designed to increase the probability of success.

Teams move from one stage of development to the next by building trust and improving communication.[6] As team members begin to listen more openly, share responsibility, and learn from each other, they lay the

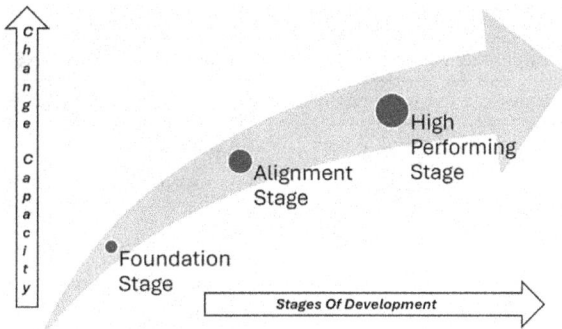

FIGURE 4.1

Our performance-driven framework of team development showing the relationship between stages of development and change capacity.

foundation for stronger collaboration and higher performance. Progress is built through small, consistent steps. At the foundational stage, trust begins with clarity and consistency. Team members need to know what's expected of them and that others will follow through. Trust grows when roles are clear, commitments are honored, and a safe space is created for open dialogue. One of the activities we explored in Chapter 1 was recognizing the power of our "trust wobbles." It's a helpful way for teams, especially in those early stages when trust is still forming, to start building stronger connections and understanding.

In the alignment stage, as trust deepens, the team focuses on establishing a shared purpose and mutual accountability. It's no longer just about doing your part but also believing others are equally committed. Teams build trust by clarifying goals, engaging in open conversations, and giving feedback with respect and transparency.

Finally, once a team begins to perform at high levels, the effective interdependency of team members takes trust to the next level. At this stage, members learn to trust each other's skills and intentions. This allows them to disagree productively, adapt quickly, and rely on each other in high-stakes situations. Trust is sustained through reflection, vulnerability, and consistent recognition of effort and contribution.

The first task in building teams is understanding where the team is in terms of its own development. The second task is to explore approaches for further growth. Table 4.1 provides a snapshot of the primary needs teams have in each stage and how they may best address the need.

TABLE 4.1

Stages of Team Development, Primary Needs, and How to Address the Needs

Stage of Development	Primary Need	How to Address Need
Foundation	• Structure • Roles • Rules • Trust	• Establish team norms. • Clarify roles and responsibilities.
Alignment	• Shared Vision • Goals	• Co-create a purpose statement with team members. • Revisit goals and progress often.
High Performing	• Learning Capacity • Sustained Engagement	• Look for opportunities to experiment or pilot new projects to promote learning. • Rotate leadership to stretch individual development. • Recognize contributions from team.

Now that we have leveled the playing field about the significance of team development, we'll focus on applying this to our five core change principles.

4.4 PRINCIPLE 1. FRAME THE EVIDENCE FOR CHANGE

4.4.1 Creating a Shared Understanding

Every successful change initiative begins with a clear and shared understanding of the challenge or opportunity at hand. This is a process that shapes how teams perceive, approach, and ultimately solve complex problems or engage new opportunities during the change journey. But framing alone isn't enough. Without genuine participation from team members, even the most well-crafted framework can miss key nuances, leaving potential untapped and outcomes uncertain.

In this section, we'll explore how effective framing, combined with high levels of participation by team members, can unlock a team's full potential. We'll engage evidence from a model of organizational practice and demonstrate how framing provides the structure and focus needed for clarity, while participation creates the energy, collaboration, and commitment that drive success. Through real-world examples and actionable insights, we'll demonstrate how these two approaches work together to build alignment, resilience, and innovation in teams facing change. When teams are empowered to co-create the framework for change, they don't just adapt; they thrive. Let's dive into the principles and practices that make this possible.

4.4.2 Why Framing during Change Is Important

Creating a frame of reference is like setting the coordinates on a map; it determines the direction, boundaries, and path for everything that follows. In organizational change, framing helps teams define the issue or challenge, understand the dynamics influencing it, and determine how to approach it effectively.[7] It's the blueprint that provides clarity, alignment, and a sense of purpose for everyone involved. However, while most teams engage in some level of framing, they often fall into the trap of focusing too narrowly, missing critical nuances across the broader system. Effective framing must be multi-dimensional and flexible, evaluating internal and external contexts, anticipating risks, and setting achievable goals.

4.4.3 Bolman and Deal's Four Frames: A Lens for Team Change

One of the most robust models for framing organizational challenges for teams is the "Four Frames" model by Bolman and Deal,[8] which details the following views.

- **Human Resource Frame.** This is the people-focused lens, emphasizing skills, participation, and psychological support—not to be confused with the HR department in organizations.
- **Structural Frame.** This refers to the organizational blueprint, examining roles, policies, and workflows that may need adjustment.
- **Political Frame.** This lens serves as a reality check on power dynamics, stakeholder influence, and potential conflicts.
- **Symbolic Frame.** This lens reflects the cultural heartbeat of the organization, addressing rituals, stories, myths, heroes, and role models. The symbolic frame answers "What does this place stand for?"

Each frame acts like a corner of a map, offering a different perspective on the terrain of change. Leaders who neglect any one corner risk navigating with incomplete information, leading to stalled initiatives or unintended consequences. In the next section, we'll provide a detailed example of these frames in action within the context of our previous example at HorizonTech.

4.4.4 Framing at HorizonTech: A Tale of Two Teams

As we shared in the opening of this chapter, HorizonTech's organizational transformation provides a vivid example of how framing can shape team dynamics and outcomes during change. Let's revisit these contrasting journeys of Team Alpha and Team Beta, using Bolman and Deal's Four Frames to understand their use of framing and resulting successes and failures. Table 4.2 provides an overview of how Team Alpha and Team Beta utilized the frames and their outcomes. It's important to understand that, according to the Bolman and Deal model, no single frame is best in all situations. Within any one frame, there are different ways to apply it. Team Alpha delivered a delayed, over-budget product that lacked innovation and left the team fractured. Team Beta not only met its goals but also exceeded expectations, delivering innovative solutions and fostering a motivated, cohesive team.

TABLE 4.2

HorizonTech's Two Teams Focus on the Four Frames

Frame	Successful Use (Team Beta)	Outcome	Unsuccessful Use (Team Alpha)	Outcome
Human Resources	Emphasized psychological safety, allowing employees to voice concerns and contribute beyond their formal roles. Regular check-ins improved relationships and engagement.	Employees felt valued and motivated, leading to higher engagement and retention. The culture of learning strengthened the team's ability to handle future challenges.	The leader focused on efficiency and execution but neglected team development. Employees were expected to deliver results without investment in their growth or engagement.	Employees felt undervalued and disconnected from the bigger picture. The lack of collaboration led to burnout and the eventual departure of key team members.

TABLE 4.2 *(Continued)*

HorizonTech's Two Teams Focus on the Four Frames

Frame	Successful Use (Team Beta)	Outcome	Unsuccessful Use (Team Alpha)	Outcome
Structural	Adopted a more flexible structure that balanced clarity with adaptability. The leader encouraged input from all members, fostering a culture of shared ownership.	A structured yet adaptable approach enabled effective problem-solving. The team delivered an innovative solution that exceeded expectations and gained company-wide adoption.	Adopted a hierarchical structure with centralized decision-making. The leader set a clear direction but discouraged broad discussions. Defined roles limited cross-functional collaboration.	While initially efficient, the rigid approach failed to adapt to emerging challenges. Small misalignments snowballed, leading to costly course corrections and delays.
Political	The team recognized the value of influence beyond formal authority. By incorporating diverse perspectives, they navigated internal challenges effectively and built consensus.	Decisions were made inclusively, ensuring alignment with organizational goals. The collaborative environment reduced resistance and improved implementation success.	No effort was made to build alliances or leverage informal networks. Decision-making authority remained with leadership, and differing perspectives were largely ignored.	Top-down decision-making resulted in limited buy-in from the team. Issues surfaced too late, and problem-solving was reactive rather than proactive.
Symbolic	The leader reinforced a compelling vision, connecting the project's purpose to the company's broader transformation. Rituals like reflective debriefs helped sustain engagement.	A strong team identity emerged, with members feeling a sense of accomplishment and purpose. This created lasting momentum for future initiatives.	The project lacked a shared narrative or deeper purpose beyond deadlines and deliverables. Employees saw their roles as tasks rather than contributions to a larger vision.	Without an emotional connection to the project, motivation declined. The final product lacked innovation, and the team's morale suffered post-delivery.

4.4.5 Ways to Engage Bolman and Deal's Four Frames

Assess an Organizational Initiative or Communication

One way to assess how well your team thinks about these frames is to ask team members to interpret an important organizational initiative or communication, using Bolman and Deal's model. We once did an exercise with 12 managers who had just received an organizational communication about an impending change to the company's hiring process. After the managers received the communication and had a chance to ask questions, we asked each one to articulate how they would translate the company message to their teams, using each of the frames in the Bolman and Deal framework. We heard 12 very different messages. For example, one manager looked at the human resources frame and suggested that a lack of training for managers would be the biggest issue in this frame. Another manager highlighted the organization's skepticism of "follow through," which he attributed to the organization's history (or symbolic), as the biggest issue. A third identified senior leadership buy-in (or political) as the most important. While there may be some truth in each of these depictions, imagine the downstream effect when managers are not aligned in how they perceive and use these frames! Without this alignment, team members across the organization could hear inconsistent or even conflicting explanations for the same initiative. This can lead to confusion about priorities, uneven levels of commitment, and competing interpretations of what success looks like. Over time, these inconsistencies can erode trust in leadership, slow the pace of implementation, and cause well-intentioned efforts to work at cross-purposes. In the worst cases, employees may disengage altogether, believing that the organization lacks clarity or cohesion in its decision-making and communication.

Practical Ways to Make Sense of the Four Frames

The exercise we just described highlights both the power and the challenge of using multiple frames to better understand these diverse dynamics. Each interpretation reveals something important. As a leader, the goal isn't to eliminate differences in perspective but to surface them, understand them, and use them to inform a more holistic approach to change. Here are some practical steps for building upon the varied responses across frames:

- **Acknowledge differences.** Begin by acknowledging that diverse interpretations are not only expected but beneficial.
- **Look for patterns and tensions.** Are several team members pointing to political concerns (e.g., buy-in, power dynamics)? Other concerns based on the frames? These patterns can surface unspoken risks or opportunities that might otherwise go unnoticed.
- **Bridge the Four Frames.** Guide the team to explore how insights from one frame might affect the others. For example, if the human resources frame reveals a professional development gap, how might that affect structural readiness?
- **Align on priorities, not uniformity.** The goal isn't to get everyone to agree on a single interpretation. Instead, help the group identify shared priorities that cut across frames.
- **Translate insights into action.** Finally, synthesize the insights into a shared narrative of understanding and action.

Engagement of a Problem-Solving Method

Another strategy that many teams find refreshing is to use Bolman and Deal's Four Frames as a problem-solving tool. Teams can be invited to analyze a current challenge or opportunity from all four perspectives: structural, human resources, political, and symbolic. But if you're really daring, try asking the team to first identify its *least-used frame* or the two frames they *default to most often*. Then, challenge them to approach the issue using the neglected frame(s). For example, a team struggling with inconsistent cross-department collaboration initially focused on structural fixes, clarifying roles, redefining workflows, and implementing new software tools. When prompted to use their least preferred frame, the symbolic frame, the team realized that what was truly missing was a shared story or sense of purpose. They created a simple narrative that emphasized "one team, one mission," celebrating small wins and shared values across departments. This symbolic shift, paired with earlier structural adjustments, dramatically improved engagement and cooperation. This kind of frame-switching often leads to creative solutions that would have otherwise been overlooked. It invites teams to step outside their habitual lens, uncover hidden agendas, and design more well-rounded, adaptive responses to complex challenges.

4.5 PRINCIPLE 2. ASSESS WITH ENGAGEMENT

4.5.1 Begin with Team Development

Organizational change is inherently complex, bringing with it uncertainty, shifting priorities, and emotional intensity. During these transitions, teams face the dual challenge of delivering results while adapting to new ways of working, communicating, and collaborating. To navigate these challenges effectively, leaders must focus on both team dynamics and levels of participation. Assessment can support team dynamics, the patterns of interaction, and communication. Participation focuses on developing the trust that shapes how a team functions, ensuring that all voices are heard and team members are actively engaged in decisions. These two elements work together: strong team dynamics create the foundation for collaboration, while participation activates that foundation to drive learning, inclusion, and innovation. Together, they are essential to building resilient, high-performing teams that can thrive through change.

4.5.2 Assessment Myths

Myths about team assessments often prevent leaders from fully leveraging their benefits. Assessments can be very powerful vehicles for discussion, learning, and action; however, when we do receive resistance, it usually comes from one of the common misconceptions about assessments.

In our consulting and leadership work, we have discovered that teams spend very little time assessing their own team dynamics. In fact, in working with hundreds of teams, it's a ratio of approximately 10 to 1: for every ten teams, only one will consider assessing their team's dynamics. Why? One reason may be that there are many team myths regarding assessment that may be hard to overcome. Let's explore some of these common myths in Table 4.3.

TABLE 4.3

False Myths about Team Assessments and Their Associated Truths

False Myths	Truths
Team assessments are so complex that you leave with not understanding anything regarding the team.	Team assessments don't have to be complex when they focus on collective behaviors, communication patterns, and shared goals, offering a more comprehensive understanding of the team.

TABLE 4.3 *(Continued)*

False Myths about Team Assessments and Their Associated Truths

False Myths	Truths
Assessments only provide static snapshots that do not reflect the evolving nature of teams during change.	Assessments can be iterative and adapted to track progress over time.
Team assessments are only necessary when issues arise.	Team assessments that proactively assess challenges *and* opportunities can uncover potential challenges early, identify strengths, and build alignment before problems escalate.
Team assessments might erode trust if they expose interpersonal tensions.	When conducted transparently and framed as opportunities for growth, assessments can strengthen trust by fostering open communication and shared understanding—and especially when facilitated by a team development professional.

4.5.3 Introducing Three Key Team Assessment Methods

Now that we have established the importance of team assessment, let's delve into this further. In our experiences working with teams, we've identified three main types of assessment methods that effectively address different team needs. Depending on the team's specific context, they may choose to focus on one method or combine two or even all three.

- **Low-Lift Assessment Methods.** Simple, flexible tools that leaders or teams can quickly design and implement, sometimes even on the spot, to assess how things are going.
- **Grab-and-Go Assessment Frameworks.** Research-based models that teams can easily adapt to fit their specific needs. These provide structure without being overly complex.
- **Comprehensive Assessment Packages.** Formal survey-based tools, sometimes available for purchase or at no cost online, that provide in-depth insights and highlight key areas for improvement.

4.5.4 Low-Lift Assessment Methods

There are countless ways to assess a team's dynamics, but don't let this overwhelm you. We're keeping it simple. The goal isn't to chase perfection; it's to gather meaningful insights that lead to better conversations, smarter decisions, and real action. A good assessment should be ongoing, multi-sourced, and most importantly useful. And while surveys and performance metrics are helpful, some of the richest insights come from more qualitative methods: tools that focus on stories, observations, and experiences rather than numbers. Think open-ended feedback, team dialogue, and plain old observation.

Here are five easy-to-use, high-impact tools leaders can use to kickstart the assessment process. No PhD required!

Quick Pulse Surveys. Think of these as the espresso shots of assessment: short, strong, and energizing. A few anonymous questions about trust, communication, collaboration, and morale can go a long way.

Example: One team used a monthly three-question pulse ("What's one thing we're doing well?" "What's one thing getting in our way?" "How supported do you feel this week?"). The answers helped the team identify a growing workload issue early, before burnout hit.

Stakeholder Conversations. Want the truth? Ask someone *outside* the team. Peer teams, supervisors, or internal clients often see what insiders miss. These conversations can reveal misalignments or highlight quiet wins.

Example: A team thought they were doing fine until a supervisor from another unit remarked, "You're great . . . but we never know what you're working on." This insight led to a quick improvement in communication and visibility—with zero added work.

Observational Checklists. Mike often adds observations about who is speaking up and who is silent to the team checklist. Or who's checked out? How are disagreements handled? This real-time lens provides a candid view of how the team truly operates.

Example: Some items we have used in our observational checklist are: Who is speaking most? Who is consistently interrupting? Who is not speaking up? Who acknowledges what others have said, etc.?

Team Reflection Exercises. After a major meeting, project, or even a tough day, pause for a "micro-retrospective." Ask: What worked? What didn't? What should we try next time? These ten-minute reflections build learning loops without derailing the day.

Example: After a chaotic product launch, one team held a quick collective reflection. From the feedback he received on what worked and what didn't, the team leader quickly realized they'd skipped key stakeholder input. The fix? A follow-up with key stakeholders that they now use before every major milestone.

Self-Designed Team Development Models. Instead of handing the team a textbook model, let them define their own. Have them describe three imagined teams: one just forming, one in the messy middle, and one high-performing and admired across the company. Then ask: Where are we now? What does success look like? What's one step we can take to get closer?

> **Example:** A team realized their ideal high-performing version included more peer coaching. Within a month, they piloted "learning partners": peer pairings designed to encourage regular reflection, feedback, and mutual support, and found their skills and morale rising together.

These tools are low-cost, low-barrier, and high-value. They ease your team into assessment without triggering eye rolls or anxiety. Table 4.4 provides more guidance on what each tool is best for and when to use it.

TABLE 4.4

Summary of Five Low-Lift Techniques and When to Use These

Technique	Focus	Best for	When to Use It
Quick Pulse Survey	Capture quick insights on morale, trust, and team health.	Teams needing regular temperature checks	Weekly or monthly check-ins to monitor team health
Stakeholder Conversation	Gather external feedback to uncover blind spots.	Teams seeking broader perspective or validation	During or after meetings to assess participation and engagement patterns
Observational Checklist	Gauge the level of engagement across all team members.	Teams where only some voices are present	During team meetings, problem-solving, or decision-making
Team Reflection	Create learning loops through short, structured reflection.	Teams building habits of continuous improvement	After key meetings, milestones, or challenging events
Self-Designed Team Development Model	Engage the team in defining their own developmental path.	Teams open to co-creating their vision for team effectiveness	During offsites, retreats, or structured team development sessions

4.5.5 Grab-and-Go: Off-the-Shelf Assessment Frameworks

If your team is ready for a deeper dive, consider using an established team development model to guide your assessment. These models offer structured insights into how teams form, function, and flourish, and they can help team members self-reflect, spot growth opportunities, and align on how to move forward. A few easy-to-use options include:

- **Tuckman's Stages of Development.**[9] Addresses team growth in stages: forming, storming, norming, performing (and sometimes adjourning).
- **Lencioni's Five Dysfunctions of a Team.**[10] Focuses on common challenges that derail teams, such as lack of trust or fear of conflict.
- **Hackman's Model of Team Effectiveness.**[11] Emphasizes conditions that enable team success, including structure, purpose, and support.

Any of these can be useful, depending on your team's goals and experiences. For example, while the Tuckman model is sometimes seen as overly simple, it's a great fit for teams newer to self-assessment. On the other hand, Lencioni's model may resonate with teams navigating interpersonal dynamics or struggling with accountability. We encourage you to explore these models in more depth to determine which one is the best fit for your team. For example, Mike asked an AI platform to help him understand what model would be best for a new team. Table 4.5 summarizes engagement of three team development models based on AI support.

TABLE 4.5

When to Use Three Team Development Models Based on aI Support

Model	Focus	Best For	When to Use It
Tuckman's Stages of Development	Stages of team formation and growth	New teams or teams going through major changes	When teams are forming, reforming, or need to understand normal development patterns
Lencioni's Five Dysfunctions	Identifying and addressing barriers to team effectiveness	Teams struggling with trust, conflict, or accountability	When interpersonal dynamics are the primary barrier to performance
Hackman's Team Effectiveness	Conditions that support team performance	Established teams wanting to evaluate or improve their overall effectiveness	When you want to assess team conditions and long-term effectiveness

4.5.6 A Simple Team Development Assessment Activity

To get started on any of these models or others, try this simple develop-ment assessment activity identified in Table 4.6.

TABLE 4.6

Suggested Activities to Engage the Team Development Models Just Introduced

1. **Introduce the Model (two minutes).** Provide a quick overview of the chosen model. Keep it high-level—just enough for everyone to understand the core idea and stages/areas it covers.
2. **Silent Reflection (two to three minutes).** Ask each team member to reflect on two questions:
   * *Which stage do you think best represents where we are now?*
   * *What behaviors, dynamics, or examples make you think that?*
3. **Quick Anonymous Vote (optional).** Invite team members to privately jot down their responses on a Post-it Note™ or digital poll. Tally the responses and show the results visually; this can uncover patterns or surprising variation.
4. **Group Discussion (five to seven minutes).** Facilitate a short discussion with questions like:
   * *Where do we agree? Where do we see it differently?*
   * *What might be helping or holding us back from progressing?*
   * *What behaviors would signal that we're growing as a team?*
5. **Wrap-up (two minutes).** Ask: *What's one small thing we can do this week to move forward as a team?* Capture a few shared actions or insights to revisit later.

To get the most value from this kind of exercise, consider bringing in an outside facilitator, like a team coach, consultant, or even an experienced peer from another team. A neutral third party can guide the conversation, surface dynamics more easily, and keep things constructive. No model is perfect, but each one can offer a shared language to talk about what often goes unspoken in teams. Combine the structure of a model with the flexibility of open dis-cussion, and you've got a recipe for insight and momentum. And again, don't forget AI! In Table 4.7, there are some prompts that might help you deter-mine which model to use, what other models to consider, as well as the pros and cons of each one. Once you've tried a prompt, ask AI what additional information would be useful in selecting or implementing a particular model given your own specific context.

TABLE 4.7

Sample AI Prompts for Team Development Model Selection

---

1. "We're a mid-sized team working in a hybrid environment and trying to improve communication and accountability. What team development model would be best to help assess where my team is in its development process?"
2. "I'm leading a newly formed cross-functional team. We're still figuring out roles and responsibilities. Which team development model would help us assess our current stage and guide our growth?"
3. "My team has been together for over a year, but we're struggling with trust and decision-making. Can you recommend a team development model that can help diagnose where we are and what to focus on?"
4. "Which off-the-shelf team development models can I use to help a remote team reflect on their collaboration and engagement levels?"
5. "We're going through organizational change, and I want to assess how my team is functioning under pressure. What model can help me understand both team dynamics and development needs?"

4.5.7 Comprehensive Assessment Packages

There are hundreds of team assessment tools available online—many free or low-cost. As consultants, we often guide clients in choosing the right one. The good news is that you don't always need a consultant to do this. With the help of AI, you can explore options yourself; it can be surprisingly easy and even fun. For example, Mitch recently worked with a client who wanted a user-friendly, validated assessment tool with strong reviews, priced under US$100 per participant. The client simply asked AI, *What is a team assessment survey that is easy to use, validated, and under US$100 per participant?*

Beyond recommending assessment tools, AI can further help you apply them to your own team and synthesize findings into a comprehensive report. Curious what would happen if we applied one to Team Alpha? Let's take a look!

> *Role: Act as a change consultant and expert on team development. Question: Apply Lencioni's Five Dysfunctions framework to identify key dysfunctions in team Alpha's dynamic and suggest potential team development practices to remedy them. Format: Summarize your answer in a table format.*

You may get a response like the one shown in Table 4.8 after attaching a description of Team Alpha.

If you're exploring validated assessments, consider a few key factors or ask AI to help you find the best fit based on your team's situation or focus area:

TABLE 4.8

Identification of What AI May Produce with a Prompt to Apply to Team Alpha, Using Lencioni's Five Dysfunctions Model

Dysfunction	Symptoms in Team Alpha	Remedial Practices
Absence of Trust	Hesitancy to share concerns	Team building, leader vulnerability
Fear of Conflict	Limited debate, stifled feedback	Ground rules for debate, structured conflict
Lack of Commitment	Decisions without buy-in	Inclusive discussions, explicit agreement
Avoidance of Accountability	Siloed work, no shared ownership	Clear expectations, regular retrospectives
Inattention to Results	Focus on tasks, not outcomes	Clear team goals, celebrate/learn from results

1. **Purpose.** What specific team dynamics or behaviors are you hoping to assess—trust, communication, roles, or decision-making?
2. **Evidence based.** Look for tools that have been tested for reliability and validity across different teams or organizations.
3. **Ease of use and reporting.** Choose an assessment that provides clear, actionable reports without requiring specialized training to interpret.
4. **Cost and scalability.** Ensure that the tool fits your budget and can scale for larger teams if needed.
5. **Expected outcomes**. Choose a well-chosen assessment that includes:
   - A clearer picture of team strengths and gaps
   - A shared language for discussing team dynamics
   - Concrete next steps for improvement
   - Increased awareness and buy-in across the team

When used effectively, a validated tool can spark meaningful dialogue, align team efforts, and accelerate growth.

4.6 PRINCIPLE 3. EMBRACE SYSTEMS THINKING

4.6.1 Systems Thinking: A Practical Approach to Navigating Team Change

Organizations are complex systems, much like teams. Every decision, action, or relationship influences the whole. That's where systems thinking comes in. A systems mindset helps teams see how different parts connect rather than focusing on isolated problems. This perspective is especially important during organizational change. Change never happens in isolation; when one part of an organization shifts, the effects ripple across teams, sometimes in expected ways but often with unintended consequences. Teams are at the center of these shifts, and how they adapt can determine whether a change effort succeeds or stalls.

Shifting priorities may create confusion, as what mattered yesterday may no longer be the focus today. Conflicting goals often emerge when teams interpret change differently, leading to misalignment. At the same time, interdependence between teams increases; decisions made in one area now have a greater impact elsewhere. Without a clear understanding of these connections, small changes can lead to larger, unforeseen challenges. For over two decades, we've applied systems thinking principles to help organizations navigate change. We've found that teams function more effectively when they recognize how interconnected they are and use systems thinking to guide their approach. Rather than reacting to problems as they arise, teams that embrace systems thinking identify patterns and recognize that cause-and-effect relationships are rarely linear. They understand that multiple interconnected factors and feedback loops can obscure direct links, making these relationships complex.

There are simple ways teams can begin building a systems mindset. One is to regularly ask, *Who else is affected by this decision, and how?* Another is to map out how changes in their team's work could create downstream effects for others. Visually sketching these links can make connections more tangible. This deeper insight enables teams to anticipate unintended consequences and address systemic challenges proactively. It also helps them adapt quickly, collaborate across functions, and make decisions that address root causes rather than just symptoms.

4.6.2 The Keys to Systems Thinking for Teams

Think of your team as part of a bigger puzzle. Each piece connects, and when one piece is out of place, it affects the whole picture. Systems thinking helps teams recognize these connections and work together more effectively, especially during change. Here are three keys that teams can use to unlock a systems perspective:

1. **Everything is connected (interconnectedness).** No team works in isolation. What happens in one department influences others. If your team struggles with a process or deadline, it can ripple across the company. Just like in a relay race, each handoff matters—when one runner stumbles, the whole team feels the impact.

2. **The whole is greater than the sum of its parts (Emergence).** Have you ever been part of a brainstorming session where one idea sparks another, and suddenly the team comes up with a breakthrough? That's emergence in action. For example, during a product design meeting, one engineer suggested a minor change to reduce packaging waste. This sparked a marketer's idea to rebrand the product as eco-friendly, which then led a supply chain manager to propose a partnership with a sustainable materials vendor. None of these ideas would have surfaced in isolation, but together, they created a breakthrough product strategy. When teams collaborate effectively, they can solve problems and innovate in ways no single person could on their own. Encouraging open dialogue and diverse perspectives unlocks new possibilities.

3. **Small actions can have big consequences (nonlinearity).** In teams, little things may make a huge difference. A small act of recognition from a leader can boost morale more than a major policy change. At the same time, large initiatives can fall flat if they don't resonate with the team. This is why understanding how change affects people—beyond just processes—is crucial for success.

A fascinating research study with 64 software development teams conducted by Faraj and Yan provides a view of the interconnectedness of systems thinking with teams. In a nutshell, these researchers identified three types of team activities:[12]

- Boundary spanning
- Boundary buffering
- Boundary reinforcement

What we appreciate about this research is that it provides new perspectives that many teams don't acknowledge. Let's take a closer look. Boundary spanning identifies the importance of reaching out beyond one's own team—often building alliances and coalitions. In contrast to boundary spanning, which is a strategy of engagement, boundary buffering is a method of disengagement to protect the team from uncertainties and disturbances from outside the team. And boundary reinforcement focuses on factors internal to the team, such as maintaining their identity and solidifying weakened boundaries. Here's an activity that's simple and robust based on this boundary framework. Mitch has shared either the essence or the full article with teams (with permission from the publisher). And he has asked them this simple question: "What insights about these three boundary activities might be applied to your team?" First, elements of surprise surface regarding two of the boundary actions: spanning and buffering. Often not giving it much thought. Second, they start identifying the relevance of applying some of this boundary work to their own team. Systems thinking at its finest!

Fixing Performance Review Inconsistencies

At a large publishing company, the finance leader approached the HR team with a challenge: performance ratings were inconsistent across the organization. Some lower-performing units were receiving disproportionate merit increases, creating fairness concerns and budget strains. A project team was put in place to come up with recommendations, with the assistance of our consulting services. Instead of simply issuing new grading guidelines, the project team used system decision mapping to analyze how performance ratings were determined across departments. A systems decision map is, in essence, a process map that focuses on the decisions affecting an outcome. In this case, individual departments and the decisions they made on merit increases for their employees.

Each department was asked to identify a decision in their process, the inputs used, and any associated assumptions on which the decision was based. The project team, made up of managers and individual contributors, mapped out the entire process using this approach, uncovering inconsistencies in how decisions were made. For example, in some departments, all the merit decisions were made by the department head, in others by the supervisors, and in a few by a mixture of both. There was significant variation in what criteria were considered for merit-based increases and the philosophies of the department on how to manage the merit budget. By the end of the exercise, the team realized that not only was there variation in approach, philosophy, inputs, and assumptions between departments on the merit decisions, but those same dynamics also existed in the decisions associated with performance ratings, the prime input for merit increases. Once the map was completed and insights generated, the team could begin to generate practical solutions that improved fairness and consistency in merit allocations. The key to success? Participatory problem-solving, where cross-functional individuals worked together to understand the system and make informed recommendations. Figure 4.2 shows the resulting decision map.

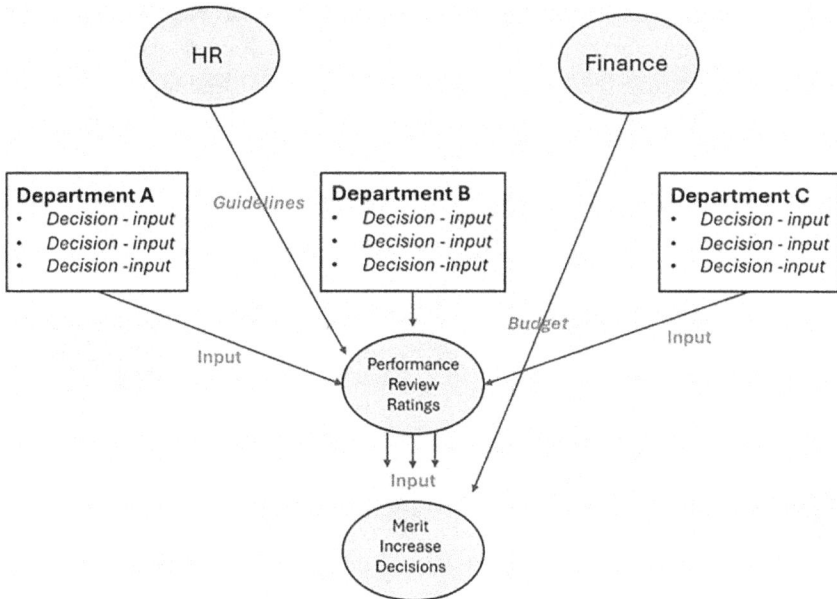

FIGURE 4.2
A depiction of the systems decision map used to improve the merit process.

Practical Systems Thinking Strategies for Teams

Here are three practical ways teams can apply systems thinking during change.

Use ideation teams to identify patterns. Too often, teams focus on fixing individual issues rather than looking at the bigger picture. Instead, create "ideation teams," small groups tasked with identifying patterns across the organization rather than just reacting to isolated events. For example, imagine a customer service team at a software company who noticed a spike in customer complaints about response times. Instead of simply adding more agents, an ideation team could analyze support tickets, customer feedback, and workflow data.

This might uncover that a new internal approval process was causing delays. One technique we like to use with ideation teams is something called the "Five Whys." Have the team examining their problem ask, "Why is this happening?" five times to uncover root causes rather than symptoms.

Implement feedback loops that lead to action. Feedback loops are essential in systems thinking because they allow teams to witness their impact and adjust in real time. But feedback is only valuable if it's used effectively. A feedback loop is a process where the outcomes of a system's actions are fed back into the system itself, influencing future decisions, behaviors, or performance, either reinforcing (positive feedback) or balancing (negative feedback) the system over time. Figure 4.3 provides a simple visual that depicts a feedback loop.

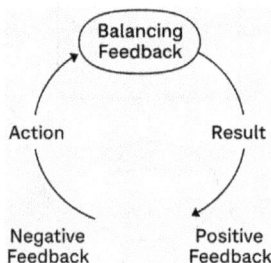

FIGURE 4.3
Depiction of a simple feedback loop.

Consider this hypothetical example. A marketing team at a retail company wanted to improve collaboration with the sales team. They introduced a biweekly feedback loop where sales provided input on how marketing materials were performing in the field. Marketing then adjusted messaging based on these real-world insights, leading to an increase in customer engagement. We recommend the following:

- **Make it frequent and easy to implement.** A quick five-minute team huddle or a pulse survey works better than a once-a-year review.
- **Ensure two-way communication.** Feedback should not just be collected but acted upon. Teams should openly discuss results and next steps.
- **Close the communication loop.** If changes are made based on feedback, let the team know what changed and why. This reinforces the value of participation.

Causal loop diagrams help teams visualize how different factors influence each other over time. By mapping these cause-and-effect relationships, teams can uncover unintended consequences, reinforcing cycles, and points of leverage for change. For example, a hospital team used a causal loop diagram to understand why staff burnout was increasing despite new wellness initiatives. They discovered a reinforcing loop: understaffing led to longer shifts, which increased stress and absenteeism, further worsening the staffing issue. Mapping this cycle helped leadership identify targeted interventions, like adjusting shift rotations and hiring temporary support. Figure 4.4 shows a causal loop diagram illustrating the relationships between change activity in an organization, leadership training on change, perceived threat, and resistance by employees. The (+) sign designates a positive relationship between the factors, meaning that when one increases, the other factor increases. As the level of change increases, so does the amount of training. The (–) signals a negative relationship, meaning when one factor increases, the other decreases. Notice that as resistance increases, the amount of change in this particular organization decreases. Finally, a loop may be a reinforcing loop (R), meaning that the loop reinforces itself. Here the amount of change results in more training. The second type of loop is a balancing loop (B). A balancing loop acts as a counterchange with behavior that counters or balances the factors. In the balancing loop, the amount of change results in perceived threat and ultimately resistance that limits the change activity.

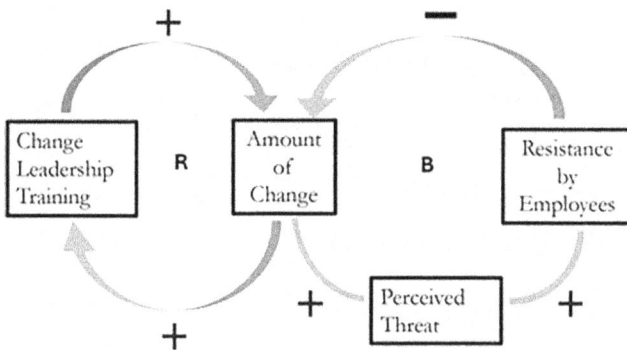

FIGURE 4.4
A causal loop diagram showing positive and negative relationships and reinforcing and balancing loops.

To facilitate this technique with a team, the team leader could follow the following steps:

1. Identify a challenge (e.g., employee burnout).
2. List key factors influencing the problem (e.g., workload, team morale, productivity).
3. Draw arrows to show how one factor affects another.
4. Identify reinforcing loops (positive or negative cycles).
5. Use insights to adjust policies or interventions.

By using these tools, teams can see beyond surface-level problems and make more informed, lasting decisions for the organization during change. Teams that apply systems thinking don't just react to change; they understand it, shape it, and drive sustainable solutions. Curious how Team Alpha could have benefited from these tools? Gilles created the following prompt to get you started:

> *Role: Act as a human resource specialist. Context: Team Alpha recently recognized that a number of its team members suffered from burnout. Some of the factors included a very ambitious product redesign, imbalanced risk-reward analysis in decision making, and an underdeveloped team with participation during meetings dominated by a few senior people. Question: Generate a causal loop diagram describing the employee burnout negative cycle and propose interventions to address root causes and end the cycle. Format: Use icons and arrows to depict the diagram.*

Try different variations and have fun with it!

4.7 PRINCIPLE 4. TARGET RESULTS *AND* OUTCOMES

4.7.1 Using Evidence-Based Approaches to Facilitate Desired Outcomes

In times of change, teams are under pressure to act quickly, make decisions amidst ambiguity, and deliver visible results. But without a clear focus on *outcomes*—the meaningful shifts in behavior, capability, or performance that change efforts aim to achieve—teams risk confusing activity with progress. This is where evidence-based approaches become essential. Grounded in credible data, research, and shared experience, they help teams cut through the noise, align on what matters most, and stay anchored in purpose rather than just motion.

Even in stable environments, integrating evidence into team decision-making can be a challenge. It requires interpretation, dialogue, and the courage to question assumptions. During change, it becomes even harder. Competing priorities, shifting agendas, and the uncertainty of transitions can easily cloud judgment. Yet it's precisely in these moments that evidence-based practices offer the greatest value, ensuring that decisions are guided by insight, not impulse.

Consider the difference between results and outcomes in teams. A team may successfully launch a new performance feedback system. That's a result. However, if that system doesn't lead to more honest conversations, increased trust, or improved employee development—the intended outcomes—then the effort hasn't delivered real value. Evidence-based approaches help teams define success in meaningful terms, identify the signals that matter, and course-correct when needed. The goal of a focus on outcomes, not just results, is to make sure what gets done truly makes a difference.

We'd like to demonstrate the significance of understanding the difference in results and outcomes with a type of team we have not yet discussed in this book: the board of directors. Many profit and non-profit organizations have one. Unfortunately, little is often done to build this team, as well as understand how they power up differences in results and outcomes. So, let's take a closer look by examining a research study by Sydney Finkelstein and Ann Mooney.[13] Here's the gist of their study. They discovered that boards need to focus more on "process" than they typically do. In this context, process means knowing how to work together as a team, understanding the power of addressing decisions comprehensively, and identifying ways to deal with destructive conflict. Before you respond with a nod and say to yourself "Well yes. This makes total sense", we'd like to present you with the reality. In the dozens of projects Mitch has done with boards, rarely has any board member or representative told him, "We need ways to build our team." Instead, he initially hears requests for helping them plan strategically or identifying ways to address their competition. Yet, if you want the board to produce a better outcome in achieving the organization's strategic vision, you first need to address whether conflict management among board members is a barrier to achieving this vision. How many boards have realized this, let alone asked for help with this? Very few!

For anyone who is helping boards plan strategically, a first step may be to frame the intervention by sharing the results of this research. A follow-up step would be to identify ways to support the board in achieving their desired outcomes by first focusing on improving their team cohesion. Team results breed productive outcomes!

4.7.2 Using Lessons from the Research Process as a Guide

In our practice, when working with teams, we rely on some of the same principles used in the sound research process. Although we don't expect organizations to invest in the rigor typically required for scholarly work, the methods used in this type of research can be instructional for understanding evidence-based inquiry. When teams use evidence to make decisions, they must ensure that the evidence is:

- Reliable
- Relevant
- Interpreted effectively.

Think of evidence like the baton in a relay race; using a poorly designed or ill-fitting baton can disrupt the team, regardless of how skilled the runners are. Reliability ensures that the evidence comes from a credible and consistent source, just as a team trusts a securely gripped baton over one that is slippery or likely to break mid-race. Relevance ensures that the evidence aligns with the specific challenge at hand; using strategies developed for sprinting might not translate well to long-distance relay races, just as a precise handoff is crucial for success in a relay but unnecessary in a solo sprint. Finally, effective interpretation requires careful consideration of context and potential biases. Two teams may receive the same baton, but based on their different strategies, training, or understanding of the track conditions, they may choose different approaches for how to carry and pass the baton on their way to the finish line. Without these safeguards, evidence can become a misleading anchor, reinforcing pre-existing beliefs rather than guiding teams toward well-informed decisions. In Table 4.9, we have identified a checklist of questions to ask when evaluating evidence using the three requirements of reliability, relevance, and interpretation. You can use AI to supplement these questions by asking it to search for relevant sources of evidence, asking if the evidence you do have relates to your specific problem, or asking if your

TABLE 4.9

Reflective Questions for Three Evidence Requirements

Requirement	Questions to Ask
Reliable Evidence Is the evidence trustworthy?	• **Where did this information come from?** Is it from a well-known and trusted source, like a respected expert, organization, or multiple reliable reports? • **Do other trusted sources say the same thing?** If you checked elsewhere, would you find similar conclusions? • **Is it up to date?** Does this information still apply, or could things have changed since it was collected?
Relevant Evidence Is the evidence applicable to the problem?	• **Does this information actually relate to our problem?** Or is it about something different? • **Is it meant for people like us?** Does it apply to our industry, team size, or type of challenge?
Effective Interpretation Are we making sense of the evidence correctly?	• **Are we just looking for what we want to discover?** Are we open to evidence that challenges our assumptions? • **Could there be another explanation?** Are we considering different ways to understand this information? • **Does this demonstrate cause and effect?** Or is it just showing that two things happened at the same time?

evidence is consistent with best practices, or if there are other explanations or practices you should consider.

4.7.3 The "What If" Checklist

As the Head of HR, one of Mike's key responsibilities was overseeing his company's annual employee survey: a massive initiative designed to capture the pulse of our workforce. Each year, his team would pour over hundreds of survey responses, searching for insights to guide organizational initiatives. On the surface, it seemed like a straightforward process: identify trends, spot gaps, and propose interventions to improve engagement, retention, and overall workplace satisfaction. But over time, they noticed a troubling pattern. Despite their best efforts, many of the initiatives launched didn't yield the results they had hoped for. Projects meant to address low morale fell flat, communication workshops didn't resolve the root causes of misunderstandings, and costly training programs showed minimal impact. The culprit? Flawed evidence.

Their survey data, while extensive, were riddled with blind spots. Was it trustworthy? Not always. Response rates were often too low to be considered representative, and the loudest voices (whether positive or negative) tended to dominate the narrative. Did it tell the full story? No. They rarely cross-checked their survey findings with exit interviews, performance data, or focus groups. Instead, they leaned heavily on single data points, treating them as absolute truths rather than pieces of a bigger picture. One year, for example, the survey results suggested that employees felt a significant lack of recognition from their managers. At first glance, the evidence seemed clear. In response, the team rolled out an expensive, companywide recognition program. Plaques, gift cards, and quarterly awards became the norm. Yet, a follow-up analysis revealed something they had missed entirely: were they asking the right question? No. The issue wasn't a lack of formal recognition but rather inconsistent day-to-day feedback from managers, a problem that their survey question hadn't even captured. They had taken the data at face value, without questioning its relevance to the real problem. This experience became a turning point for Mike. It highlighted the critical importance of evaluating evidence systematically, ensuring that it is credible, representative, and viewed through multiple lenses. Over time, his team adopted defined strategies for assessing evidence, such as:

- **Checking where the information came from.** Were our data truly reflective of the full workforce, or just the most vocal groups?
- **Looking for patterns instead of isolated insights.** Were we seeing the same themes in exit interviews and performance reviews?
- **Asking for different perspectives to challenge our assumptions.** Were managers and employees aligned in their perceptions of recognition?
- **Making sure the data actually apply to our decisions.** Were we solving the right problem, or just reacting to surface-level feedback?

The lesson was clear: poor evidence leads to poor decisions, no matter how well-intentioned the intervention. And as leaders, it's our responsibility to approach evidence not as an absolute, but as a puzzle, one that requires multiple pieces to form a complete picture.

4.7.4 The Bias and Complexity Trap

One of the biggest threats to effective team participation when evaluating evidence is bias. Teams should discuss and integrate *bias mitigation strategies* to improve the ability to interpret evidence. Awareness of cognitive biases like confirmation bias or recency bias can help individuals examine evidence more holistically. Structured decision-making processes and the participatory practice itself are also effective mitigation strategies. In Table 4.10, we have provided some common biases to consider when interpreting evidence.

TABLE 4.10

Common Bias Traps That Teams Need to Consider When Interpreting Evidence for Decisions or Solving Problems

Bias Type	Description	Example	One Way to Address
Confirmation Bias	The tendency to seek out, interpret, and remember information in a way that confirms preexisting beliefs while ignoring contradictory evidence.	A leadership team believes remote work decreases productivity. When reviewing survey data, they focus only on negative comments about remote work while dismissing positive feedback that suggests employees are more productive.	Actively look for information that challenges your assumptions rather than only what supports them.
Availability Bias	The tendency to rely on information that is easiest to obtain rather than seeking a full, objective view of the data.	If a team leader recently dealt with a high-profile employee burnout case, they might assume burnout is a companywide crisis, despite broader data showing that most employees report high engagement.	Rely on comprehensive data and statistics rather than recent examples.
Anchoring Bias	The tendency to rely too heavily on the first piece of information encountered (the "anchor") when making decisions.	If an initial employee survey suggests that pay dissatisfaction is the biggest problem, the team may become fixated on salary issues, even when later evidence shows that career development opportunities are actually the bigger concern.	Encourage independent assessments before finalizing decisions to counterbalance initial anchors.

(Continued)

TABLE 4.10 *(Continued)*

Common Bias Traps That Teams Need to Consider When Interpreting Evidence for Decisions or Solving Problems

Bias Type	Description	Example	One Way to Address
Groupthink	The tendency for teams to value agreement and cohesion so highly that they avoid conflict, suppress dissenting views, and overlook alternative solutions.	If a majority of a team believes a new training program is effective, dissenting voices may hesitate to challenge the conclusion, even if the data suggest otherwise.	Invite different viewpoints and create an environment where dissent is welcomed.

There are so many other biases that can affect decision-making and problem-solving on teams. We encourage teams to use the following well-researched practices to mitigate these biases.

1. **Encourage diverse perspectives** to challenge assumptions.
2. **Cross-check multiple data sources** before making decisions.
3. **Assign a "counter point advocate"** in discussions to question dominant views.
4. **Pause before acting** to ensure that decisions are based on a comprehensive, unbiased set of evidence.

Complexity can also be a barrier to evaluating evidence. Often, evidence in the form of a conclusion or interpretation of something occurs over time and can get distorted. When the evidence being considered has multiple aspects, it helps to "chunk" it and examine each aspect separately before considering the whole. We use a practice borrowed from good research, where we ask team members to break up the evidence into all the aspects they can think of and then evaluate the relevance of each aspect given the current context. Ask the question: "What aspect is most impactful to this situation, or what aspect would have the most influence on this problem or decision?" In addition, we recommend the following to deal with complex evidence:

1. **Assign different lenses to the evidence**. Different team members bring unique perspectives that can reveal hidden insights. For example, we have used role engagement here effectively. You can assign team members different roles, like the analyst who looks at trends and patterns, the skeptic who challenges assumptions, and the end user who considers the impact.
2. **Use outside facilitators or coaches to assist with evidence evaluation.** This can be extremely helpful when the evidence being considered is contentious or when there is the presence of self-interest. Think of the role a mediator plays in resolving disputes.
3. **Prioritize actionable insights**. Not all data are equally useful; focus on what drives action. You can ask, "What pieces of this evidence are most relevant to our objective?" Using a decision matrix can also be helpful. A decision matrix is a structured tool that helps teams evaluate multiple options based on set criteria to make objective, data-driven decisions. It assigns weights to different factors and scores each option, allowing teams to compare choices side by side. It helps teams stay objective, reduce bias, and make complex decisions easier to manage. We have provided a hypothetical example of a decision matrix in Table 4.11.

TABLE 4.11

Example of a Hypothetical Decision-Making Matrix That Has Been Completed

Criteria	Weight (1–5)	Option A Gift Card	Option B Public Awards	Option C Manager Feedback Training
Cost	5	5 (low)	4 (moderate)	3 (higher)
Impact on Morale	4	3	4	5
Ease of Implementation	3	5	3	4
Sustainability	4	2	3	5
Total Score	-	52	50	62 (Best Option)

Step-by-step setup for your decision matrix:

1. Assign a weight to each criterion based on importance. Higher weights indicate more important factors.
2. Rate each option for every criterion using a consistent scale (e.g., 1 to 5, where 1 = Poor and 5 = Excellent).
3. Multiply the rating by the weight for each criterion. For example, if Gift Cards have a Cost rating of 5 and Cost has a weight of 5, then: 5 (rating) × 5 (weight) = 25 points.
4. Repeat for all options across all criteria.
5. Sum up the weighted scores for each option to get a total score. For example, gift cards: Cost = 5 ×5 =25, impact on morale = 3 × 4 =12.
6. Compare total scores.

AI can be your ally in conducting an objective and independent analysis of your data. It can be a particularly useful tool for leaders to analyze complex data retrospectively and understand what went well or went wrong with their teams. Do you think Team Alpha was subject to one of the four types of bias? Gilles asked AI using the following prompt:

> *Role: Act as a team facilitator. Context: Team Alpha completed a Strengths, Weaknesses, Opportunities, and Threats (SWOT) analysis and here are their key findings: #Strength: bold, ambitious vision for a new product; #Weakness: get distracted by external input; #Opportunity: work harder, move faster; #Threat: let decision making slow down the project. Question: First, generate a list of questions to help the team uncover whether they were vulnerable to Confirmation Bias, Availability Bias, Anchoring Bias, or Groupthink Bias. Then, based on the information provided in the context, determine the type of bias most likely affecting the team.*

It looks like Groupthink Bias was likely affecting Team Alpha!

4.7.5 The Power of Evidence-Based Approaches in Organizational Change

In times of organizational change, uncertainty can cloud judgment—not just for leaders but for entire teams. When decisions are driven by instinct, tradition, or the loudest voice in the room, teams risk acting on incomplete or inaccurate information. Evidence-based decision-making gives teams a structured, objective approach that cuts through ambiguity, enabling them to evaluate options collectively and choose actions with the highest likelihood of success.

The strength of this approach depends on the process behind it. Teams must ensure that evidence is reliable, relevant, and interpreted in a way that incorporates multiple perspectives. This shared discipline helps teams avoid common pitfalls, such as confirmation bias or oversimplifying complex challenges. It also fosters transparency, as everyone can see the link between data, reasoning, and the decisions being made.

When teams embrace these principles during change, they do more than just make better decisions—they develop a culture of trust, shared accountability, and continuous learning. These are all critical outcomes. These not only improve their ability to navigate the current change but also strengthens their resilience for the challenges ahead.

4.8 PRINCIPLE 5. SUSTAIN WHAT WORKS

4.8.1 Sustaining High-Performing Teaming during Change

High-performing teams are cultivated through intentional practice, shared learning, and a deep commitment to continuous improvement. These teams thrive not on occasional success but on daily habits that build trust, fuel adaptability, and anchor them through complexity. In changing environments, especially, they stand out as essential drivers of transformation. They can learn faster, adapt more effectively, and help carry the organization forward when others may struggle. Throughout this chapter, we've highlighted the connection between team development and change capacity. That link becomes most evident when we observe high-performing teams in action during periods of disruption. They remain grounded in purpose, maintain cohesion under pressure, and evolve in response to new demands. What sets them apart is how they learn. Research consistently shows that teams engaging in structured learning behaviors such as debriefing after key events, openly discussing mistakes, and reflecting on shared experiences outperform those that do not.[14] Teams with a strong learning culture solve problems more creatively, communicate more openly, and sustain higher levels of engagement. Mike has witnessed the power of this learning culture throughout his career, beginning in the military and continuing in complex organizational settings. The teams where he felt most committed were not necessarily the ones with the fewest problems, but the ones where learning was alive, where feedback was welcomed, growth was visible, and progress was shared. These experiences point to a deeper truth: when learning becomes the norm, performance becomes sustainable.

4.8.2 Continuous Feedback as a Foundation for Growth

In high-performing teams, feedback isn't reserved for formal reviews; it's woven into everyday interactions. These teams use feedback as a continuous loop, helping them recalibrate in real time, strengthen relationships, and stay aligned with evolving goals.[15] It's the difference between noticing a small shift in the wind and adjusting your sails and waking up to find your ship off course. Sustained performance depends on these timely course corrections. Feedback can take many forms: peer insights, stakeholder input, informal conversations, or structured reflections; the most resilient teams embrace all of them. Leaders play a key role in setting the tone by normalizing feedback as a positive, routine part of team life. Whether through quick check-ins, anonymous pulse surveys, or reflection prompts during meetings, feedback must be practical, safe, and actionable. In our work, we've used tools such as team surveys, peer feedback exercises, and leader-facilitated retrospectives to foster open dialogue and continuous improvement.

Here are some simple ways teams can embed feedback into their routines:

- Use a quick, one-question check-in at the end of key meetings (e.g., "What worked well? What needs adjustment?").
- Dedicate five minutes at the end of the week for each member to share one success and one challenge.
- Rotate a "feedback facilitator" role each month to prompt reflection and capture insights. The feedback facilitator's job is to listen for opportunities in the team discussion to ask team members to reflect on their process. The facilitator, for example, might ask the team questions like *What did we do well during that meeting?* or *What would we do differently next time to improve our dialogue?*

Create a team dashboard with rotating feedback indicators. These feedback indicators can vary from month to month. For example, the dashboard might be focused on feedback regarding solution orientation one month and seek feedback on improvement ideas the next month. The idea is to get feedback from peers, clients, or collaborators on a variety of areas. For example, one team displayed weekly feedback scores from client interactions alongside internal ratings of communication and workload balance. Over time, this helped them spot trends and intervene before issues escalated. When feedback becomes a habit, it fuels a cycle of learning that sustains performance long after the initial push for change.

4.8.3 The Pulse Check and the Pulse Survey

Instead of waiting for a crisis to surface concerns, high-performing teams use **pulse checks and pulse surveys** to stay ahead of problems. While the two terms are often confused, they serve different purposes: a **pulse check** offers an immediate, informal read on team sentiment—like taking the room's temperature in real time—whereas a **pulse survey** is a short, structured tool that gathers measurable, often anonymous data over time, making it easier to spot trends and track progress.

Pulse surveys, typically under ten questions, can be deployed monthly or quarterly to assess morale, collaboration, and emerging challenges. Keeping core questions consistent allows teams to track trends, identify shifts, and intervene before small problems escalate. To evaluate the results, look at both the direction and magnitude of changes over time. Use AI and simple data visualization tools, such as line graphs, to identify trends and fluctuations. A sudden dip in scores may signal an urgent issue, while gradual shifts can highlight slow-building tension or disengagement.

Pulse checks, while less formal, can give teams quick insight into shifts in perception caused by recent events and are best used to prompt immediate discussion or small course corrections. Importantly, whether using pulse surveys or pulse checks, teams should discuss the results together to co-interpret the data and co-create next steps. You can even use AI to help you design a pulse check or survey for any team focus area of interest. Table 4.12 provides a sample of a pulse check focused on engagement.

TABLE 4.12

Sample Pulse Check Focused on Engagement

1. "How energized do you feel about our work this week?"
2. "Do you feel clear on our most important priorities right now?"
3. "How connected do you feel to the rest of the team this week?"
4. "How open is the communication within my team this week?"
5. "Do you have what you need to do your best work this week?"

4.8.4 The Pre-Post Survey

Another type of survey that we recommend is a "pre-post survey," typically given at the beginning and at the conclusion of the change process. The pre-post surveys, unlike the pulse, are a more exhaustive survey designed to provide more detail. Table 4.13 represents a basic pre-post survey that can be used to measure the level of collaboration on a team during a change initiative. The "pre" part of the survey engages baseline data; these are then compared after a period of time with the "post" results.

TABLE 4.13

Sample Pre-Post Survey

Thank you in advance for taking the time to complete this survey. The purpose of this assessment is to measure team collaboration before and after the change initiative. Your honest feedback will help us understand how collaboration evolves over time and identify areas for improvement.

- **Pre-Survey:** Complete before the change initiative begins.
- **Post-Survey:** Complete after the change initiative concludes.

Each question should be rated on a **five-point scale:**
  1. **Team members communicate openly with one another.**
     (1—Strongly Disagree, 2—Disagree, 3—Neutral, 4—Agree, 5—Strongly Agree)
  2. **There is a strong sense of trust among team members.**
     (1—Strongly Disagree, 2—Disagree, 3—Neutral, 4—Agree, 5—Strongly Agree)
  3. **Team members actively listen to different perspectives before making decisions.**
     (1—Strongly Disagree, 2—Disagree, 3—Neutral, 4—Agree, 5—Strongly Agree)
  4. **Collaboration across different roles is encouraged.**
     (1—Strongly Disagree, 2—Disagree, 3—Neutral, 4—Agree, 5—Strongly Agree)
  5. **We work effectively as a team to solve problems.**
     (1—Strongly Disagree, 2—Disagree, 3—Neutral, 4—Agree, 5—Strongly Agree)
  6. **Everyone on the team shares information in a timely manner.**
     (1—Strongly Disagree, 2—Disagree, 3—Neutral, 4—Agree, 5—Strongly Agree)
  7. **Team members feel comfortable providing constructive feedback to one another.**
     (1—Strongly Disagree, 2—Disagree, 3—Neutral, 4—Agree, 5—Strongly Agree)
  8. **There is a shared understanding of team goals.**
     (1—Strongly Disagree, 2—Disagree, 3—Neutral, 4—Agree, 5—Strongly Agree)
  9. **I feel that my contributions to the team are valued.**
     (1—Strongly Disagree, 2—Disagree, 3—Neutral, 4—Agree, 5—Strongly Agree)
  10. **I am confident in my team's ability to collaborate effectively during this change initiative.**
     (1—Strongly Disagree, 2—Disagree, 3—Neutral, 4—Agree, 5—Strongly Agree)

The baseline can be supplemented with the pulse survey throughout the change process. To evaluate the results, begin by identifying patterns across key dimensions. Look for high and low scoring areas, as well as inconsistencies between subgroups (e.g., leaders vs. staff). Use averages to get a sense of consensus versus divergence. Visual tools like bar charts or spider graphs can help surface insights quickly. Most importantly, share and discuss the findings with the team to build shared awareness and align on areas for improvement. The goal is not just measurement but also collective reflection and action. For example, Figure 4.5 provides a simple schedule leaders can use to integrate both types of surveys for feedback. The length of the change initiative will influence the interval timing of each survey, but a general rule of thumb is not to have more than two surveys within 30 days. Too many surveys risk exhaustion and degrading of the responses. This figure demonstrates the possible scheduling of pre-post and pulse surveys during a change initiative.

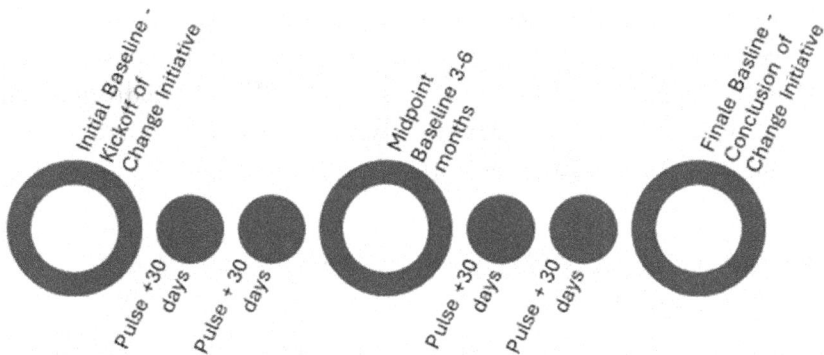

FIGURE 4.5
Demonstration of the possible scheduling of the pre-post and pulse surveys.

4.8.5 Peer Feedback Rounds

When feedback is only top-down, team members may disengage. Peer feedback fosters ownership and accountability. In peer feedback rounds, team members share one strength and one improvement area for each other in a structured, judgment-free setting. Picture a team where feedback is delivered like a friendly coffee-break conversation rather than a tense performance review. For example, once a month, each team member shares one strength and one area for improvement for their peers during a team session. To eliminate any initial awkwardness, we recommend using a team coach to kick things off until the team finds its rhythm. The team coach should be external to the team (either someone outside the team or outside the organization)—someone with basic facilitation skills. It's important that these sessions have some basic rules to keep them supportive. Some basic rules we use when coaching these sessions are as follows:

- Keep feedback constructive, not critical; focus on helping teammates grow.
- Assume positive intent; everyone is working toward the same goal.
- Keep discussions professional, not personal; focus on behaviors and outcomes, not personalities.
- Commit to a structured approach (like start, stop, and continue mentioned earlier in the chapter) or Situation—Behavior—Impact (SBI). This SBI approach uses a description of the situation where the team member would describe the context (situation), what was observed (the behavior), and identify how it affected the team or outcome (impact). Mike used this activity in his coaching practice with individuals and teams. It is effective at separating fact from assumptions and identifying how those assumptions color perception.

4.8.6 Reflection as a Sustainability Mechanism for Continuous Improvement

High-performing teams use structured reflection to assess their actions and make informed adjustments. Research has found that team reflexivity, where teams collectively reflect on their processes and adapt their working methods, leads to better decision-making and overall performance.[16] Teams engaging in regular reflection significantly improve shared mental models, leading to stronger coordination and more effective collaboration.[17] Reflection is such a simple concept, but we're amazed by how few teams actually use it. Imagine a team that doesn't just move from one task to the next but actually takes time to figure out what worked, what didn't, and how to do it better next time. This deliberate process of reflection strengthens team cohesion, enhances adaptability, and ensures that past experiences drive future success. Two basic techniques that we use in all of our work are "personal reflection journals" and the "what if" activity.

Personal Reflection Journals

Personal reflection journals are a great way for team members to examine how they show up on a team and reflect on how they react to other team members' behaviors. We're often asked by leaders or team members we're coaching, "How do I journal in a way that would be useful?" We encourage them to write journal entries at least once a week. At the beginning of the week, they can simply identify their intentions for the week. For example, they might choose one or two things they will do differently, such as "I will show up to my staff meetings five minutes early" or "I will give one piece of feedback to my direct report this week." At the end of the week, they can reflect on how they did against that intention. What prevented progress? What were some positive outcomes? Another way these journals can be helpful is to have each team member keep a weekly journal reflecting on their contributions, challenges faced, and lessons learned. Periodically, they share insights with the team to foster collective learning. This activity will increase trust among team members and foster more open dialogue. We have seen teams' perceptions of inclusion and trust increase as a result of these activities.

"What If?" Reflection Scenarios

Here, during monthly reflection meetings, the team explores "What if?" scenarios (e.g., "What if we don't agree on an approach during this change initiative? Or what if organizational priorities change?) to anticipate and prepare for potential challenges. Table 4.14 provides a set of instructions and some questions that can be used for this activity.

TABLE 4.14

"What If" Scenario Instructions

---

1. **Choose a scenario.** As a team, select a relevant challenge, opportunity, or situation you want to reflect on. This could be related to a recent project, a change initiative, or team dynamics.
2. **Brainstorm "What If" questions.** Think of various *What If* scenarios that could impact the situation. For example, you could ask, "What if we approached this challenge differently?" or "What if we face an unexpected obstacle?
3. **Discuss and document responses.** As a team, explore the possible outcomes, strategies, and actions for each scenario.
4. **Reflect and apply insights.** Identify key takeaways from the discussion and determine actionable steps moving forward.

Trying to learn from the failure of Team Alpha described in the beginning of this chapter, the leadership of HorizonTech decided to sit down with the team and reflect on what they could have done differently. They attached the information in Table 4.2 to their go-to AI assistant and then asked the following:

> *Role: Act as a leadership coach. Question: Based on the attached information about Team Alpha, generate various "What If" scenarios as questions, such as "What if we had approached this challenge differently?", to help the team assess what other strategies they may have taken in tackling this project to improve team performance.*

These questions and follow-up discussions helped Team Alpha understand the gaps in their approach and provided key insights for future projects at HorizonTech, emphasizing the importance of communication, collaboration, and adaptive strategies. As a bonus, the leadership team recognized the value AI could have in helping its teams continuously self-assess and identify gaps early on. As a result, they implemented the concept of an AI coworker on each of their teams who is responsible for facilitating regular evaluation of team development, assessment of team performance through various frames, audit for potential bias in decision-making, and analysis of pulse survey results.

By embedding continuous feedback and reflection into team practices, organizations can sustain high-functioning team behaviors beyond the initial phases of change. Rather than relying on individual leaders or short-term initiatives, a commitment to continuous feedback, participatory engagement, and structured reflection ensures that teams remain agile, aligned, and effective long into the future.

4.9 KEY TAKEAWAYS

4.9.1 The Three Instruments for Change

Teams are a vital link in the change environment because they act as a mechanism for alignment between the organizational level and the individual level. Let's review what we've covered in this chapter about fostering high-performing teams through the three instruments for change.

Self as the Instrument for Change

- **Intentional Participation.** Individuals play a crucial role by actively engaging in team processes, offering diverse perspectives, and contributing to team development.
- **Reflection and Feedback.** Personal commitment to self-assessment and openness to feedback strengthens participatory practices and inclusion within the team.

Team as the Instrument for Change

- **Alignment and Development.** Teams serve as the bridge between individual efforts and organizational strategy, requiring clear alignment between the purpose of the change and actions team members take.
- **Participatory Practice.** Effective teams intentionally monitor and refine how participation occurs; they use feedback loops to enhance decision-making and problem-solving.
- **Capacity Building.** Team development is an ongoing process, with success depending on the team's ability to adapt, collaborate, and leverage the strengths of all members.

Organization as the Instrument for Change

- **Systemic Support.** Organizational context, work culture, and structures shape how teams operate and develop, influencing the adoption and effectiveness of participatory practices.
- **Strategic Alignment.** Organizations must ensure that team efforts align with broader strategic goals and values, providing support and resources for participatory decision-making.
- **Enabling Environment.** The organization's commitment to fostering team development and participatory practice is essential for sustained change, requiring ongoing evaluation of system dynamics and alignment across all levels.

By viewing change through these three interconnected lenses, leaders can ensure that individual contributions, team dynamics, and organizational systems work in concert to drive effective, sustainable transformation.

4.9.2 The Five Principles of Change

To help you reflect on this chapter, we have compiled a list of self-assessment questions and tools mentioned in this chapter for the five change principles in Table 4.15.

TABLE 4.15

Self-Assessment Questions and Tools Related to Participatory Teams

Principles of Change	Self-Assessment Questions	A Highlight of Tools Introduced in This Book to Address These Self-Assessment Questions
Frame the Evidence for Change	How clearly does the team understand the purpose and urgency of the proposed change? Are team goals aligned with the organization's broader strategic vision?	• **Communication Tools.** To engage town halls and visual aids to clarify goals and expectations. • **Surveys.** To assess alignment and address gaps. • **Bolman and Deal's Four Frames.** To clarify challenges/opportunities from multiple lenses—human resource, structural, political, symbolic—so teams comprehensively frame change needs and purpose.
Assess with Engagement	To what extent are diverse team perspectives included in diagnosing challenges? How well does the team assess its readiness to adopt new processes or behaviors?	• **Pulse Surveys/Anonymous Feedback.** To gather honest, wide participation data to reveal how engaged and prepared the team feels for change. • **Tuckman, Lencioni, and Hackman Models.** To help teams self-reflect and benchmark readiness and engagement using established frameworks for team development.
Embrace Systems Thinking	Have we mapped how team priorities interact with other departments or systems? Are the unintended consequences of team decisions proactively addressed?	• **Ideation Teams and "Five Whys."** To surface patterns and root causes across boundaries to reveal interconnected impacts. • **Feedback Loops.** To make impact visible; enable real-time adjustment and organizational learning. • **Causal Loop Diagrams.** To help teams visualize reinforcing/feedback cycles and identify unintended consequences.

TABLE 4.15 *(Continued)*

Self-Assessment Questions and Tools Related to Participatory Teams

Principles of Change	Self-Assessment Questions	A Highlight of Tools Introduced in This Book to Address These Self-Assessment Questions
Target Results *and* Outcomes	Do team goals balance short-term deliverables with long-term capacity building? Are leading indicators (e.g., collaboration quality) tracked alongside lagging results?	• **Evidence Evaluation Checklists.** To ensure data used to set goals and evaluate progress are trustworthy, relevant, and well-interpreted. • **Bias Mitigation Checklists.** To guide teams to counter cognitive biases that can distort outcome focus.
Sustain What Works	What mechanisms ensure the sustained adoption of new team behaviors after an initiative? How regularly does the team evaluate progress and adapt its approach?	• **Pulse Check Surveys.** To track ongoing engagement and flag issues early, supporting sustained behavior change. • **Pre-Post Surveys.** To measure collaboration and impact over time. • **Peer Feedback Rounds, Reflection Journals, "What If?" Scenarios.** To drive continuous learning and adaptation in team routines.

NOTES

1 Hackman, J. R. (1998). Why teams don't work. In *Theory and research on small groups* (pp. 245–267). Springer US. & Hackman, J. R. (2002). *Leading teams: Setting the stage for great performances.* Harvard Business School Publishing Corporation.

2 Garcia, J. (2022, March 29). *Common pitfalls in transformations: A conversation with Jon Garcia.* McKinsey & Company. https://www.mckinsey.com/capabilities/transformation/our-insights/common-pitfalls-in-transformations-a-conversation-with-jon-garcia

3 Higgins, M. C., Weiner, J., & Young, L. (2012). Implementation teams: A new lever for organizational change. *Journal of Organizational Behavior, 33*(3), 366–388.

4 Goodman, E., & Loh, L. (2011). Organizational change: A critical challenge for team effectiveness. *Business Information Review, 28*(4), 242–250.

5 Drexler, A. B., Sibbet, D., & Forrester, R. H. (1988). The team performance model. In R. W. Brendan & K. Jamison (Eds.), *Team building: Blueprints for productivity and satisfaction* (pp. 45–61). NTL Institute for Applied Behavioral Science.

6 Feitosa, J., Grossman, R., Kramer, W. S., & Salas, E. (2020). Measuring team trust: A critical and meta-analytical review. *Journal of Organizational Behavior, 41*(4), 325–348. https://doi.org/10.1002/job.2436

7 Howard, C., Logue, K., Quimby, M., & Schoeneberg, J. (2009). Framing change. *OD Practitioner, 41*(1).

8 Bolman, L. G., & Deal, T. E. (1999, January 1). Four steps to keeping change efforts heading in the right direction. *Journal for Quality and Participation*, 6–11.

9 Tuckman, B. W. (2001). Developmental sequence in small groups. *Group Facilitation*, (3), 66.

10 Lencioni, P. M. (2010). *The five dysfunctions of a team: A leadership fable*. John Wiley & Sons.

11 Cavanaugh, K. J., Logan, J. M., Zajac, S. A., & Holladay, C. L. (2021). Core conditions of team effectiveness: Development of a survey measuring Hackman's framework. *Journal of Interprofessional Care, 35*(6), 914–919.

12 Faraj, S., & Yan, A. (2009). Boundary work in knowledge teams. *Journal of Applied Psychology, 94*(3), 604–617.

13 Finkelstein, S., & Mooney, A. (2003). Not the usual suspects: How to use board process to make boards better. *Academy of Management Executive, 17*(2), 101–113.

14 Tannenbaum, S. I., & Cerasoli, C. P. (2013). Do team and individual debriefs enhance performance? A meta-analysis. *Human Factors, 55*(1), 231–245. https://doi.org/10.1177/0018720812448394

15 Gabelica, C., Van Den Bossche, P., De Maeyer, S., Segers, M., & Gijselaers, W. (2014). The effect of team feedback and guided reflexivity on team performance change. *Learning and Instruction, 34*, 86–96.

16 Yang, M., Schloemer, H., Zhu, Z., Lin, Y., Chen, W., & Dong, N. (2020). Why and when team reflexivity contributes to team performance: A moderated mediation model. *Frontiers in Psychology, 10*, 3044.

17 Kneisel, E. (2020). Team reflections, team mental models and team performance over time. *Team Performance Management: An International Journal, 26*(1/2), 143–168.

5

Address Toxic Work Cultures: Use for Any Work Culture Shift

5.1 CHAPTER PREVIEW

While we focus on the erosion of toxic cultures in this chapter, the same methods can be used for any kind of workplace culture change. By leveraging our five principles of change, leaders can systematically address ways to transform an organization's or work team's culture. This applies to whether it's fostering innovation, enhancing a culture of safety, elevating customer service, breaking down those infamous team silos, developing leaders, or, as we share in this chapter, eroding a toxic work culture. Here, we walk through how leaders can identify the impact of toxic behaviors, take focused actions to improve the environment, and make those improvements last. Kusy and Holloway's national study of toxic workplaces and behaviors identified how damaging toxic work cultures can be. One quote from a participant in the study nailed it this way: "The day this person left our company is considered an annual holiday."[1] Toxic behaviors not only corrode day-to-day relationships but also act as powerful accelerants of change resistance. When negativity, incivility, or bullying go unchecked, employees are far more likely to resist new initiatives—not because of the change itself, but because of a lack of trust in those leading it.

Eroding toxic behaviors opens the door to more productive teams and a healthier organization. We'll explore how to make the shift. It's the stuff of office lore and water cooler tales, but not in a good way. This chapter takes you on a candid exploration of why work culture is the backbone of a thriving organization and how to fix it when things go awry. Along the way, we'll take a few breaks from focusing on toxic cultures and dive into how different approaches and activities we share that can be applied to other key work

DOI: 10.4324/9781003622925-5

culture challenges beyond toxic behaviors. For example, considering the current market trends, how can we tap into new ways of innovating? Or, another example might be, how can we get our team members involved in blending two work cultures during an upcoming acquisition?

Think of this chapter as a user manual for navigating and improving workplace dynamics when mired in toxic, unproductive behaviors. These behaviors don't just ruin morale; they hurt individual performance, derail teamwork, and can even erode organizational productivity, as well as sink your organization's bottom line, whether you are a profit or non-profit organization. The good news is that these toxic work cultures can be identified, managed, and uprooted. For those mired in a toxic work culture, we'll help you reduce the drama, ease the tension, increase performance, and get a good night's sleep along the way!

5.2 A CRITICAL INCIDENT OF A TOXIC WORK CULTURE

Imagine you're the captain of a ship, but the crew is bickering, the sails are in tatters, and the passengers are complaining about the food. That's the metaphorical scenario the chief medical officer of a large medical center found herself in when she called Mitch to figure out why their team of physicians and nursing staff seemed to be running aground. The symptoms of trouble were hard to ignore, including high turnover, more sick days than a flu season, reluctance to work overtime, physicians not referring patients to their own colleagues, and patient satisfaction scores taking a deep dive. Our initial "culture check-up" revealed what we could only describe as a slow-boiling stew of disrespect leading to a disruptive work culture, which many on the team labeled as "toxic." People were behaving badly, and no one was holding them accountable. Disrespect was spilling over into patient care, leaving patients and their families feeling they were second-class. One of the more shocking discoveries was the trend of lateral and vertical abuse. Nurses were at odds with nurses, and doctors were bickering with each other: all an indication of lateral abuse.[2] The prevalence of lateral abuse can be as high as a whopping 80% in some settings.[3] As well, there was vertical abuse in which the charge nurse was admonishing unit nurses without clear feedback; and physicians were joining the fray with condescending behavior with nurses. To make matters worse, this unprofessional behavior was sometimes happening right in front of patients and their families, leaving them less confident in the care they were receiving. And who could blame them? Trust is hard to build when the people in charge of your health are lobbing passive-aggressive comments instead of collaborating. We'll explore these types of critical incidents in this chapter from the perspectives of each of the principles of change.

5.3 PRINCIPLE 1. FRAME THE EVIDENCE FOR CHANGE

5.3.1 Leveling the Playing Field for Any Workplace Culture Transformation

Ah, "organizational culture" or "workplace culture"—a phrase that gets bantered about, sometimes without really understanding how it gets its power. You've probably heard it referred to positively and negatively:

- "Our organizational culture is amazing!"
- "Our culture? Ugh, don't get me started."
- "Our team culture is just another management fad."
- "Leaders keep talking about work culture, but do they *really* model it?"

So, exactly what *is* "organizational culture?" Think of it as the DNA of your workplace: the shared values, beliefs, norms, and practices that shape how people think and act, influencing decision-making and organizational outcomes.[4] Table 5.1 identifies our cheat sheet of work culture.

Reviewing those values, beliefs, norms, and patterns that guide how things really get done, we'd like to frame what we mean by "organization" in the context of improving work cultures. Think of an organization as a group of people united by a common purpose. It might be the entire company, a scrappy department, a high-powered team, or even a tight-knit division.

TABLE 5.1

Work Culture Cheat Sheet

• **Values.** "What matters to us."
• **Beliefs.** "Why these values matter."
• **Norms.** "The unspoken rules of the road."
• **Practices.** "The patterns of behavior that show us what's really going on."

Work culture leaves a bigger mark than most people realize, especially when it turns toxic. And a bad work culture can spread faster than a nasty email thread. In fact, research shows that a toxic work environment is the number one reason people quit: ten times more powerful than salary![5] Our approach to culture change isn't just about detoxing bad workplaces (though that's a great place to start).[6] It's a flexible game plan for any cultural shift at work, whether you're aiming to level up customer service, break down silos between teams, or grow leaders who inspire. Whatever the goal, a better workplace is within reach with the right strategy. We present this strategy in terms of our five principles of change. You might be wondering why we haven't slapped a formal definition on "toxic" yet. Mitch has worked with thousands of leaders regarding eroding toxic work cultures; he has found that when we ask them what "toxic" means, they don't hesitate to share their thoughts. And they nail it with accuracy along with stories that are concrete and real. Don't worry; we'll define it soon. But first, we want to show you just how powerful a toxic culture can be (in all the wrong ways), get you reflecting on your own experiences, and have you come up with your own workable definition.

Keep the Spotlight on the Positive, but Gently Highlight the Impact When It's Absent

While it's tempting to frame any workplace culture change process on what's wrong, focusing on what's right can spark momentum, especially at first when you are trying to engage stakeholders in this culture change initiative. But don't overdo the positive; you need to recognize strengths and expose areas for improvement. Even in the face of toxic behaviors, highlighting the power of a respectful work culture is important.[7] Sharing clear examples and insights, both from the team's experiences and research, provides a showcase of what can happen when respect is eroded. A respectful work culture isn't necessarily about being nice; it's about treating everyone with professionalism and dignity even when disagreements arise. For example, when giving feedback to a colleague, focus on encouraging behavior change—not proving you're right. Research over the past two decades has demonstrated that respect boosts well-being, team performance, and organizational success. It increases joy as well. In fact, joy has been the subject of recent research at the University of California, Berkeley.[8] The study with 22,000 participants in 22 countries discovered that "micro-acts of joy" resulted in:

- **26%** greater well-being
- **23%** more optimism
- **27%** improved happiness
- **34%** increased engagement of others.

So, what exactly are "micro-acts of joy?"

- **Doing something kind and unexpected.** Buy someone behind you (whom you do not know) a cup of coffee at your local coffee shop.
- **Celebrate another's joy.** Talk to someone about a situation that makes *them* happy.
- **Shift your perspective.** Recall a frustrating moment. Write three positive things about this experience.

If you are new to this concept of micro-acts of joy or are running out of ideas, you can always ask your favorite artificial intelligence assistant for inspiration! Simply ask, for example: *Act as an organizational researcher. What are micro-acts of joy that are appropriate in my professional setting to boost my team's morale?* Below are just a few of the many examples that AI may return as identified in Table 5.2.

Remember, these small, joyful actions aren't just feel-good fluff; they're catalysts for boosting well-being, optimism, happiness, engagement, *and* productivity. When we have shared these statistics with clients, we've seen many spontaneous, humorous reactions. First, they're floored that scientists have actually studied joy. Yes, there are people measuring happiness like they're gold nuggets! Second, they're amazed that joy isn't just a nice-to-have but actually packs a punch regarding improved performance. And third, they realize, "Hey, I can do this!" Let's face it, joy works. Science says so. And now, we do too, as you will see demonstrated later in this chapter.

TABLE 5.2

Examples of AI Responses to the Prompt of Micro-Acts of Joy

Offer to help with a task, bring in coffee, or check in on someone who seems stressed.
Share a funny (work-appropriate) meme or light anecdote at the start of a meeting.
Begin meetings with a quick "one good thing" round where everyone shares a recent positive moment.

Target the Behavior, Not the Person

Here's where we need to tread carefully: bad behaviors don't always mean bad people. It's the behavior we want to change, not the person's personality, which, quite frankly, is quite difficult to change. Think of it this way: no one is always a jerk (well, okay, *almost* no one). Most people have their moments. Frame the behavior in this way, and you might be surprised how much people can change. After all, as psychologists like to say, behaviors can evolve, but personalities? They're pretty set in stone. There can be a fine line when addressing negative behaviors in the heat of the moment, at a time when emotions easily dominate over reason. Taking a step back allows you to assess the situation with a clearer perspective and separate the behavior from any personal feelings you may have about the individual. Need an impartial point of view as you try to craft a measured response? Gilles leverages AI to get objective feedback, for example, by performing tone and sentiment analysis. Sentiment analysis assesses whether words or sentences are generally associated with positive or negative feelings. It is often used to analyze social media content. Sentiment analysis helps to identify problematic elements and suggest more neutral alternatives in your response. Here's how you might engage AI in sentiment analysis: *Act as a data scientist. Based on the attached document, perform a sentiment analysis and assess the overall tone. Then highlight examples of two very positive and two very negative passages.*

Sentiment analysis can be a powerful tool to guide and frame change initiatives, especially when focusing on these two key instruments of change: self and the team.

1. *Self as the instrument for change.* If the sentiment analysis shows that many individuals in the organization have negative feelings about the change, that's not a sign to abandon the initiative. Instead, it's a signal for leaders to lean in. This insight gives you a starting point:
   - Acknowledge the concerns and emotions people are experiencing.
   - Show that leadership is listening and willing to understand these concerns.
   - Use this understanding to guide communication and engagement efforts.

   In short, negative sentiment doesn't mean failure; it means you have a clearer roadmap for where to begin building trust and momentum.

2. *Team as the instrument for change.* For larger organizations, analyzing sentiment by teams (such as departments, divisions, or business units) helps you spot where support is most needed.
   - Are there teams that are highly resistant?
   - Are some groups more optimistic than others?

This targeted insight allows leaders to focus their efforts where they'll have the greatest impact, tailoring communication, resources, and leadership support to the specific needs of each team.

5.3.2 A Primer on Disruptive Behaviors

Whether you call it disruptive, toxic, uncivil, disrespectful, or plain old bullying, the name doesn't matter nearly as much as ensuring everyone in your organization understands what it means. Think of disruptive behavior as a pebble tossed into a calm lake. The ripples don't just stop with one splash; they spread out, disturbing the entire surface. The Healthy Workforce Institute (HWI), which works with organizations to improve workplace culture from disrespectful to respectful, offers a framework for identifying disruptive behaviors. Through Mitch's partnership with the HWI, he embraces their call to break down toxic behaviors into three factors. Table 5.3 describes the factors associated with disruptive behaviors as identified by the HWI.[9]

This simple framework helps teams and organizations define disruptive behaviors in ways that are easy to spot and address. Recognizing the problem is the first step toward resolving it. Looked at another way, we view

TABLE 5.3

The Three Telltale Factors of Disruptive Behaviors Identified by Dr. Renee Thompson, CEO of the Healthy Workforce Institute

Factor	Description
Targeted	There's usually a person (or group) who has been earmarked to receive the barrage of disrespectful behaviors.
Harmful	Intent doesn't matter. It's not about what you meant; it's about how it lands. (Picture someone saying, "I was just joking!" after stepping on your toes—still hurts, right?)
Repeated	Everyone has bad days, but if it happens over and over, it's no longer a "Monday mood"; it's a pattern.

toxic behaviors as "a pattern of inappropriate and disruptive actions that seriously debilitate individuals, teams, and organizations."[10] The keyword here? *Pattern.* Everyone has their moments, but when bad behavior keeps popping up, it's no longer a one-off; it's toxic. And this just doesn't happen one-on-one. Consider when a group targets others; this is sometimes called "mobbing." In addition, our study identified three primary "flavors" of toxic behavior: shaming, passive hostility, and team sabotage.

Shaming. Behaviors associated with shaming occur in public or private. Imagine being called out for a mistake to embarrass you, make you feel "small," or to draw attention to you in a condescending kind of way. Shaming behaviors include things like humiliating others, either one-on-one or in public. In other circumstances, it's about taking a little *too* much joy in pointing out a colleague's mistakes. Another instance is when feedback is given, but it is less about helping the person and more about flexing your muscles of righteousness. It's about "dressing someone down" just because you can or you feel more important.

Passive hostility. This is anger wearing a polite disguise. Passive hostility (a.k.a. passive-aggressive behavior) may involve taking sly "pot-shots" at someone. At times, it's about using sarcasm that's less witty and more . . . ouch. Another is spreading rumors that travel faster than an office email chain full of gossip. And finally, "backstabbers" smile sweetly while sharpening the metaphorical knife.

Team sabotage. This is tantamount to workplace "vandalism." These are actions designed to hurt others, all in the name of self-interest. Examples include seeking revenge and meddling in ways that derail a team or individual. Of course, some behaviors don't fit neatly into one bucket; they may spill over all three. Yelling, verbal abuse, rudeness, and teasing that hit below the belt are the workplace equivalent of throwing a wrench into the gears. A summary of these behaviors can be found in Table 5.4.

TABLE 5.4

Summary of Toxic Behavior Domains

Domain	Examples
Shaming	Humiliating others, pointing out mistakes unnecessarily, and giving condescending feedback to appear "righteous."
Passive Hostility	Passive-aggressive actions, potshots, hurtful sarcasm, spreading rumors, and "backstabbing."
Sabotage	Retaliation, meddling to bring others down for personal gain.

Here's a jaw-dropper from Mitch's study: 94% of the 900+ research participants reported they've worked with a toxic person in the last five years.[11] That's almost everyone! And at every presentation or keynote Mitch has given, he's asked the same question: "Have you worked with a toxic person in the past five years?" Guess what? The audience response is eerily consistent: 95% (or more!) raise their hands and nod knowingly. Here's where it gets really interesting. When we follow up with this question, "Why does this keep happening?," we often receive these responses:

- *Management does nothing.*
- *It's just part of the culture here.*
- *They've got power or expertise—better not cross them or rock the boat.*
- *It's not on management's radar screen.*

Now, whether or not these things are *actually true* is almost beside the point. What matters is this: these are perceptions, and perceptions spread through an organization's culture like gossip at the water cooler. (And just like gossip, they're hard to contain once they start!)

5.3.3 The Cost of Toxicity

It's important to frame *any* culture change around hard data because sometimes people interpret any change around respect as attending "charm school." Mitch titled his 6th business book, *Why I Don't Work Here Anymore: A Leader's Guide to Offset the Financial and Emotional Costs of Toxic Employees*. Why? Toxic work cultures push people out the door. The numbers don't lie. A mega-study on workplace incivility by Porath and Pearson found that 12% of people quit due to exposure to bad behavior.[12] In Mitch and Elizabeth's study, a whopping 51% reported that they were likely or very likely to quit. That's more than half your team potentially saying, *I'm out of here!* According to recent research by the Society for Human Resource Management, toxic work cultures cost businesses a staggering $2 billion per day.[13] Yes, you read that right—*per day*. Let's break this down:

- $1.2 billion per day is due to lost productivity.
- $828 million per day comes from absenteeism, with an average of 1.5 days off per person.

Interpolating these statistics and integrating them with Mitch's research study beckon this. Toxic work behaviors, when unchecked and allowed to continue, result in lost revenue of a minimum of 6% of total organizational compensation. So, for example, if your organization is spending $10,000,000 in annual compensation, toxic work behaviors are costing your organization $600,000 annually. And this is a most conservative estimate. If toxic behavior were a leaky faucet, this would be the equivalent of leaving it running full blast 24/7 × 365. Toxicity in the workplace doesn't just hurt people. It drains morale, productivity, and the bottom line. It's like having a bad apple in the fruit bowl: leave it there long enough, and the whole batch starts to spoil. The good news? Once you frame how big the problem is, you can start tackling it head-on.

Toxicity also impacts customer service in so many ways. Let's peel back the curtain and go beyond statistics for a moment. Christine Porath and Christine Pearson didn't just crunch numbers; they uncovered fascinating perspectives that align with what we've seen with thousands of clients. Here are some insights that might make you go, *Wow!* Customers are far less likely to buy from a company when they experience an uncivil employee, whether the behavior is directed at them or someone else.[14] Witness someone getting reprimanded in front of them? Many customers say "Nope!" and take their business elsewhere. Here's a real-life example: during one of Mitch's business trips, as he was waiting for a flight, he saw the pilot storm out of the gate bridge and absolutely *unload* on the gate agent. Mitch had no idea what sparked the meltdown, but the person sitting next to him, a complete stranger, turned and said, *I'm never flying this airline again!* He was visibly upset, and honestly, so was Mitch. That airline didn't just lose a customer; they lost a potential brand ambassador. When it comes to understanding the catastrophic ripple effects of disruptive behaviors, no industry has done its homework quite like healthcare. The Joint Commission has been the gold standard in quality improvement and patient safety for over 22,000 healthcare organizations. The Commission has spent years diving deep into the problem. And what they've uncovered is enough to make anyone's pulse race:

- **67%** of healthcare workers reported witnessing disruptive behaviors that led to adverse patient outcomes.
- **71%** of those adverse outcomes were medical errors.
- **27%** of those errors tragically ended in patient mortality.[15]

Let's pause for a moment. How can something as seemingly "soft" as a bad attitude have such deadly consequences? Unfortunately, these numbers aren't just casual findings; they're backed by hundreds of studies, including personal experiences. In a recent keynote address, Mitch shared a real-life example that hit home for many. He talked about how toxic behaviors like public shaming can short-circuit someone's ability to think critically, leading to errors and poor service. A woman in the audience chimed in, sharing how her husband, a nurse, hesitated to clarify a questionable medication order with a certain physician. Instead, he consulted two other doctors. Why? "Because he didn't want to get yelled at or shamed in front of others," she said. Cue a roomful of nodding heads. Then, another individual raised her hand and reported that she was a surgeon. She proudly declared, "I have to be shaming and intimidating in the surgical suite to demand perfection." Then she posed this question (or more like an ultimatum). "Dr. Kusy, would you go to a surgeon who isn't perfect?" Feeling the heat, Mitch responded, "Doctor, I would want to go to a surgeon who, if they're about to make a mistake, the team feels comfortable enough to call it out without fear of retribution." The room went silent. It's not just anecdotal. A study of 13,653 patients found that surgeons with more complaints about unprofessional behaviors were significantly more likely to have patients with medical and surgical complications (p <0.001).[16] The message? Toxic behaviors put patients' lives on the line. And it's not just healthcare. Toxicity creeps into every industry, impacting not only performance but also workplace well-being. A McKinsey study of 15,000 employees in 15 countries revealed a stark connection: organizations with high burnout levels exhibited eight times more toxic behaviors than those with low burnout levels.[17] Specifically, the researchers found that 52.5% of those organizations that reported burnout also reported high levels of toxic behaviors; only 6.9% of those organizations that reported burnout had low levels of toxic behaviors.

Burnout and toxicity are like two toxic best friends fueling each other in a vicious cycle. And here's a revealing statistic: 70% of employees would turn down a job in an organization with a reputation for a toxic culture, and a higher paycheck would not even be tempting.[18] That's right. Better pay isn't enough to gloss over a bad work culture. As one might say, "Money can't buy happiness . . . or workplace civility."

Just as you should dive into hard data about toxic work cultures, leaders need to bring that same energy when gathering data for any type of culture change. And to help discover evidence of toxicity in your specific setting, use

AI to track down this evidence. Let's assume, for example, that your organization recently completed an employee satisfaction survey. You could try the following prompt after attaching your survey results:

> *Role: Act as an HR consultant. Question: Analyze the attached open-ended responses and quantitative results of our employee satisfaction survey for indications of toxic behaviors or toxic workplace dynamics. Highlight any recurring themes, including evidence of effective and ineffective behaviors. Summarize your findings and suggest areas and methods for further investigation.*

Next up. Let's roll up our sleeves and tackle how to identify and manage uncivil work cultures. Get ready for practical tools and actionable insights!

5.4 PRINCIPLE 2. ASSESS WITH ENGAGEMENT

5.4.1 The First Month of Work with the Design Team

Just as in strategic planning initiatives (Chapter 3), think of the design team as the architects of change. They begin their work roughly within the first month of the cultural transformation. This is a group of interdisciplinary leaders and influencers ready to shape the foundation of your new culture. Typically, the design team formation occurs within the first month of this culture change initiative. These folks will plan, inspire, and even dig through past organizational data to figure out what's been holding the organization or team back from a successful culture shift. Notice we said "team" in addition to "organization," as this process can be used to change the culture of one or several teams who might go through the process together, as well as entire organizations. For the sake of brevity, we refer to "organization" as incorporating any iteration of this, whether it's one or multiple teams, a department, a division, or the whole system. This design team works much like the one we talked about in the strategic planning chapter, with the same purpose of creating a strategic direction but with a slightly different focus. It's all about aligning efforts and driving the vision forward.

Ideally comprised of members from various disciplines and hierarchical levels, this design team is responsible for initiating the culture change process. As the team's name implies, they design it from soup to nuts, so to speak, in much the same way the design team functions in strategic planning. Over the following two to six months, the design team is actively involved, taking on a series of key responsibilities as outlined below:

- **Share the need for change**. Start with the facts (e.g., survey data, focus groups, culture change surveys, exit interviews). Show why creating a new workplace culture isn't just a "nice to have," but something we absolutely need.
- **Identify historical patterns**. Look at past data (e.g., turnover rates, customer feedback, grievances). Anything that calls out, "Ah, here's what needs fixing!"
- **Create a game plan for additional data needed**. Determine what additional information is needed to fully understand the situation.
- **Model the way**. Leaders, if you're still acting like "jerks," stop. Be the change you want to see. One of the aspects often overlooked in this first phase is that leaders need to "model the way," based on the research from Kouzes and Posner.[19] Researcher Robert Sutton also has discovered that it is difficult to extol the virtues of culture change around toxic behaviors when leaders are acting as "jerks."[20]
- **Design the process**. Collaborate with other key influences and keep it transparent.
- **Start conversations early**. Share what the design team knows so far. This builds anticipation for positive change.
- **Include "naysayers."** These are the people who raise their hand and say, "This won't work." Or "We've been through this one too many times already. What makes this different now?" Why do we include them? Because sometimes they're the first to spot a pothole on your road to success. And here's the bonus: if you can win them over, they might just become your loudest cheerleader. Listen to their objections. Don't take it personally. Use their feedback to make the process stronger.
- **Engage stakeholders**. Who needs to be engaged and in what ways? Who has influence and can champion this effort, address questions, interpret results, and share the vision? Get those people on board the design team!

AI can be a powerful ally here to quickly analyze large quantities of data, extract qualitative and quantitative metrics, and synthesize data into information and insights. It can identify gaps in your dataset and help you design employee surveys to gather fresh information that can validate, or invalidate, your hypotheses of what's really occurring. AI can also draft effective communications for you, supported by data and references relevant to your organization and its employees. Building on our previous prompt example for analyzing employee satisfaction surveys, you could ask your AI assistant any of the follow-up questions listed in Table 5.5.

TABLE 5.5

Sample Questions for Data Analysis Using AI

Purpose	Prompt
General Exploration	• What is the most prevalent negative theme in the survey comments? Are there particular words, phrases, or complaints that keep surfacing? • Which teams, locations, or levels reported the lowest satisfaction? What's unique about their environment?
Comparisons and Patterns	• How do scores differ across departments, teams, or demographic groups? • Are there any teams with consistently strong scores despite challenging circumstances? What are they doing differently? • Are people reporting similar issues in exit interviews or grievance records?
Relationships and Alignment	• Where do survey data and turnover data align or diverge? What could explain the difference? • Do teams with frequent reports of incivility or low trust/morale also report higher absenteeism or customer complaints?
Drilling Down on Toxicity-Related Issues	• Which survey questions most strongly correlate with low overall satisfaction or intent to leave? • Are negative comments clustered around specific leaders or management styles? • What are the most common descriptors people use when talking about their managers/peers?
Looking for Hidden Spots	• Are there groups with low participation in the survey—are they less comfortable or more cynical about speaking up? • Is there a mismatch between how managers rated the culture versus individual contributors? • Are there positive "official" survey scores but consistently negative comments? What might people feel unable to say directly?
Formulating Hypotheses	• What are three possible root causes for the most common disruptive behaviors? • If we were to run a focus group with employees in the lowest-scoring department, what clarifying questions would we ask? • If toxic behavior is present, where is it most likely originating—peer-to-peer, supervisor-to-employee, or top-down?

Finally, after reviewing and consolidating your findings into one document, you can attach it and ask AI for a high-level summary and suggested next step as follows:

> *Role: Act as a project manager. Context: Attached is a document summarizing our analysis of our employee satisfaction survey data. Question: Write a concise executive summary that highlights the main findings, key patterns, and probable root causes of toxicity uncovered. Follow with a brief, actionable remediation plan. Prioritize two or three high-impact interventions that address the most urgent issues and propose a timeline for next steps. Style: The summary and plan should be written for senior leaders—focused, direct, and suitable to be shared as a standalone briefing.*

Isn't it nice to have an assistant always ready to help?

5.4.2 Work with the Design Team during the Next Two to Six Months

Now it's time to roll up your sleeves and start the real work. Here, we figure out the expectations and actions to build a culture of respect and productivity. This could involve leadership training, coaching, or team development activities. Consider framing the change as helping stakeholders understand why this culture change is important, with assessment and engagement as creating a blueprint of what's going on. All this typically happens within two to six months of the start of the cultural transformation. Table 5.6 identifies the key responsibilities associated with this assessment phase and how to accomplish these. This approach is not limited to turning around a toxic culture; it applies to any culture change effort. Mitch has used this assessment process for the past 25 years, engaging strong evidence supporting the need for change.

TABLE 5.6

How the Design Team Assesses with Engagement, with Application to Any Culture Change Initiative

Responsibilities	How It's Done
Collect baseline data	Understand where you are
Share the results and design best practices	Help others spot the cracks in the wall (and the opportunities to fix them).
Engage in learning opportunities that produce successful outcomes	Design and pilot the change. For example, start with leaders before scaling to all staff.

5.4.3 Collecting Baseline Data Is the Start of Your Blueprint for Success

Collecting baseline data provides a blueprint for success. Collecting data doesn't have to be boring. Surveys are great, but you can also get rich details from focus groups, interviews, or even exit interviews. For instance, Mitch once surveyed a team about toxic behaviors, and the results weren't pretty. To enrich the data from the surveys, he also conducted focus groups. Other clients have started with focus groups to identify critical areas of concern, followed by a survey based on these results. No matter what you do, it's important to collect data: both quantitative *and* qualitative. Then, share the data and allow people to discuss these results. Engagement is key. Table 5.7 is a quick peek at 12 of the most common toxic behaviors—a good place to start. Begin the discussion with simple, open-ended questions such as:

* "How does respect show up on our team?"
* "Do any of these 12 behaviors get in the way of respect around here?"

These kinds of questions in interviews or focus groups can give you a real sense of what's happening beneath the surface. Then, once you have some insights, you can roll out a more formal survey to dig even deeper. The key? Start small, stay curious, and be ready to learn.

TABLE 5.7

Snapshot of the 12 Most Common Toxic Behaviors and Their Prevalence from the Kusy and Holloway Study.[21] Use This to Inspire Your Own Survey or Focus Group Questions

Behavior	% Response
Protects their territory	99%
Points out everyone else's mistakes	95%
Distrusts others' opinions	94%
Can't handle feedback	93%
Clueless about their own toxicity	91%
Is passive-aggressive	90%
Takes potshots at others	83%
Meddles in teamwork	83%
Monitors team behaviors ruthlessly	76%
Loves sarcastic remarks	75%
Humiliates others	69%
Wields authority to punish	66%

We've found that these 12 behaviors make a great benchmark for gathering insights on workplace culture. A smart way to dig deeper? Use AI to generate thoughtful, open-ended questions to uncover what's really happening in your organization. As an example, below is a set of probing questions we've generated with AI around ten toxic behaviors:

1. **Territorialism:**
   - "Have you ever noticed team members getting a little too protective of their responsibilities?"
   - "How did that impact collaboration and team dynamics?"
2. **Mistake Highlighting:**
   - "How does calling out mistakes—big or small—affect morale on your team?
   - "Any moments stand out?"
3. **Distrust of Opinions:**
   - "Have you ever felt like your ideas weren't taken seriously?"
   - "How did that shape the way you contribute?"
4. **Handling Feedback:**
   - "How does your team typically react to constructive feedback?
   - "Do you see any common patterns in how it's received?"
5. **Toxicity Awareness:**
   - "Do people recognize when they're bringing negativity into the workplace?
   - "Can you think of a time when someone lacked that awareness?"
6. **Passive-Aggressiveness:**
   - "What's the most common passive-aggressive behavior you see at work?
   - "How does it impact communication and teamwork?"
7. **Team Dynamics:**
   - "How does the team dynamic shift when someone takes little jabs at others?
   - "Or gets too involved in everyone's work?"
8. **Surveillance and Monitoring:**
   - "Does strict oversight make the team more productive or just more stressed?"
   - "What kind of work environment does it create?"
9. **Sarcastic Communication:**
   - "When does sarcasm cross the line from humor to something that hurts?"
   - "How does it shape team interactions?"

10. **Humiliation and Authority:**
    - "Have you ever seen authority used to embarrass or punish someone?"
    - "What effect did it have on the team?"

These questions can help uncover important cultural patterns. With AI's help, you can refine them even further to fit your team's specific needs.

5.4.4 A Few Words of Wisdom

To get started on this journey, think of assessment as introducing a new way of thinking; even small first steps can make a big difference. Like giving someone a nudge to recognize respectful behavior or inspiring a leader to embrace the process, it's about sparking change and not over-promising. Here are some tips, from our experience as consultants and from research on effective culture change, to help you begin the process of meaningful culture change:

- **Small Tests of Change**
  In any change initiative, we suggest starting with "small tests of change" before expanding. To establish cultures of respect, consider nudging someone to embrace kindness, or helping a leader realize that sarcasm isn't a leadership strategy, or even supporting a three-month pilot study.
- **Numbers + Stories = Key Learning**
  Share key statistics and then sprinkle in a relatable anecdote or two. This approach brings meaning to the culture change process.
- **Brief, but Mighty Discussions**
  Don't drown people in data. Share your findings in digestible chunks, starting with leaders. Show them how respect isn't about being "nice"; it's about driving better results. Highlight one or two shocking statistics (like the 99% of respondents who saw protection of their turf as the #1 toxic behavior or the 12% of targets of disruptive behaviors who quit) and invite them to discuss these research results. Combine these statistics with your own organization's or team's survey that revealed similar or contrary patterns.

Culture change is hard, but it's also rewarding. Start small, aim big, and remember that it's okay to laugh along the way, as long as the laugh is not at the expense of any one person or group. After all, respect and productivity thrive in a workplace that doesn't take itself *too* seriously.

5.5 PRINCIPLE 3. EMBRACE SYSTEMS THINKING

5.5.1 The Compact of Professional Behaviors

While there is a myriad of methods for engaging systems thinking here, one that Mitch has facilitated is the *Compact of Professional Behaviors.* Think of this as a team's constitution; it outlines what behaviors people always and never want to experience or witness. It's not dictated from above; it's created by the team itself. Mitch has engaged this strategy through his work with Dr. Renee Thompson, CEO, Healthy Workforce Institute.[22]

1. **Gather the team or teams.** Bring as many team members as possible into a room for a 45-minute brainstorming session, but with a twist. Think of this as a mini town hall, but with Post-It Notes™ instead of long-winded speeches. The "room" can be virtual or face-to-face. Mitch has facilitated this process with anywhere from one to three teams in one room.

2. **Split flipchart pages into "Always" and "Never" zones.** Set up flipcharts labeled at the top with "ALWAYS want to experience" and "NEVER want to experience." Again, this can be done virtually or in a physical room.

3. **Let the brainstorming begin**. Give everyone a pad of Post-It Notes™ and encourage them to write down *one* behavior they "ALWAYS want to experience" and one behavior they "NEVER want to experience." Quantity over perfection is the name of the game here. At first, some may be reluctant to participate; others may believe they are done after they post one sticky note. Not so! Read on. Here we see the self as the instrument of change demonstrated in what each stakeholder identifies on their Post-It Notes™.

4. **Include and collaborate.** Encourage participants to go to the flipchart pages and include ideas from others if they believe this is a behavior that they have witnessed but have not yet captured. The reason is that

themes are number-based. All of a sudden, participants "get it" and start contributing madly! Here, we see the power of the team as the instrument of change come alive.

5. **Consider multiple teams.** We've had up to three teams working in the same room at once. Each team still creates its own *Compact*, but the cross-pollination of ideas is invaluable. People wander, chat, borrow ideas (with permission!), and spark fresh thinking. Turns out, it doesn't just take a village; it takes a few villages swapping tips at the town square!

6. **It's not over yet!** For those who missed the session, don't worry. We're bringing the flipchart pages back to the team area. Alternatively, it can be done virtually. Over the next seven to ten days, we invite everyone to add their own gems to the list. And here's where the magic kicks in: people start nudging each other, like cheerleaders on the sidelines, to jump in and contribute. Before you know it, the activity takes on a life of its own: buzzing, humming, and gathering momentum. Engagement at its absolute finest! Figure 5.1 provides an example of a couple flipchart pages for the "Always" and "Never" activity during the first ten minutes of the 45-minute activity. Figure 5.2 demonstrates multiple flipchart pages at the 45-minute mark.

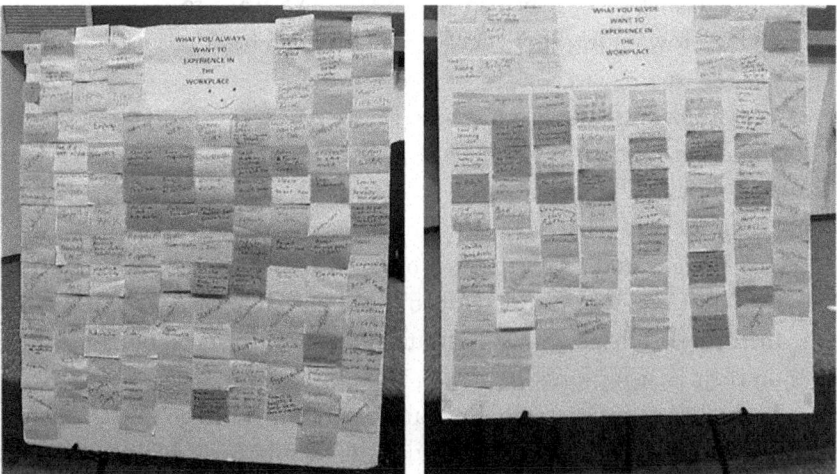

FIGURE 5.1
The first ten minutes of results for the "Always Want to Experience" and "Never Want to Experience" activity through the engagement of the Healthy Workforce Institute.

FIGURE 5.2
The results of the "Always Want to Experience" and "Never Want to Experience" at the 45-minute mark through the engagement of the Healthy Workforce Institute.

7. **Review and cluster into themes.** The design team then clusters the sticky note responses into themes based on repetition—a surefire way to identify the biggest priorities. Table 5.8 is an example of themes we have extracted from work with recent clients.

TABLE 5.8

Sample *Compact* Themes Extracted from Work with Several Clients at the Healthy Workforce Institute

Always	Never
Acknowledge contributions.	Interrupt others.
Provide constructive feedback.	Use sarcasm.
Celebrate team wins.	Gossip or spread rumors.
Show empathy in tough situations.	Shame others publicly.
Collaborate on problem-solving.	Dismiss diverse opinions.
Help out a team member in need.	Roll your eyes at anyone.
Make an effort to understand different viewpoints.	Show favoritism.

8. **Draft the compact and share.** Once the themes are analyzed, the design team drafts the first rendition of the *Compact of Professional Behaviors*, which is shared with staff for their review, revisions, and ultimate confirmation. At this point, the team is heavily involved in revising this latest draft. An example of the *Compact of Professional Behaviors* is demonstrated in Figure 5.3. Please note that the blank bullets are provided to protect confidentiality and anonymity.

HEALTHY WORKFORCE INSTITUTE   Sample Compact of Professional Behaviors

Our Commitment: We are all responsible for creating a healthy, professional, and respectful workplace focused personal well-being, the patient experience, and....BLANK FOR PURPOSES OF CONFIDENTIALITY.

How We Make This Commitment Happen:

Recognize and Appreciate.

- Give credit liberally without expected returns.
- Apologize with genuineness to restore trust.
- Model psychological safety.
- BLANK FOR PURPOSES OF CONFIDENTIALITY.
- BLANK FOR PURPOSES OF CONFIDENTIALITY.

Demonstrate Professionalism

- Engage professionally including how we dress and how we allow others to finish speaking.
- Be punctual for work shifts, patient care sessions, or any interactions where time is critical.
- BLANK FOR PURPOSES OF CONFIDENTIALITY.
- BLANK FOR PURPOSES OF CONFIDENTIALITY.

Openness and Understanding of Differences

- Consider new ideas and practices; ask ourselves "why not?" to new ideas.
- Go out of our way to understand and respect differences—if we don't know, ask.
- Engage in "cultural humility"--being aware of our own personal biases, understanding cultural and religious differences and barriers, and learning from these different cultures.
- BLANK FOR PURPOSES OF CONFIDENTIALITY.
- BLANK FOR PURPOSES OF CONFIDENTIALITY.

What We Don't Support:

Overt Incivility

- Gossiping about others—whether true or not!
- BLANK FOR PURPOSES OF CONFIDENTIALITY.
- BLANK FOR PURPOSES OF CONFIDENTIALITY.

Covert Incivility

- Ignoring others or not including them in conversations / meetings as a means of retaliation.
- Shaming others in public or private in passive ways with the intention of hurting others.
- Having *keyboard courage*: Using social media to criticize without talking with the person.
- BLANK FOR PURPOSES OF CONFIDENTIALITY.

Destructive biases

- Not realizing the impact of "isms": sexism, favoritism, nepotism, racism, classism, ableism.
- Not making an effort to understand transgender and LGBTQ+ perspectives.
- BLANK FOR PURPOSES OF CONFIDENTIALITY.

FIGURE 5.3

Example of *Compact of Professional Behaviors* Extracted from Work with the Healthy Workforce Institute; Revised and Adapted for Purposes of Confidentiality.

9. **Add some humor!** This activity is fun! Picture someone jotting down "Don't steal my lunch from the fridge" on a sticky note under "Never." It may sound small, but these moments bring authenticity and camaraderie to the process.

You can leverage AI to make the process a lot easier on you, from automatically extracting dominant themes from everyone's input to synthesizing them into a *Compact of Professional Behaviors* that is consistent with your organization's existing policies and even formatting the content to fit your favorite template! Try the following prompt:

> *Context: Attached is a document containing a list of behaviors our employees Always want to experience or Never want to experience in the workplace. It also contains information about our organization's values and HR policies. Role: Act as an HR manager. Question: Synthetize themes from the provided context into a Compact of Professional Behaviors that is consistent with our organization's values and policies. Style: Format the document with three distinct sections: 'Our commitment,' 'How we make this commitment happen,' 'What we don't support.'*

If you're like most leaders, you might be getting a bit of that "Oh no, is the *Compact of Professional Behaviors* just going to be another plaque on the wall?" feeling. Don't worry. It's not! When we dive into the *Sustainability Culture Change Plan* in the section "Sustain What Works," you'll see how this isn't just fancy words frozen in time but extends the reach of the *Compact of Professional Behaviors*.

5.5.2 Values-Based Team Performance: A Serendipitous Finding!

One great finding from the *Compact of Professional Behaviors* is how it's helping with performance management. Both staff and leaders have told us it's been really useful—so much so, they've started using parts of it in their own performance reviews.

The process is simple:

> Each employee picks one norm from the *Compact* that they want to improve. This becomes part of their annual review. While some organizations may refer to these as "norms" of behavior, other organizations may use different terms. For example, at 3M Corporation, they refer to these as "leadership attributes."

There are a few key benefits:

- Employees helped create the *Compact*, so they're already engaged.
- They choose a behavior that matters to them.
- Because they're involved and see the value, they're more committed.

It's a win-win for everyone!

5.6 PRINCIPLE 4. TARGET RESULTS *AND* OUTCOMES

5.6.1 Professional Development: Extended Training Sessions Are "Dying on the Vine"

Over the years of designing and running professional development programs (or "training" sessions as they are commonly referred to), we've seen a strong shift toward shorter learning sessions. Today, more than 90% of our clients prefer sessions that last no longer than two hours at a time. As one client put it, "Long sessions are dying on the vine." At the Healthy Workforce Institute, Dr. Renee Thompson engages this model of short training opportunities. Adults tend to focus better in shorter bursts, and with so much training now happening online, anything longer than two hours, even with breaks, can feel overwhelming. If longer sessions are needed (and sometimes they are), it's important to sprinkle within these sessions with action-oriented activities that have direct application to the work environment. With that in mind, this section focuses on learning programs that can be delivered effectively in two hours or less. Here, we segment professional development into two categories: staff development and leadership development. We will also demonstrate how each can breed results and outcomes. Table 5.9 provides a visual of this distinction.

As a summary, here are the highlights:

- **Results.** The immediate, visible actions (like using a new feedback model or reducing gossip)
- **Outcomes.** The long-term changes that happen because of these actions (like better teamwork or improved performance)

Both results and outcomes are important to determine the impact of these activities. Results show if the skills are being applied, while outcomes reveal the broader long-term impact.

TABLE 5.9

Examples of Results versus Outcomes for Staff Development and Leadership Development Opportunities

Activity	Possible Results	Possible Outcomes
Staff Development		
How to Give Effective Feedback Without It Feeling like a Root Canal	Use of the four-phase feedback model	Team becomes more effective.
Tackling Gossip: A Simple Fix with Big Wins	Reduction of team gossip	More time spent with customers
The Art of the Apology: Because "Sorry" Shouldn't Be So Hard	Less passive-aggressive behavior	Increased team member support for other team members
		Improved team performance
The Standout Thank-You Note: The Often Forgotten Strategy	Team members receive affirmation.	Extension of respect to students
Leadership Development		
Coaching to Improve Respect: Brief and Focused	Leaders show respect.	Enhanced patient experiences
A Fresh Take on the Exit Interview: Moving a Dinosaur That Is Extinct	HR uses the new interview model.	Fewer employees leave the company.
How to Avoid Hiring Toxic People: Simple Strategies That Get Results	The recruiting team uses a guide during interviews.	More employees stay with the company.

5.6.2 Sample Professional Development Activities

This section highlights some go-to professional development ideas that have worked wonders in helping our clients and their teams implement their new norms, once the final draft of the *Compact of Professional Behaviors* is complete. Think of these activities as training, in-service seminars, or even brown-bag lunch learning. Here, we provide a snapshot of the content— short and sweet descriptions to get your creative juices flowing. The design team would tailor these to fit the vibe of the new culture you're building.

5.6.3 Sample Staff Development Venues

How to Give Feedback without It Feeling like a Root Canal

Starting a tough conversation can feel daunting. To provide feedback, we suggest using our template of the *Intro-Behavior-Impact-Toss Back Model (IBIT).*

Dr. Renee Thompson of the Healthy Workforce Institute says to "Script It" ahead of time for each part of the conversation. Notes help!

1. **Intro.** Clear and Respectful Right from the Start.
   Begin on a professional note. Think of it as setting the stage—calm and without any drama. Don't use long positive intros that set the stage for "the axe is about to fall."
2. **Behavior.** Skip Any Judgmental Words.
   Stick to the facts. State what is happening; describe it. Instead of "You shamed me in public," you might consider, "You rolled your eyes while I was speaking."
3. **Impact.** Highlight Why This Is Important.
   This is where you point out why the behavior matters. Bonus points if you tie it to some hard evidence, the team's purpose, or the organization's vision.
4. **"Toss Back."** Get Their View.
   Here's your chance to pass the ball. Ask for their perspective. You might not have all the facts; this keeps the conversation two-sided.

Mike recently used this with a client. It was powerful, swift, and delivered results.

Intro. I'd like to talk with you about some observations I've had at the last few meetings.

Behavior. You often interrupt others when they are expressing a perspective. I notice it most often in team meetings.

Impact. When this happens, it makes me feel that you don't care about other opinions.

Toss Back. You may not realize the impact of this behavior. How might we shift this?

The trickiest part? Starting the conversation. Some leaders pile on so much positive fluff right from the beginning that the real feedback (when it arrives) feels like a stealth attack. Others come in way too strong, leading with the proverbial sledgehammer. Both approaches tend to flop. That's why we share conversation starters and encouragers in Table 5.10.

Need to customize this model to your own situation? AI is here to help! Gilles generated the following prompt and questions to get you started:

TABLE 5.10

Here Are Some Examples of Conversation Starters and Encouragers, Using the *Intro-Behavior-Impact-and-Toss-Back Model (IBIT)*

Intro (I)	"I've noticed something in our recent meetings that I'd like to talk about. I'll share my thoughts, and I'd love to hear yours too."
	"We've run into a few challenges recently, and I'd like to work together to find a better way forward."
	"Can we chat about what happened this morning?"
	"It seems like we have different ideas about the customer service situation. I'd like to share my concerns and hear your thoughts."
	"I've noticed something in our recent meetings that I'd like to talk about. I'll share my thoughts, and I'd love to hear yours too."
Behavior (B)	"I noticed you rolled your eyes just now."
	"In the last few team meetings, you've raised your voice at me in front of others."
	"You mentioned that I don't know what I'm talking about."
Impact (I)	"A patient mentioned noticing this and I'm worried about how it might affect our reputation."
	"It makes me feel hesitant to share my thoughts in meetings."
	"Other team members brought this up after hearing it, and it's becoming a concern."
Toss Back (T)	"Can we find a time to discuss this?"
	"Is everything okay?"
	"I'd like to talk this through—does now work for you?"

Role: Act as a corporate psychologist. Context: """insert here or attach a supporting document, e.g. past email communications""". Then ask one of the questions from Table 5.11.

Tackling Gossip: A Simple Fix with Big Wins

Gossip is the junk food of workplace communication. Tasty in the moment, but bad for you long-term. Research[23] backs this up:

- 90% of people gossip, and 21% do it regularly.
- Each employee spends an average of 65 hours a year gossiping.

Why do we do it? Blame the psychological principle of "secondary gain." Gossip feels good because it bonds us to others, but not in a good way. Imagine a group huddling together, shaking their heads, and saying, "Can

TABLE 5.11

Suggested AI Questions to Help You Implement the *Intro-Behavior-Impact-Toss Back (IBIT)* Model. Notice how AI responds to each specific question.

How AI Can Help	Example Questions	Example of Short AI Response
Drafting and Personalizing Conversations	*Question: AI, help me draft a respectful Intro-Behavior-Impact-Toss Back message about a colleague interrupting me in meetings.*	I noticed you often interrupt me in meetings. I'd appreciate having space to finish my thoughts before responding.
Scenario Practice	*Question: AI, simulate a difficult conversation using IBIT where I address a team member's chronic lateness.*	I've noticed you often arrive late to our meetings. This affects our ability to start on time and stay on track. How do you see this situation?
Sentiment and Impact Analysis	*Question: AI, analyze this draft message for tone and potential impact. Does it sound constructive and respectful?*	The tone of your message is constructive and respectful, focusing on the behavior and its impact rather than the person.
Suggesting Timing and Venue	*Question: AI, is it better to have this conversation over email or in person, given the context?*	Given the sensitivity, it's best to have this conversation in person to allow for open dialogue and immediate feedback.

you believe what she said to her boss?" It's like being part of a team, but the kind of team that wears negativity on their shirtsleeves. What happens when the toxic person everyone gossiped about leaves? That bond built on bad vibes crumbles, leaving the team unsure how to relate positively. Gossiping has been their shared language! So, how do you break free? It's easier said than done, but here's a simple approach. We suggest sharing something like this:

> I know I've been part of these conversations in the past, and honestly, they don't make me feel great. Moving forward, I'll step away from these discussions.

Notice how this doesn't call others out. Instead, you're focusing on your own actions—less finger-pointing, more self-accountability. If you want to flip the script entirely, try "positive gossip," according to Stanford researcher Dr. Jamil Zaki. Instead of tearing people down, share good stories about them with the same energy you'd bring to regular gossip. Imagine the impact of this shift! One strategy Mitch has shared during professional development seminars related to gossip involves helping people understand the negative impact of something called the *fundamental attribution error.*[24] This occurs when we assume that someone's actions are due to their personality or character, rather than their situation. But when we do the same thing, we often blame the situation, not ourselves. For example, a group might gossip about someone who frequently interrupts, saying that the person is rude or disrespectful. But if we interrupt, we might say it's because we were just trying to clarify something or correct a misunderstanding. By learning about this bias, team members can better understand their own behavior and be more thoughtful before judging others. It also helps reduce gossip and encourages a more respectful, understanding team environment. To synthesize this section on gossip, we see eroding the power of gossip as the result and improving team performance as the outcome.

The Art of the Apology: Because "Sorry" Shouldn't Be So Hard

In the research that led to one of Mitch's books, *Breaking the Code of Silence: Prominent Leaders Reveal How They Rebounded from Seven Critical Mistakes,*[25] he uncovered something fascinating (and a little awkward): most people are terrible at apologies. Their apologies are either over the top or so half-hearted they might as well not bother. The issue? Most folks just don't know how to apologize effectively. Through the research that led to this book, Mitch and his co-author, Dr. Louellen Essex, discovered some amazing things about the apology. First, we take a little commercial break to share that our research is based on a Western culture model, so if your team is ready to dive into this learning opportunity, you'll want to frame it with that perspective in mind. And if there are participants with experiences from other cultures, engage them to share their perspectives. We all win with this kind of dialogue. Second, not only do team members get better at smoothing over workplace hiccups, but they also report that their newfound apology skills transfer to improved team outcomes. Suddenly, they're nailing apologies with friends, spouses, and significant others. Third, and probably most importantly, it supports the work of the *Compact of Professional Behaviors.* Think of it this way: an effective apology is like a reset button for relationships. It clears the air, repairs the damage, and makes room for better communication: all in the results domain. For the outcome domain, improved apologies make room for achieving team performance goals more quickly and effectively because team members don't have a chip on their shoulders.

Here are the nuts and bolts of the apology. Most people think they're nailing it, but often, they're doing the equivalent of a "sorry, but . . . I'm not really sorry." You've heard it before: "I apologize, *but*." That little "but" undoes the entire apology, turning it into an excuse as identified in Table 5.12. The right way? Consult the second section of the table in which the person apologizing takes full accountability—no buts, no qualifiers. It's like building a bridge back to trust. If your apology feels genuine, people are more likely to meet you halfway. Think of apologies as the content for a professional development workshop. Done well, they mend fences, build credibility, and show you're human (just like everyone else). And if your team or organization has developed a *Compact of Professional Behaviors*, it's likely to improve your workplace norms.

It's not rocket science, but it *is* the kind of honest communication that can rebuild trust faster than you'd expect.

TABLE 5.12

The Two-Step Erroneous Way Most People Apologize, with Failure Many Times

Ineffective apology:	**No Ownership** "I apologize [or "I'm sorry"] for [behavior inserted here]." **The Excuse** "But I was [insert the reason here]."
Effective apology:	**Own What You Did (Concrete and Past Tense).** Say exactly what happened. No dancing around it, no vague statements. For example, *Over the past three weeks in team meetings, I've been raising my voice and throwing out stats that, honestly, I skewed in my favor. That was wrong.* **Acknowledge the Impact.** Don't skip this step; it's the icing on the cake. Be clear about how your actions affected others. For example, *I know this has made you lose confidence in me as a leader, and that's on me.* **Say You're Sorry.** Keep it simple and genuine; no "but" allowed. For example, *I'm sorry for this behavior. I regret how I handled things.* **Share Your Plan to Do Better.** This is where you bring it home. Outline exactly how you'll fix things and invite others to help hold you accountable. For example, *I plan to work on this by changing my behavior. If I get too intense or intimidating in a meeting, I'd like you to interrupt me and call me out. If you're not comfortable doing that, I hope you'll let me know privately.*

The Often Forgotten Thank-You Note

It seems that, to many, the thank-you note is a relic of the past. In an incredible research study by McVanel and Zalter-Minden, we have learned that it has new uses in creating a culture of respect. She looked at how employees want to be recognized. She discovered:[26]

- 95% reported, "tell me thank you."
- 92% said, "tell me specifically what I did well."
- 88% shared, "write me a thank-you note."

We take the important work from McVanel and Zalter-Minden and transform it into a brief professional development workshop. People love stories, and we tell this next one at the opening of these workshops. Let's step back in time when Mitch had been interviewing for a leadership position at American Express. As he was being interviewed, he saw all these "VIP" (Values In Practice) cards all over the place. Mitch asked about this and was told that when someone witnesses a colleague engaging in one of the four values of the organization, they have an opportunity to recognize this. Essentially, they scribe a handwritten note and give it to the person. At first, Mitch thought this was a bit hokey. Well, long story short . . . Mitch was hired and his opinion changed when he received his first VIP card, and then his second, etc. What an amazing feeling this was! It also spurred on new results like increased respectful behaviors. It also provided clear outcomes: team members working more effectively with each other on the same team (intra-team development) *and* teams working more effectively with other teams (inter-team development). There's solid evidence for the value of recognition. For example, employees who reported that managers who were exceptional at recognizing them were 40% more engaged.[27] We have integrated the content regarding the power of recognition into several professional development workshops. It's easy, applicable, and effective.

5.6.4 Sample Leadership Development Venues

Coaching: Engaging a Singleness of Focus on Respect

Now that we have identified and described the primary vehicles for staff development, let's look at leadership development as a way to reinforce the good work in which staff have been engaged, as well as to help navigate tough situations. That's where leadership coaching comes in. Picture it as your GPS for workplace respect: staff need to have their efforts reinforced as well as supported. Leadership coaching is a primary way of doing this.

Here are three ways to make coaching more accessible and impactful:

1. **Short, Bite-Sized Coaching Sessions (Spot Coaching)**
   We have found tremendous success with quick, focused 30-minute sessions; these can work wonders, especially if the leaders show up prepared with a specific issue or opportunity they want to tackle.

2. **Virtual Coaching**
   Many established and emerging platforms provide virtual coaching at a reasonable cost. It's efficient, cost-effective, and easy to fit into a busy schedule. While AI cannot fully understand the complexity of human emotions or the context of each unique situation, it is also available 24/7 to guide an employee through various scenarios without fear of judgment or retaliation:

   • Questioning and self-reflection. Try this: *Act as a leadership coach and always respond to my inputs with coaching questions instead of answers. I need to address a team member's chronic lateness.* Response: *What do you think might be contributing to your team member's chronic lateness, and how have you addressed it with them so far?*

   • Virtual scenarios to practice your own coaching skills. Try this: *Act as a disrespectful employee who is meeting with their manager (me) for their annual performance review.* Response: *Yeah, I know we have to do this review, but honestly, I don't see the point. Every year it's the same thing-just a checklist so you can say you did your job. I get my work done, and if you have a problem with how I do it, maybe you should be clearer about what you actually want.*

   • Brainstorming to spark new ideas. Try this: *Act as a business consultant. Context: I am faced with the following problem related to low employee morale: """"insert here"""". Question: Give me 5 different options worth considering to try and resolve, or at least mitigate, this problem.* Response: *Prioritize transparent communication, Promote work-life balance and well-being, Recognize and celebrate achievements, Foster open feedback and support channels, Invest in professional development and growth*

3. **Group Coaching (A Hidden Gem)**

   Group coaching is rarely used (unfortunately). Here, leaders from the same team or different teams bring a challenge, a question, or an opportunity—everyone learns from the solutions. It's cost-effective, fosters camaraderie, and often sparks ideas leaders hadn't even thought about. Plus, there's something powerful about realizing you're not the only one dealing with difficult situations or even positive opportunities.

4. **A Coaching Model**

   There are hundreds of coaching models available. One simple and effective option is the **W-C-A Coaching Model** (*Wins* → *Challenges* → *Accomplishments*). It begins by asking participants to state ahead of time their opportunities and challenges to help them gear up for the session. On the basis of the context, we sometimes like to start on a high note by asking participants to celebrate their **Wins**—those recent successes or positive developments worth acknowledging. Next, we explore their **Challenges**—the factors that are slowing things down or creating obstacles. Finally, we hand the keys to the staff member, letting them steer by asking what **Accomplishments** they want to discuss during the session. This quick, three-step structure is effective whether you're connecting virtually or chatting over a cup of coffee. Leaders often tell us it puts a fresh spin on coaching that is doable, simple, and impactful. One suggestion is to use AI to identify which coaching approach may serve your needs best. Provide specific context information and apply relevant prompts, as we have demonstrated many times in previous chapters. It's easy to try and produce many variations of coaching models as identified in Table 5.13. Please note that the coaching models identified are acronyms, which are explained in great detail by AI.

A Fresh Take on the Exit Interview

The exit interview is like a dinosaur, whose time has long passed us by. In the exit interview, you're gathering clues about why someone's leaving your organization. Many times it's the result of a poor work culture. Traditionally, HR handles this process right before or as the employee walks out the door. Surprisingly, that timing might not be ideal, especially if the reason for leaving rhymes with "toxic boss." Think about it. Even after resigning, people might be nervous about sharing the real story. If they've been dealing with a

TABLE 5.13

A List of Coaching Models in Acronym Form Generated by AI. This Shows the Wide Range of Effective Coaching Approaches Available

Coaching Model	Distinctive Steps	Special Focus
GROW	Goal, Reality, Options, Will	Action-oriented, widely used
OSKAR	Outcome, Scaling, Know-how, Affirm & Action, Review	Solution-focused, strengths-based
CLEAR	Contract, Listen, Explore, Act, Review	Contracting/coaching relationship
FUEL	Frame, Understand, Explore, Lay out a plan	Outcomes/action
STEPPA	Subject, Target, Emotion, Perception, Plan, Action/Adapt	Emotional awareness

difficult, toxic boss, they might worry about repercussions—a bad reference, a whisper campaign to the new employer, or something even worse. One person we spoke with in our research study shared this about her toxic boss: *I'm not giving them the truth. I'll tell them what they want to hear and just move on. You never know what they might say to my new employer.* Here's an idea to shake things up that participants in Mitch's research study shared: delay the exit interview by three to four months. By then, the person is settled in their new job and far enough removed from your organization to feel more comfortable speaking candidly. How do you make this work?

1. ***Extend the invitation***. Before they leave, the HR professional asks if they'd be open to a follow-up interview down the road.
2. ***Provide key questions***. Share the questions in advance so they know what to expect.
3. ***Share how this may improve the organization***. Let them know this isn't just for gossip; it's about improving your organization and addressing potential cultural issues.
4. ***Identify themes***. Once the interview is conducted, collect the themes from the exit interviews and share these in a roundtable kind of fashion with key leaders. Learn from this. Begin changing your culture as a result.

The result of this process is likely to be a better understanding of obstacles to a respectful work culture. The outcome when actions are taken as a result of

TABLE 5.14

A Sampling of Exit Interview Questions (Three to Four Months Post-Exit)

1. What prompted you to leave the organization?
2. Did you share these concerns with anyone while employed here?
3. Is there anything we could have done differently to have kept you on board?
4. How would you describe the leadership you experienced here (i.e., your boss and other leaders)?
5. Now that you're at a new organization, do you have any fresh insights or comparisons to share?

themes extracted is that turnover and recruiting costs decrease as well as individual and team performance increases. This approach adds some breathing room and creates an environment where they're more likely to share meaningful insights. And no, the boss should never conduct the exit interview. Even if you're short on HR staff or have none, find someone respected and objective to handle it. Sharing the results with key stakeholders—especially the boss' boss—is a critical step to ensure that any problems aren't swept under the rug. Table 5.14 provides some top questions to ask someone during this delayed exit interview approach.

A Simple Method to Avoid Hiring a Toxic Employee

Recruiting is a lot like dating. First impressions sometimes matter, but if you only focus on the charm offensive, you might miss the warning signs. Here's a quick (and true) story to prove the point with names changed for purposes of confidentiality and anonymity. Aiko was interviewing for a high-level VP position. She flew in from across the country, strolled off the plane, and met Dave, the executive assistant, at baggage claim. Dave, being the consummate pro, politely informed Aiko that there had been a small tweak to the interview schedule and asked if he could explain this before the hiring manager (Kim) showed up. Aiko, however, brushed him off and offered to wait until Kim showed up. I guess Aiko was saying that she would reserve her A-game charm for Kim. When Kim showed up, Dave was left scratching his head and thinking, *Is this our future VP? Yikes.* What Dave saw was the classic "kiss up, kick down" personality—a toxic cocktail that could poison an entire workplace. Aiko was engaging and complimented Dave in front of Kim. And that's what Kim saw: a top candidate. Now, you might be wondering, "How do I spot someone like Aiko before we hire her?" Sure, you could hire an organizational psychologist (like Mitch!), roll out a battery of psychological tests, and spend a fortune dissecting their personality. Or you could save yourself the time and budget by using a simple, no-cost hack: the *Recruiting Cue Sheet*. Think of it as a secret decoder ring for spotting hidden red flags. This tool broadens the evaluation process beyond the formal interview team. Instead, it brings in people who interact with the candidate in casual settings—receptionists, drivers, cafeteria staff, you name it. These everyday encounters give you a peek behind the curtain to see how the candidate behaves when they think no one important is watching. How a candidate treats the people who may not be regarded as influential says a lot about how the candidate may treat everyone. Before the candidate arrives, hand out a short cue sheet to anyone who might cross paths with them. Keep it simple. It could include questions like:

1. Did the candidate say hello or strike up a conversation?
2. Did they show any signs of our organizational values (or at least basic decency)?
3. Would you actually want to work with this person?
4. Were there any red flags?

These casual moments can be more revealing than an hour-long grilling in a conference room. The best part? This method doesn't just help you weed out potential bad hires; it also reinforces your company's values. It shows your team that every person and interaction matter and that your organization values respect at every level. So, next time you're recruiting, remember: it's not just about who shines under the spotlight. It's about who shows up in the shadows. After the interview, be sure to check in with those who may have crossed paths with the candidate.

Are You a Toxic Protector?

Another brief staff development opportunity we have provided is to share the notion of the toxic protector.[28] These are those individuals who enable toxic behaviors in others, either knowingly or unknowingly. Picture this: a toxic employee is like a thunderstorm, wreaking havoc across the workplace, while the toxic protector is the umbrella shielding them from accountability. Why do toxic protectors exist? Sometimes it's a social connection (kids at the same school, coffee buddies). Other times, it's because the toxic person is a high performer; maybe they're bringing in revenue or have unique expertise, and you don't want to rock the boat. Regardless of the reason, the protector's actions allow the bad behavior to continue unchecked. So, how do you address this? Instead of going straight to the storm (the toxic individual), talk to the umbrella (the toxic protector). And use the same **Intro + Behavior + Impact + Toss Back** (IBIT) feedback model we suggested engaging with toxic people. Why is this so powerful? Our research demonstrated that people are more apt to provide feedback to a toxic protector than to the actual toxic person. It's less threatening and less volatile.

Here's an example of a conversation with a toxic protector.

- **Intro.** *I'd like to talk about something I've observed.*
- **Behavior.** *When you consistently overlook Sam's disrespectful comments in meetings...*
- **Impact.** *it creates an environment where others feel uncomfortable speaking up.*
- **Toss Back.** *How do you think we can address this together?*

This approach shifts the focus and accountability to the protector, who often has the power to influence the toxic person's behavior.

5.7 PRINCIPLE 5. SUSTAIN WHAT WORKS

5.7.1 The Sustainability Culture Change Plan

In this cultural transformation, we estimate the next set of actions around the six-month mark and beyond. One of the best ways to keep a culture change going strong is through a team approach developed by the Healthy Workforce Institute called the *Sustainability Culture Change Plan*. Think of it as the engine that keeps the train of progress chugging along, developed and fine-tuned by the Healthy Workforce Institute. At the heart of this initiative is the *Sustainability Culture Change Plan*—a living, breathing document. It's like a dynamic recipe for culture change, with new ingredients added and tweaks made as needed. This "recipe" ensures that everyone keeps stirring the pot to sustain the positive momentum. The team itself should be a small group of up to 12 representatives with different perspectives, roles, and ideas coming together regularly to make the newly established norms from the

Compact of Professional Behaviors even richer. Essentially, this plan maps out the "baby steps" along the way, making the big changes feel more like a series of manageable sprints instead of a marathon. It's all about steady progress—more like dipping your toes in, step by step, until you're swimming laps. For the initiative to really thrive, we recommend having two co-chairs who will guide the team, which meets for just an hour each month—short, sweet, and efficient. The primary reason for two co-chairs is that if one cannot make a meeting, the meeting still goes on. The key to success? Keep it simple: focus on no more than two goals at a time. You don't want to juggle so many goals that you drop the ball—or worse, all the balls. As the team reaches its goals, they can set new ones and keep the momentum going. Clients affirm this simple but powerful model, reporting incredible results. The bottom line? Slow and steady wins the race. Figure 5.4 demonstrates a sample, completed *Sustainability Culture Change Plan.* Note that as time goes on, the plan keeps

HEALTHY
WORKFORCE

Healthy Workforce Institute
Sustainability Culture Change Plan

Goal	Tactics / Action	Responsible Party	Status	Outcome/Results	Expected Completion Date
STRENGTHENING THE ORGANIZATION					
Build action teams to promote new culture	Share top strategies for culture change with a team outside the dept. Share at each monthly meeting.	Two action team members	Review mid-month. Pilot it for 6 months.	Colleagues reported began using these strategies successfully.	3rd quarter.
Create virtual learning in the organization.	Teams piloted intranet repository of resources to support leaders in setting standard of professionalism.	Design team	Continuous updating will be done.	Improved Compact behaviors. HR reported 10% grievance reduction	By end of year.
EQUIPPING FRONTLINE LEADERS					
Include staff onboarding experience.	Leaders assign a coffee "buddy" to new staff. "Buddy" introduces them to leaders in "coffee chat" times.	Co-chairs of action team will promote this.	1st and 2nd quarter on a pilot basis	10% reduction in turnover in the first 6 months of employment	Assess & extend as this is a pilot.
Improve leader coaching	New coaches attend "coach-the-coach" pilot program	All coaches	2nd quarter	Pilot has not been completed	Ongoing
STRENGTHENING THE TEAM					
Establish team expectations of respect	Discuss at team meetings examples of the Compact reinforces professionalism; discuss obstacles	Team leaders	Ongoing	Staff report a significant engagement of the Compact	3rd quarter
Improve staff feedback	Leader shares with staff a new behavior learned. Share with team	Team leaders	Piloting this	Staff are now using these new behaviors	Piloting
Reinforce the new culture in newsletter	Two successes are featured each month. Q & A column is added for additional engagement	Co-chairs of the goals team	Still piloting	There's now a positive buzz about the culture change process	Piloting

FIGURE 5.4

Sample page from several of the *Sustainability Culture Change Plan*; extracted, adapted, and revised to protect confidentiality.

being enhanced with new goals and actions, along with old ones accomplished and noted (it's very important to keep these accomplishments front and center!). Initially, Mitch distributes a bland *Plan* and, if needed, shares examples to catalyze the initiative.

When it comes to figuring out if something worked, there are two main ways to look at it: *quantitative data* (numbers, charts, and stats) and *qualitative data* (stories, observations, and feedback). Think of it like this—numbers primarily give you the "what," while words mainly give you the "why." Further, in terms of individual style, some leaders love stats; others are all about the stories. What's important to understand is that both are important and both are data! Here are two ways to measure success:

- The Multiple Baseline Design
- The Retrospective Evaluation

5.7.2 The Multiple Baseline Design: Staggering Measurements over Time

Imagine you're trying to roll out a new skill-training program across your team. Perhaps one of the staff development or leadership development programs we shared earlier? You may not be able to put everyone through the training program all at once. So, why not take advantage of this? Evaluate the program at various times. Sounds simple? Well, it actually is, provided that you use this opportunity to measure baseline data for all participants. That's basically what the *Multiple Baseline Design* is about. Here's how it works:

1. **Baseline Check**. You start by measuring where everyone stands right now (think of it as a pulse check before any interventions occur).
2. **Roll Out Gradually**. Participants receive the training over time in various groups. Group 1 gets the training first, while Groups 2 and 3 wait (but continue to collect baseline data). Then you compare the "before" and "after" scores for Group 1. If Group 1 improves but the others don't, you're onto something!
3. **Repeat**. Next, Group 2 receives the training, while Group 3 continues collecting baseline data. Measure again. If Group 2 also shows improvement, it's looking like your training program is effective.

Is it proof? Not exactly. We're not medical researchers testing a new cancer drug here. But it's pretty strong evidence that your program is making a difference. Unless Group 1 magically got a big raise (and that's why they're suddenly performing better), it's safe to say your intervention is working. The beauty of the *Multiple Baseline Design* is that you can recalibrate and tweak your approach before rolling it out to the rest. We have used this method with hundreds of clients, with an amazing response from leaders. Basically, "Wow! This is easy and effective!" Other comments relate to the fact that "We're providing the learning opportunities at staggered points in time anyway. Why not take advantage of this. And we did!" Figure 5.5 demonstrates this method as applied to a recent professional development program focused on providing effective feedback to colleagues exhibiting disruptive behaviors, as part of the culture change initiative. We gave them a pre-test to assess how effective participants were at providing feedback (the baseline); 60 days later, we gave them the same test to determine their skill level now (the post-test). The results indicated that each group improved. A 120-day post-test sustained these positive results. You can replace the behavior or performance indicator on the y-axis with something else that fits your needs. This makes the evaluation method flexible and useful in different situations, as discussed throughout this chapter.

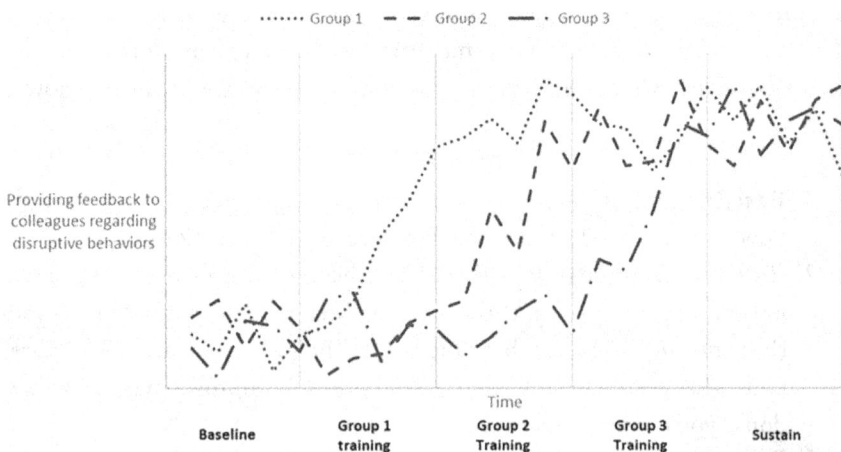

FIGURE 5.5
Demonstration of the multiple baseline design in providing feedback to colleagues regarding disruptive behaviors.

5.7.3 The Retrospective Evaluation: The "Hindsight" Method

Another straightforward way to evaluate success is the *Retrospective Evaluation*. It has the likeness of a "before-and-after" snapshot, but with a twist: we ask people to reflect on what they knew before and after the program, but both of these (before and after) are done *after* they've completed it. Confused? Let us explain. The whole idea behind this is to avoid something researchers call *response shift bias*—basically, having a different frame of reference before and after the learning event. Imagine you attend a workshop on how to erode the power of gossip. Before the workshop, one of the survey items asked, on a scale of 1 to 5, "How much do you know about eroding gossip?" You confidently think, *Oh, while I may not know everything about this, I do know a fair amount.* So, on a scale of 1 to 5, with 1 being the lowest and 5 being the highest, you give yourself a 4 (not knowing everything but still knowing a lot). Then you attend the workshop and realize, *Wow, I barely scratched the surface on understanding and eroding the power of gossip.* So, if you were to now give yourself a score after attending the learning event, you would realize you were really a 2 before the learning, not a 4. That's response shift bias. Your "before" perspective changes because you now know what you *didn't* know. Humbling, right? In a nutshell, here's how it works. Refer to Table 5.15 for a sample of this retrospective evaluation. It doesn't matter too much which performance indicators you choose for each item. As long as they are clear and focus on specific behaviors, they can be used in many different situations, not just for addressing a toxic work culture. In this box, notice that after participants completed the learning program, we asked them to rate their knowledge in two ways:

1. **Pre-learning Knowledge**. How much did you know *before* the program?
2. **Post-learning Knowledge**. Now that you've finished the program, how much do you know?

This approach helps cut through inflated self-perceptions, giving us a more accurate picture of the learning impact. Let's share a real, live example here. Mitch recently worked with a client on a program about eroding toxic work cultures. After the training, participants reflected on their knowledge before *and* after, using this retrospective evaluation. The results were

TABLE 5.15

Sample Retrospective Evaluation Instrument of a Recent Culture Change Program

Retrospective Evaluation
Please rate your knowledge of each of the items below. We ask that you consider two important benchmarks: Your knowledge *before* attending this module. Your knowledge *after* completing this module. Please rate your "before" and "after" experiences as if you are looking back in time — even before you attended the training. This means you are reflecting and writing both your "before" and "after" responses now, based on your current perspective. Hence, the term "retrospective evaluation." Your responses are confidential and anonymous; only aggregate data will be shared. Please circle the response that best describes your rating. Thank you.

Rating Key:
1 = No knowledge
2 = Limited knowledge
3 = Adequate knowledge
4 = Good knowledge
5 = Excellent knowledge

I understand how to:	My knowledge *before* this module	My knowledge *after* the module
1. Engage the five conflict management styles.	1 2 3 4 5	1 2 3 4 5
2. Apply systems thinking to my leadership.	1 2 3 4 5	1 2 3 4 5
3. Create a more positive work culture.	1 2 3 4 5	1 2 3 4 5
4. Provide meaningful feedback that works.	1 2 3 4 5	1 2 3 4 5
5. Erode the power of gossip.	1 2 3 4 5	1 2 3 4 5
6. Avoid hiring a disruptive individual.	1 2 3 4 5	1 2 3 4 5
7. Design an effective work culture	1 2 3 4 5	1 2 3 4 5
8. Reward performance more successfully.	1 2 3 4 5	1 2 3 4 5
9. Erode the role of the toxic protector.	1 2 3 4 5	1 2 3 4 5

startling! Please refer to Figure 5.6 to see the results demonstrated in a histogram format. This retrospective evaluation showed us the big wins *and* the remaining challenges, so they could keep improving. It's a simple, effective way to measure success—like shining a flashlight into both the achievements and the cracks.

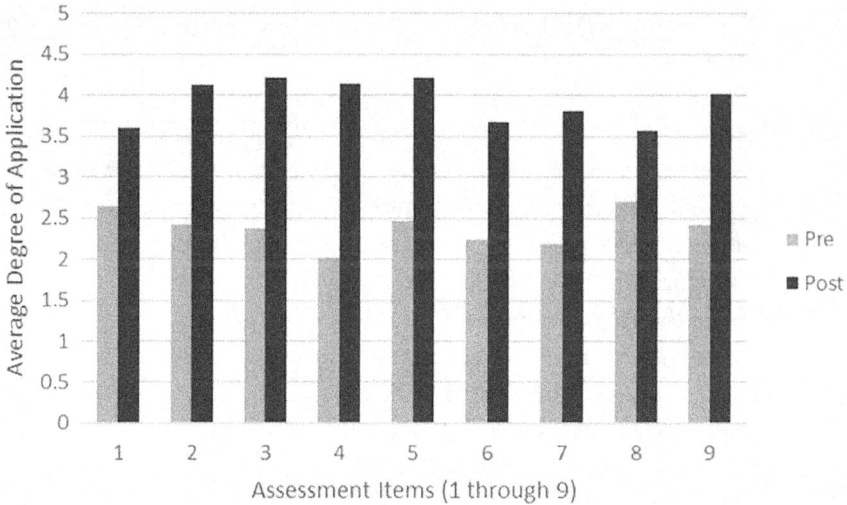

FIGURE 5.6
Histograms demonstrating completed retrospective evaluation with results.

In this section, we have shared two powerful evaluation strategies to demonstrate how to assess dimensions of culture change. These demonstrate not only learning and behavioral changes, but also areas requiring focus for future development. If you don't evaluate, you don't know!

5.8 KEY TAKEAWAYS

5.8.1 The Three Instruments for Change

This chapter focused on six phases of workplace culture change. While we engaged the one example of moving from a toxic to a respectful workplace culture, we shared how this phased process can be used for other culture change initiatives. Let's review what we've covered through the three instruments for change:

1. **Self as the Instrument for Change**
   - **Model respectful behavior.** Individuals play a pivotal role in shifting workplace culture by embodying respect, professionalism, and empathy, even when addressing negative behaviors or conflict.

- **Practice reflection and positive framing.** Employees and leaders should reflect on their own contributions to culture, leverage strengths, and use positive framing (such as micro-acts of joy) to boost morale and engagement.
- **Leverage tools for self-awareness.** Using tools like sentiment analysis and AI feedback can help individuals assess their own communication and emotional impact, providing opportunities for growth and more effective engagement.

2. **Team as the Instrument for Change**
   - **Foster participatory practice.** Teams are essential for aligning individual and organizational goals, and their effectiveness hinges on intentional participatory practices: monitoring how and when participation occurs and ensuring all voices are heard.
   - **Target behaviors, not people:** Teams should focus on addressing and changing specific behaviors rather than labeling individuals, which supports a healthier, more collaborative environment. The *Compact of Professional Behaviors* is a good example.
   - **Utilize data to guide team interventions.** Analyzing sentiment and engagement at the team level helps identify pockets of resistance or optimism, enabling targeted support and tailored interventions for maximum impact.

3. **Organization as the Instrument for Change**
   - **Align work culture with strategy:** Organizational culture—defined by shared values, beliefs, norms, and practices—must be intentionally shaped to support strategic goals, whether that's fostering innovation, safety, or customer service.
   - **Support systemic change:** Organizations must provide the structures, resources, and leadership necessary to sustain respectful, high-performing cultures and to uproot toxic behaviors systemwide. The *Sustainability Culture Change Plan* is a great example.
   - **Measure and sustain progress:** Ongoing assessment of culture (through tools like multiple baseline design, and the retrospective evaluation) and reinforcement of positive behaviors are critical for maintaining momentum and ensuring lasting transformation.

By viewing culture change through these three interconnected lenses, the chapter demonstrates how individuals, teams, and organizations each have distinct yet complementary roles in eradicating toxic behaviors and building a foundation for high performance and resilience.

5.8.2 The Five Principles of Change

In Table 5.16, we have compiled a list of self-assessment questions and tools mentioned in this chapter for the five change principles to help you reflect on your own work culture.

With these strategies in hand, you're ready to tackle toxic cultures head-on. Just remember: cultural change isn't a sprint; it's more like a marathon with occasional hurdles. But the payoff? A thriving, engaged workplace where people actually *want* to show up on Monday mornings, get a better night's sleep, and experience improved performance.

TABLE 5.16

Self-Assessment Questions and Tools Related to Culture Change

Principles of Change	Self-Assessment Questions	A Highlight of Tools Introduced in This Book to Address These Self-Assessment Questions
Frame the Evidence for Change	Are we highlighting the positive impacts of respect in the workplace? Have we identified patterns in turnover, sick days, employee grievances, and/or satisfaction scores?	**Identify Positive Impact.** Focus on the benefits of respect: well-being, performance, joy. **Culture Check-Up.** Assess turnover, sick days, employee grievances, satisfaction scores to reveal underlying issues.
Assess With Engagement	Are we focusing on strengths to inspire engagement, rather than dwelling on weaknesses? Have we gathered specific examples of toxic behaviors and their impact on employees?	**Strengths Check-Up.** Focus on strengths and successes to foster positive change. **Analysis of Areas for Improvement.** Identify results from assessments and interpret for action.
Embrace Systems Thinking	Have we defined non-negotiable behaviors to set clear boundaries? Do we have consensus on expected behaviors in the workplace?	**"Always" and "Never" Activity Leading to the *Compact of Professional Behaviors.*** Create consensus on expected behaviors. **Perspectives on What Is Non-negotiable.** Link to the organization's values.

(Continued)

TABLE 5.16 *(Continued)*

Self-Assessment Questions and Tools Related to Culture Change

Principles of Change	Self-Assessment Questions	A Highlight of Tools Introduced in This Book to Address These Self-Assessment Questions
Target Results *and* Outcomes	Are we developing staff skills in communication, empathy, and conflict resolution?	**Staff Development.** Enhance skills in communication, empathy, and conflict resolution.
	Are our leaders modeling respectful behavior, accountability, and empathy?	**Leadership Development.** Focus on modeling respectful behavior, accountability, and empathy.
Sustain What Works	Do we have a detailed plan for sustaining positive changes over time?	**Sustainability Culture Change Plan.** Develop an engaged plan for sustaining positive changes over time.
	Are we tracking changes in behavior across different teams or departments over time, as needed or relevant?	**Multiple Baseline Design.** Track changes in behavior across different teams or departments over time.
		Retrospective Evaluation. A method to avoid response-shift bias.

NOTES

1 Kusy, M., & Holloway, E. (2009). *Toxic workplace! Managing toxic personalities and their systems of power.* Jossey-Bass.

2 Waschgler, K., Ruiz-Hernández, J. A., Llor-Esteban, B., & Jiménez-Barbero, J. A. (2013). Vertical and lateral workplace bullying in nursing: Development of the hospital aggressive behaviour scale. *Journal of Interpersonal Violence, 28*(12), 2389–2412.

3 Bambi, S., Foà, C., De Felippis, C., Lucchini, A., Guazzini, A., & Rasero, L. (2018). Workplace incivility, lateral violence and bullying among nurses: A review about their prevalence and related factors. *Acta Medica, 89*(Supplement 6), 51–79. https://doi.org/10.23750/abm.v89i6-S.7461

4 American Psychological Association. (2023). *APA dictionary of psychology.* https://dictionary.apa.org/

5 Sull, D., Sull, C., Cipolli, W., & Brighenti, C. (2022, March 16). Why every leader needs to worry about toxic culture. *MIT Sloan Management Review.*

6 Kusy, M., & Holloway, E. (2010). Detox your workplace: A culture of respect can add to our company's bottom line. *Marketing Health Services, 30*(3). https://aura.antioch.edu/facarticles/54

7 Seppala, E., & Cameron, K. (2015). Proof that positive work cultures are more productive. *Harvard Business Review, 12*(1), 44–50.

8 Hart, J. (2016). The science of well-being reveals health benefits: Greater Good Science Center, University of California, Berkeley. *Alternative and Complementary Therapies, 22*(6), 266–268.

9 Thompson, R. (2025). *Enough! Eradicate Incivility & Bullying in Healthcare.*

10 Kusy, M., & Holloway, E. (2009). *Toxic workplace! Managing toxic personalities and their systems of power.* Jossey-Bass.

11 Kusy, M., & Holloway, E. (2009). *Toxic workplace! Managing toxic personalities and their systems of power.* Jossey-Bass.

12 Porath, C., & Pearson, C. (2013). The price of incivility. *Harvard Business Review, 91*(1–2), 114–121.

13 Mauer, C. (2024, August 8). *Incivility's cost to employers: $2 billion per day.* www.shrm.org.

14 Porath, C., & Pearson, C. (2013). The price of incivility. *Harvard Business Review, 91*(1–2), 114–121.

15 Rosenstein, A. H., & O'Daniel, M. (2008). A survey of the impact of disruptive behaviors and communication defects on patient safety. *The Joint Commission Journal on Quality and Patient Safety, 34*(8), 464–471.

16 Cooper, W. O., Spain, D. A., Guillamondegui, O., Kelz, R. R., Domenico, H. J., Hopkins, J., Sullivan, P., Moore, I. N., Pichert, J. W., Catron, T. F., Webb, L. E., Dmochowski, R. R., & Hickson, G. B. (2019, June). Association of coworker reports about unprofessional behavior by surgeons with surgical complications in their patients. *JAMA Surgery, 154*(9), 828–834.

17 Brassey, J., Herbig, B., Jeffery, B., & Ungerman, D. (2023). *Reframing employee health: Moving beyond burnout to holistic health.* McKinsey Health Institute.

18 MacLellan, L. (2018, November 27). The surprising fragility of a powerful perk: Company culture. *Quartz at Work.*

19 Kouzes, J. M., & Posner, B. Z. (2023). *The leadership challenge* (7th ed.). Jossey-Bass.

20 Sutton, R. I. (2018). *The asshole survival guide: How to deal with people who treat you like dirt.* Harper Business.

21 Kusy, M. (2017). *Why I don't work here anymore: A leader's guide to offset the financial and emotional costs of toxic employees.* Routledge/CRC Press.

22 Thompson, R. (2025). *Enough! Eradicate Incivility & Bullying in Healthcare.*

23 Grosser, T., Kidwell, V., & Labianca, G. J. (2012). Hearing it through the grapevine: Positive and negative workplace gossip. *Organizational Dynamics, 41*, 52–61.

24 Healy, P. (2017, June). The fundamental attribution error: What it is and how to avoid it. *Business Insights, Harvard Business School Online.*

25 Kusy, M., & Essex, L. (2005). *Breaking the code of silence: Prominent leaders reveal how they rebounded from seven critical mistakes.* Lanham, MD: Taylor Trade Publishing/Rowman & Littlefield Publishing Group.

26 McVanel, S., & Zalter-Minden, B. (2015). *Forever recognize others' greatness: Solution-focused strategies for satisfied staff, high-performing teams, and healthy bottom lines.* BPS Books.

27 Littlefield, C. (2022, October 25). A better way to recognize your employees. *Harvard Business Review.* Harvard Business School Publishing. https://hbr.org/2022/10/a-better-way-to-recognize-your-employees

28 Kusy, M. (2017). *Why I don't work here anymore: A leader's guide to offset the financial and emotional costs of toxic employees.* Routledge/CRC Press.

6

Lead Change Now. What Are Your Next Steps?

6.1 CHAPTER PREVIEW

In this chapter, we're rolling up our sleeves and turning everything you've learned so far into a practical action plan. By now, you've explored the five core change principles and the three instruments for change as well as discovered a toolbox of practical strategies. Now, it's time to apply what you've learned to your unique situation and build a personalized roadmap to success. How do you transform a collection of ideas into a cohesive plan that your team can support? The jump from abrupt change to concrete action can stop even the most seasoned leaders in their tracks! That's why we've broken the process down into a straightforward, three-step method that we describe in section 6.3. You'll discover how to kick off meaningful conversations around the five principles of change, uncover those hidden assumptions that often trip teams up, and build alignment from day one.

Along the way, we'll show you how to turn dialogue into genuine engagement, using focused questions and hands-on tools (with a dash of AI magic to keep things fresh and insights flowing). Next, we'll tackle the nitty-gritty work of finding clarity amid uncertainty and setting thoughtful priorities. To avoid getting stuck in the weeds, we'll use practical frameworks like the Stacey Matrix to map out how much clarity or uncertainty exists around your challenges—ranging from straightforward, well-defined issues to highly ambiguous, messy situations.

Then, we'll bring in the Cynefin Framework to help you sort and sequence your next moves, even when things get complicated. And don't worry if these

DOI: 10.4324/9781003622925-6

tools aren't familiar to you: no prior experience needed! We'll walk through each one step by step, using a real-world scenario to show you how it all comes together.

Finally, you'll see how to transform this newfound clarity and focus into a concrete, prioritized action plan—one that energizes your team, builds momentum, and gives everyone a clear sense of what's next. By the end of the chapter, our goal is for you to walk away with a simple, adaptable roadmap for turning your vision into action, as well as the confidence to keep tweaking and improving it as you move forward. Ready to lead your team into meaningful change, one well-chosen action at a time? Let's dive right in.

6.2 CRITICAL INCIDENT: "WRITER'S BLOCK"

Meet Soren (fictitious name and scenario), Director of Operations at InnovateTech Solutions. After nearly 20 years in tech, Soren isn't exactly a stranger to navigating change, but right now, his plate is overflowing. The company's shiny new strategic plan has handed him three big visions: ramp up AI adoption, spark new waves of innovation, and drag those old, clunky processes into the modern era. Soren knows better than to try leading this charge all by himself. He can see the market is shifting, technology is evolving, and if InnovateTech is going to keep up, it's going to take a team effort. So, what does he do? He grabs hold of the five change principles, along with the practical tools from this book, and gets his team equipped for the change to come. Here's Soren's challenge. It's one thing to rally the troops and gather ideas; it's another thing to turn all that enthusiasm into a clear, actionable plan. Soren is a huge believer in open dialogue and making space for every perspective around the table. Still, as he settles in to outline next steps, he's hit with that classic leadership speed bump: "Where on earth do I even start?" There it is—the blinking cursor syndrome, also known as writer's block. If you've been there, you know the feeling. The good news? You don't have to untangle it alone. We're about to walk you through some simple steps to help Soren (and you) tackle even the most daunting situation with clarity and confidence. Let's get to it!

6.3 A THREE-STEP APPROACH TO ACTION

To assist Soren and lead his team to success, we have developed a three-step approach that brings together powerful solutions for decision-making under uncertainty:

1. **Create alignment through structured dialogue**. Organize team conversations around the five change principles. By steering discussions with targeted, thought-provoking questions anchored to each principle, teams can surface underlying assumptions and build alignment from the start about the problem and the approach—an essential first step before applying any decision-making model.

2. **Provide clarity through rigorous analysis.** Once the team is aligned, apply robust tools, such as those presented in this book and the Stacey Matrix we'll introduce shortly, to evaluate the nature of each change principle as *Clear, Complicated, Complex, or Chaotic.* This analysis highlights which areas are ready for immediate action and which ones require deeper exploration.

3. **Drive action with thoughtful prioritization.** Use the Cynefin Framework to prioritize your actions. With this tool, you can spot those quick wins, flag where immediate action is critical, and tailor your approach to match the complexity of each challenge. No more one-size-fits-all solutions! Then, bring in AI tools to tie it all together, creating a comprehensive plan that blends smart prioritization with the evidence-based practices we have covered in this book.

By following these steps, Soren can transform ambiguity into coordinated action, ensuring his team can move forward with purpose, cohesion, and the flexibility needed to navigate change successfully. Next, we'll dive into each one of these steps and share practical templates for each one.

6.3.1 Create Alignment through Structure

To kick things off, Soren's first order of business is figuring out just how well his team understands *what* this new strategy actually means for them and for the organization as a whole. From past experience, he's learned that starting an honest, meaningful conversation about such a big, complex topic is no easy feat. That's why he's looking for a smarter way in. Taking a cue from the practical examples throughout this book, Soren decides to anchor the discussion around the five principles of change. Breaking things down this way turns a daunting, abstract challenge into smaller, more manageable bites. For each principle, Soren prepares thoughtful questions; these are real conversation starters meant to spark reflection, dig beneath the surface, and get everyone truly engaged. Why lead with questions? Because the right questions can shake people out of autopilot, open up dialogue, get them to think critically, and maybe even challenge the old ways! But here's where things get interesting: Soren isn't just fishing for answers. He wants to uncover the "why" behind their responses, to surface hidden assumptions that might be shaping their thinking without them even realizing it.

There's another bonus to structuring the conversation around the five change principles; it naturally steers the team toward specific, practical tools they can actually use to tackle each one. Soren doesn't want the team sitting back and waiting for marching orders; he wants everyone to play an active role in figuring out *how* to bring the new strategy to life. To help with this, he lines up a set of practical, evidence-based tools from the book, each tailored to a specific change principle. This way, the team isn't stuck in theory; they're equipped to explore concrete options and can smoothly transition from thoughtful discussion to real, impactful action that moves the change forward. Let's take a look at the questions and tools Soren came up with in Table 6.1.

Keep in mind, this table is just a springboard. Soren wants his team to come up with their own questions and add even more tools and practices to the list, including some that are already common practice in their organization. With his pre-work done, Soren is ready to gather his team together in the situation room. He schedules a two-hour collaborative workshop structured in three phases, each aligned with one of the three steps to action.

First Phase of the Two-Hour Workshop

The first phase of the workshop is designed to let ideas flow and spark real conversation. Soren is confident that genuine insights will emerge through these lively discussions. But he also knows that simply running down the list questions isn't enough. He needs to assess where the team is ready to move forward and where they still need to dig deeper. He's watching for alignment on two key fronts. First, alignment around the "*what*": are team members'

TABLE 6.1

Examples of Questions and Tools Associated with Each Change Principle to Help Leaders Define Their Change Situation and How to Tackle It

Principles of Change	Defining the WHAT	Defining the HOW
Frame the Evidence for Change	• How clear are the decision-making boundaries regarding these goals? Are there any "off-limits" areas, like budget constraints or technology limitations, that haven't been communicated? • To what extent do InnovateTech's employees understand the "why" behind boosting AI adoption, nurturing growth and innovation, and revamping outdated processes?	• Vroom-Yetton-Jago Decision-Making Model to assess expertise, commitment, and time constraints[1] • AI-powered thematic analysis to identify common concerns and clarify the "why", and data analysis to identify patterns and insights from customer feedback, support issues, and social media posts
Assess with Engagement	• How effectively has Soren gathered input from his team regarding the current state of AI adoption, innovation efforts, and process efficiency at InnovateTech? • To what extent are diverse voices and perspectives included in the assessment process to understand the challenges and opportunities related to these strategic goals?	• Critical Incident Technique (CIT) to analyze past successes and failures related to similar initiatives[2] • Max-Mix Groups to ensure that diverse perspectives are included in the assessment process
Embrace Systems Thinking	• How well does Soren's team understand the interconnectedness of AI adoption, innovation, and process revamp with other departments and functions within InnovateTech? • To what extent has Soren's team considered the potential ripple effects and unintended consequences of these strategic goals on the broader organizational ecosystem?	• Causal Loop Diagrams to visualize the interconnectedness of different factors influencing the strategic goals • Rich Picture Mapping to create a shared understanding of the system dynamics from multiple perspectives

TABLE 6.1 *(Continued)*

Examples of Questions and Tools Associated with Each Change Principle to Help Leaders Define Their Change Situation and How to Tackle It

Principles of Change	Defining the WHAT	Defining the HOW
Target Results *and* Outcomes	• To what extent are the success metrics for these strategic goals aligned with the organization's mission, vision, and values, ensuring they contribute to a larger purpose? • How clearly has Soren defined the meaningful outcomes that AI adoption, innovation, and process revamp should create for InnovateTech, beyond simply delivering on metrics?	• Key Performance Indicators (KPIs) and Target Dates to identify explicitly what will be measured for each goal and establish clear timelines for outcomes • Transition Tracker Board to encourage ongoing documentation and recognition of tangible behavioral and mindset shifts
Sustain What Works	• What mechanisms are in place to continuously monitor and evaluate the progress and impact of AI adoption, innovation, and process revamp initiatives at InnovateTech? • How will Soren ensure that lessons learned from these initiatives are captured, shared, and used to inform future strategic planning efforts?	• Team Reflexivity to collectively reflect on processes and adapt working methods • Appreciative Inquiry to focus on existing strengths and positive aspects related to the strategic goals

answers lining up, or are they all over the place? Is there a team consensus around the assumptions underlying these responses? Some of these assumptions, which could have a major impact on the team's success, are included in Table 6.2.

This tells Soren just how united the team is on the bigger picture and whether everyone genuinely understands—and stands behind—the same vision for change. Second, alignment around the "*how*": which tools are people naturally gravitating toward as they think about tackling or responding to the change in strategy? Are there certain tools the team believes will really help clarify or test their assumptions? This helps Soren understand whether the team believes that they have the right tools and resources to confidently navigate and implement the new strategy.

TABLE 6.2

Examples of Assumptions in the Workshop

Categories	Assumptions
AI Adoption	• The current technology infrastructure can support seamless integration of AI solutions. • AI adoption will lead to measurable productivity improvements within the first quarter.
Growth and Innovation	• Sufficient market demand exists for new products or innovative services that the team is planning to launch. • Existing employees will generate high-impact innovative ideas with minimal outside consulting or additional budget.
Revamp of Processes for Efficiency	• Current bottlenecks in processes are due primarily to outdated technologies rather than people or culture. • Updated processes will not have unintended negative impacts on customer experience or compliance.

When there's strong alignment on the "*what*" and the "*how*," it indicates a well-developed principle; it's like a green light to start moving forward decisively. Otherwise, it's probably best to hit pause, gather more information, and work on building that principle up before charging ahead. To understand why alignment is such a critical step, consider the following analogy. Imagine each team member as an individual grid, with the two axes representing the "*what*" and the "*how*." Stack these grids on top of one another, and you've got your team. If everyone is pointing in different directions, or even slightly misaligned, the openings in the grids don't line up. You can try and shine light through, but it gets blocked, leaving the team in the dark. As soon as you start orienting the grids along a common direction, however, those openings begin to line up, and boom! Light comes pouring right through, bringing clarity and illuminating the path ahead, as illustrated in Figure 6.1.

That's the magic of alignment: when everyone's perspectives are structured and oriented to let understanding and insights shine through for the whole team. Just remember, you can't have alignment without structure in the first place—otherwise, there's nothing to line up!

You can infuse fun and energy into this team exercise by incorporating a few engaging strategies while also tapping into AI tools to streamline and enrich the process.

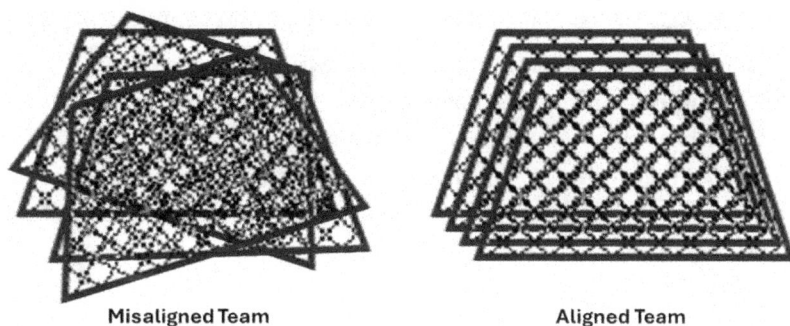

Misaligned Team   Aligned Team

FIGURE 6.1
Illustration of team alignment.

Gamification and Interactivity

Making the workshop fun and engaging doesn't just lift the energy in the room; it also gets everyone actively involved, turning participation into a team sport instead of just another checkbox.

- **Team challenges**. Transform the assessment into a virtual escape room, where teams must solve a series of puzzles or complete tasks related to the assessment topics to "unlock" the next stage until they "escape" by finishing all stages. This format encourages teamwork, quick thinking, and engagement while making the assessment process both fun and memorable.
- **Interactive polls**. Take advantage of virtual collaboration platforms to hold live polls during sessions. Real-time responses and instant visual feedback can energize the conversation, showcasing the team's diverse viewpoints and levels of agreement in a fun, interactive format.

Collaborative AI Tools

These smart assistants can supercharge brainstorming sessions, lift the blind-folds to reveal new perspectives, and help teams explore different scenarios, sparking fresh conversations and making it easier for everyone to jump in with new ideas.

- **AI-powered brainstorming**. Use AI to generate ideas, prompts, and thought-provoking questions or scenarios that spark deeper discussions.

This approach enables team members to build and expand on one another's suggestions, promoting creativity and innovation.

- **Playing out different scenarios with AI**. Set up scenario-generating activities where AI simulates different stakeholders' reactions. This allows the team to consider various perspectives and engage in problem-solving with a bit of theatrical flair, keeping the exercise lively and thought-provoking.

6.3.2 Provide Clarity through Analysis

After 45 minutes of lively discussion within the workshop, Soren can sense that the team is finally aligned. It's as if they're all ready to flip the switch and let the insights flood in. Don't be fooled, though: alignment isn't the same as agreement; it just means everyone is viewing the situation through the same lens and under the same light, even if they each have their own judgment and opinions about it. Now comes the important part: capturing what's surfaced in the discussion and pulling it all together into a clear, collective picture of where the team stands. Soren wants a method to not only analyze and synthesize their collective thinking but also make it easy for everyone to visualize and interpret the results at a glance.

Enter the Stacey Matrix.[3] This is a nifty conceptual framework by Ralph Stacey that helps leaders and managers navigate the complexities of organizational change and decision-making. Stacey introduced his matrix as a way to help organizations navigate uncertainty, change, and conflict. It categorizes situations on the basis of two axes: the level of certainty—how clearly cause and effect are understood—and the degree of agreement—how much stakeholders align on both the problem and potential solutions. The matrix divides scenarios into four quadrants: Clear (**High Certainty, High Agreement**), Complicated (**Low Certainty, High Agreement**), Complex (**Low Certainty, Low Agreement**), and Chaotic (**High Certainty, Low Agreement**), as shown in Figure 6.2. Each quadrant suggests a different approach to management and problem-solving, guiding leaders on how to adapt their tactics effectively.

Second Phase of Two-Hour Workshop

Using a whiteboard or digital collaboration tool, Soren draws the Stacey Matrix as shown in Figure 6.2. To make the exercise a bit less abstract, he further defines its axes as Agreement about the "what" (i.e., what specifically

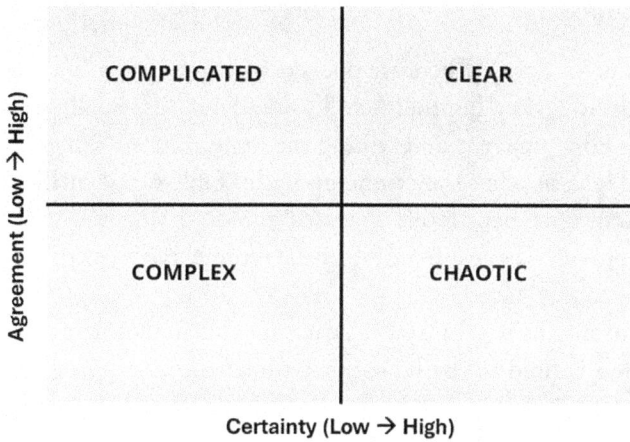

The Stacey Matrix diagram shows a four-quadrant matrix. The vertical axis is labeled "Agreement (Low → High)" and the horizontal axis is labeled "Certainty (Low → High)". The four quadrants are: COMPLICATED (top left), CLEAR (top right), COMPLEX (bottom left), and CHAOTIC (bottom right).

FIGURE 6.2
The Stacey Matrix and its four quadrants.

are we asked to deliver) and Certainty about the "how" (i.e., what specific tools are at our disposal to tackle this challenge and how effective they would be), which they discussed and defined during the first phase of the workshop. He invites the team to weigh in on each change principle, sparking an open conversation about where they stand on agreement and certainty. He asks the group questions like, "Do we agree on our understanding of the new strategy?" and "How confident are we in our ability to drive the new strategy forward with the tools at our disposal?"—all grounded in their earlier discussions. As the team works together to position each principle on the matrix, patterns start to emerge. Some principles are clear-cut: the team feels good about the strategy's goals and sees them as aligned with the organization's bigger mission. They're on board with the tools, too—at least when it comes to maintaining clarity over time. That means Soren has the green light for framing the case for change. But not everything is so straightforward. The team is more divided when it comes to questions like, "Are we really ready for such a major shift?" and "Who's going to drive the change—or push back on it?" There's also skepticism about whether the tools are truly objective or just ticking a box; after all, people might nod along even if they're not completely convinced, just to appear supportive. This hands-on approach not only helps Soren and the team pinpoint the nature of each principle—it also builds understanding and buy-in, since everyone has a hand (quite literally!) in shaping how they'll tackle the new strategy.

Analysis Reporting

The takeaway for Soren? There are pockets where the team can jump straight from analysis to action, but there's still work to do—especially when it comes to assessing how prepared and willing the organization really is for change. Let's take a look at what they came up with: Table 6.3 identifies the team's certainty and agreement levels captured earlier during the workshop, and Figure 6.3 provides a corresponding visual representation of the change principles in the Stacey Matrix.

Isn't it amazing how a little bit of structure and analysis can bring so much clarity? Soren is fired up by how quickly his team is progressing. With the

TABLE 6.3

Example of Team Assessment of Each Change Principle within the Four Quadrants of the Certainty and Agreement Matrix

Principles of Change	Certainty About the "HOW"	Agreement About the "WHAT"
Frame the Evidence for Change	High	High
Assess with Engagement	Low	Neutral
Embrace Systems Thinking	High	Low
Target Results *and* Outcomes	Neutral	High
Sustain What Works	Neutral	Low

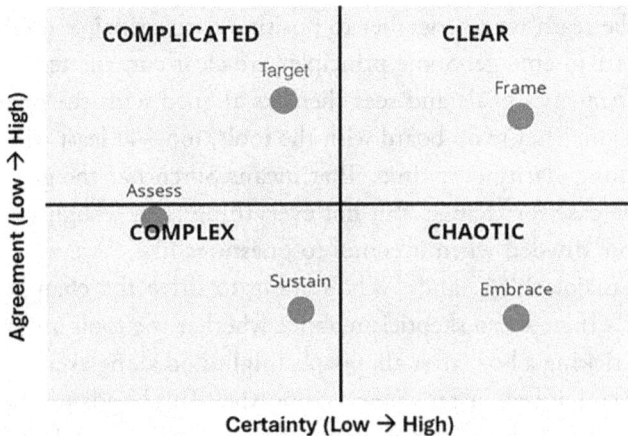

FIGURE 6.3

Visual representation of team assessment using the Stacey Matrix.

Stacey Matrix filled out, they have a clear understanding of the nature of each change principle and a solid grasp of the current landscape. The big question now is: where do they focus their energy first? They are about to define the answer to that question as they kick off the third and last phase of the workshop.

6.3.3 Drive Action through Prioritization

While every principle matters, Soren senses that there are some quick wins ripe for immediate action, while other areas will call for a slower, more deliberate approach and careful planning before jumping in. He's on the hunt for a framework that will help them cut through the noise, nail down their top priorities, and lay the foundation for a concrete, actionable plan.

Luckily for Soren, the Stacey matrix shares similarities with other complexity-based models like the Cynefin Framework.[4,5] This handy decision-making guide helps leaders analyze the complexity of the situation they're dealing with and, more importantly, decide how to respond based on that complexity. It's all about making sense of messy, fast-moving environments so you can steer clear of the common trap: throwing simple solutions at complicated problems. By understanding the context first, leaders can avoid wasted time and resources and make smarter, more effective decisions.

Third Phase of the Two-Hour Workshop

For Soren and his team, Cynefin is the perfect companion piece to their Stacey Matrix exercise, helping them zero in on what to tackle next and the best way to go about it. Since this framework is unfamiliar to many— including Soren's team—we'll begin with a brief review of how to apply the Cynefin Framework for effective prioritization:

1. **Clear Quadrant (High Certainty, High Agreement)**:
   - **Action**. Follow best practices and standard operating procedures. No need to reinvent the wheel here; the relationship between cause and effect is evident.
   - **Prioritization**. Tackle these items first to achieve quick, reliable wins. These tasks can typically be delegated, ensuring efficient execution without overthinking or delay.

2. **Complicated Quadrant (Low Certainty, High Agreement):**
   - **Action**. Engage experts or specialists and conduct a thorough analysis. While solutions exist, they require in-depth knowledge and expertise to assess.
   - **Prioritization**. Focus on research, expert consultation, and diagnostic activities. Wait for expert recommendations to make informed decisions and identify appropriate solutions.
3. **Complex Quadrant (Low Certainty, Low Agreement):**
   - **Action**. Encourage pilot projects, safe-to-fail experiments, and collaborative exploration. Solutions are not immediately apparent and will surface through iterative approaches.
   - **Prioritization**. Support actions that foster collective sense-making and adaptive learning, keeping adaptability at the forefront. Be patient; let the process drive you.
4. **Chaotic Quadrant (High Certainty, Low Agreement):**
   - **Action**. Stabilize the situation with immediate, decisive action. Focus on actions that establish order and agreement quickly, such as implementing strong leadership and clear communication.
   - **Prioritization**. Act quickly, make rapid decisions, and prioritize stabilization over analysis. Once grounded, transition into the Complex or Complicated quadrant for further analysis.

By combining the Stacey Matrix just completed in Figure 6.3 with the Cynefin Framework, Soren and his team can now create a more targeted plan and set priorities more strategically across the five change principles.

Introducing Prioritization Scores

As a group, they review the principles and discuss a method to assign them priority scores, taking into account the certainty and agreement levels from the Stacey Matrix as well as the sense of urgency highlighted by the Cynefin Framework. They agree that principles falling within the clear and chaotic domains—where certainty is high—should be given the highest priority, as they require immediate attention and response. Meanwhile, principles situated in the complicated and complex domains should receive lower priority since these areas need additional time and resources for analysis and experimentation, including input from subject-matter experts. The team comes up with the following scoring table in Table 6.4.

TABLE 6.4

Example of Prioritization Weights across the Four
Quadrants of the Certainty and Agreement Matrix

Assessment Results	Priority Score
If Certainty is Low	+ 0
If Certainty is Neutral	+ 0.75
If Certainty is High	+ 1.25
If Agreement is Low	+ 0
If Agreement is Neutral	+ 0.5
If Agreement is High	+ 0.75
Total Score	0 to 2

Seems complicated? Think of it like a recipe. The team starts with all the necessary ingredients, but creating the final dish is about finding the right balance of flavors—just like adjusting spices and seasonings. The exact measurements aren't as crucial as achieving the right blend for your personal taste. Similarly, Soren and his team focus on the relative importance of each principle rather than the specific scores themselves. What truly matters is that this step allows them to tailor the framework to their unique situation, including time, budget, and other resource constraints, and prioritize actions accordingly. To help you develop your own scoring table, Gilles used AI to identify five key factors that can impact prioritization:

- **Timeline and Urgency**
  - **Tight deadlines**. Issues needing immediate attention—such as crises—should be prioritized in the *Chaotic* or *Clear* domains, where fast stabilization or execution is critical.
  - **Flexible timeline.** For projects with more lenient deadlines, the *Complex* or *Complicated* domains may be prioritized, allowing room for experimentation or thorough expert analysis.
- **Organization Size**
  - **Large organizations**. With more layers and stakeholders, decision-making can be slower, increasing the need for consensus and raising the priority of issues in the *Clear* and *Complicated* quadrants.
  - **Small organizations**. Greater agility often makes it easier to address *Complex* or *Chaotic* situations, as quick action and experimentation are less burdensome.

- **Organizational Culture**
  - **Risk-tolerant cultures.** Organizations that encourage innovation and learning from mistakes may prioritize *Complex* actions, such as pilot programs and experimentation.
  - **Stability-oriented cultures.** Environments that value predictability and standard procedures are more likely to focus on *Clear* or *Complicated* actions, emphasizing expert solutions and best practices.
  - **Communication style.** Open and collaborative cultures are often more adept at identifying disagreement, which is key for properly addressing *Complex* or *Chaotic* scenarios.
- **Resource Availability**
  - **Abundant resources.** Enable more investments in experimentation, in-depth analysis, or consulting with experts, supporting *Complex* and *Complicated* actions.
  - **Limited resources.** Drive focus on quick wins in the *Clear* domain or urgent stabilization in the *Chaotic* domain, with less room for error or extensive analysis.
- **Nature of the Change**
  - **Technical change.** Typically falls within the *Clear* or *Complicated* domains, where established solutions or expert input can address the issue.
  - **Adaptive or work culture change.** Often involves deeper shifts in values, beliefs, or behaviors, and usually fits the *Complex* or *Chaotic* domains—requiring experimentation, sense-making, and adaptive approaches.

Soren can now compute a priority score for each change principle as shown in Table 6.5.

TABLE 6.5

Priority Scores of the Five Change Principles

Principle	Frame the Evidence for Change	Assess with Engagement	Embrace Systems Thinking	Target Results *and* Outcomes	Sustain What Works
Priority Score	2.0	0.5	1.25	1.5	0.75

The results couldn't be clearer: three change principles emerge as the team's highest priority items. They are:

1. Frame the Evidence for Change
2. Target Results *and* Outcomes
3. Embrace Systems Thinking

Et voilà! By applying the right tools at the right time, pinpointing the highest priority change principle for your team has never been easier! Truly a game changer for any leader facing complex change challenges. By zeroing in on the principle that requires immediate focus, Soren can concentrate his team's energy and resources where they will have the greatest impact, avoiding the pitfalls of trying to tackle everything at once. This clarity allows him to outline specific, targeted actions that address the core issues, ensuring that the strategy is not only robust but also easy to implement. Moreover, a plan anchored in a clearly prioritized principle is inherently more defendable. Soren can confidently articulate the rationale behind his choices, drawing on aligned stakeholder insights and data-driven analysis to back up his approach. Through this participatory process, he not only secures buy-in from the team and leadership but also ensures smoother execution, as everyone understands the "why" and "how" behind the plan, ultimately steering the organization toward successful outcomes with precision and purpose.

Regular Review and Update Cycle

What if you're not starting from square one like Soren and have already made progress on your change journey? No worries—you can still use this framework by revisiting the five change principles with an eye toward the future. Ask yourself: is there still uncertainty around each principle? Does the team agree on whether further action is needed? In fact, it is good practice to regularly review and update your assessment and scores as new challenges emerge, resources evolve, and your environment shifts.

6.3.4 Bring It All Together

With ten minutes left in the workshop, Soren and his team are now ready to draft an action plan, pulling together the tools they have identified and the recommendations from the Cynefin framework. Too little time? Not at all!

With AI, it can literally write itself! Soren compiles his team's data and analysis from the workshop into a document, attaches it to his favorite AI tool, and uses the following prompt that Gilles generated to conclude the process:

> *Role: Act as a change consultant and expert in organizations. Context: Our team has completed a self-assessment and identified three change principles as our top priorities using the Stacey Matrix and Cynefin framework: 1- Frame the Evidence for Change (Clear quadrant), 2- Target Results and Outcomes (Complicated quadrant), 3- Embrace Systems Thinking (Chaotic quadrant). The assessment results, along with a list of recommended tools for each principle, are described in the attached document. Question: Using the provided context, generate an action plan that describes how the team should proceed with respect to these three change principles by combining what you know about the Cynefin framework with the list of tools provided. Envision what a successful implementation could look like for the team.*

Next, let's examine the action plan that AI crafted for the team.

The Action Plan

1. **First Priority: Frame the Evidence for Change**
   Before anyone can rally behind a strategy, they need to understand—and believe in—the "why." Here, the team is united behind the new direction and confident in their ability to articulate the rationale for it. That confidence is Soren's launchpad for action. Here are the suggested next steps:
   - **Clarify boundaries**. Use Vroom-Yetton-Jago to define what is "in scope" for each goal (AI adoption, innovation, process revamp). Communicate any "off-limits" or non-negotiable areas at the outset.
   - **Build the case**. Run AI-powered thematic analyses on internal data (surveys, support tickets, exit interviews) and external data (market trends, benchmarks) to articulate the "why" with data-driven clarity.
   - **Synthesize and summarize**. Create a concise "evidence wall" or dashboard that allows team members to see the case for change at a glance.
   - **Communicate consistently**. Share the evidence and rationale widely; ensure that every team member can articulate why the strategy matters.

2. Second Priority: Target Results and Outcomes

With the team on board, attention shifts to defining success. Here, the path is less obvious because, while everyone agrees that it is critically important, opinions diverge widely about how and when to measure and report progress. The team will need to consult experts, use robust analysis, and iterate as they learn:

- **Define Success Metrics**. Engage stakeholders and subject-matter experts to set meaningful KPIs and clear targets for each initiative (not just adoption counts, but, e.g., "% of work automated by AI," "number of new products launched," and "cycle time reduction").
- **Diagnostic Deep-Dive**. Conduct root-cause analyses for barriers to results; use tools like cause-and-effect diagrams or expert workshops.
- **Set Milestones**. Create phased targets (immediate, intermediate, and long-term outcomes) aligned with strategic objectives.
- **Monitor and Adapt**. Use the Transition Tracker Board to visually track adoption, success stories, and "small wins." Feed learning back into the plan.
- **Communicate Progress**. Routinely report outcomes to all stakeholders; adjust tactics based on data, not assumptions.

3. Third Priority: Embrace Systems Thinking

Complex change rarely unfolds in a straight line; it can be rather chaotic, with small actions producing surprising, outsized ripple effects across the organization. The team learned about interdependency-mapping tools during the workshop but they disagree about where to apply them and what to look for. It's essential to act fast and build a shared understanding to drive the team from chaos toward order. Here is how:

- **Identify issues and interdependencies**. Establish a temporary "systems response task force" to quickly map emergent issues and surface interdependencies (e.g., how does AI adoption ripple through operations, Information Technology, and human resources?).
- **Take decisive action to tackle the main "pain points"**. Identify key "pain points" or bottlenecks causing chaos (misalignment, conflicting processes, communication breakdowns) and implement "stop-the-bleed" actions (temporary process freezes, priority resets, or communication blitzes) to try and stabilize the situation.
- **Map the system**. Use Causal Loop Diagrams and Rich Picture Mapping in cross-functional workshops to make hidden connections and feedback loops visible.

- **Iterate with experiments**. Launch a few rapid, safe-to-fail pilot projects (e.g., test a new workflow in a single department and observe ripple effects).
- **Sense and respond**. Set up real-time feedback channels (Slack, stand-ups, retrospectives) to monitor signals, adapt, and capture learning on the fly.

What Success Looks Like

As a result of executing the proposed action plan, the team can aim to achieve the following outcomes:

- **Everyone knows the "why," "what," and "where the boundaries are."** There is no confusion about the imperatives or areas out of scope. Communication is crisp, consistent, and evidence-based.
- **Results and outcomes are clearly defined, measured, and communicated**. Barriers to outcomes are surfaced and addressed quickly. Progress is visible, recognized, and celebrated.
- **Initial chaos is tamed: Urgent issues are stabilized, and teams are no longer overwhelmed**. Teams have system-wide visibility and quickly adapt to new information. The organization transitions from reactive firefighting toward proactive, system-aware learning and adaptation.

What's Next?

By leveraging AI, Soren turned theoretical frameworks into practical, actionable steps for his organization in no time. "The best strategies are lived, not laminated," Soren reminds his team as they leave the situation room. The tools are set; the priorities are clear. Now, they are ready to write InnovateTech's next chapter—one deliberate action at a time. *What about the other principles?* one team member asks. Prioritization isn't about neglecting what's not immediately at the top of the list; it's about thoughtfully staggering actions to maximize impact given finite resources. For Soren's team, this means they can get started on executing high-priority tasks from day one, focusing their energy where it matters most, such as the change principles of highest need. Meanwhile, Soren can begin strategizing on how to address the lower-priority principles, ensuring that no aspect is left behind. Gilles has found that this approach allows teams to build momentum and achieve quick wins, setting a strong foundation for tackling subsequent challenges. It's a strategic balance, ensuring that every part of the plan receives attention at the right time, ultimately driving holistic and phased progress for the organization.

6.4 NOW IT'S YOUR TURN!

Looking back on how far the team has come in just two hours, Soren can't help but appreciate how the three-step approach to action planning we just covered helped streamline what could easily have turned into an overwhelming and crippling task. Instead of getting bogged down in uncertainty and complexity, the team followed a clear, structured approach that simplified every step and brought everyone onto the same page. With visual aids, interactive tools, and open communication, Soren created an environment where every team member felt heard, valued, and empowered to contribute. This collaborative spirit was the secret sauce, enabling Soren to steer his team through the twists and turns of real organizational change with confidence. By weaving together big-picture principles and practical action steps, the team moved from scattered ideas to united execution. Now, with a shared sense of purpose and clear priorities, Soren and his crew aren't just coping with change—they're running with it, ready to make a lasting impact across the organization. Like Soren, you may be a leader embarking on strategic change. Remember, no change is perfect right out of the gate. It's about learning, adapting, and keeping that forward momentum. And with the right tools, you can feel confident that you can tackle any obstacle along your journey. So, how will *you* take the first step?

6.5 KEY TAKEAWAYS

6.5.1 The Three Instruments for Change

This chapter provides a practical three-step approach to action planning by integrating individual contributions, team dynamics, and organizational frameworks:

1. **Self as the Instrument for Change**:
   - **Build Personal Understanding.** Use questions structured around the five change principles to clarify what the new strategy means for each person.

- **Leverage AI for Analysis.** Apply AI-powered analysis to illuminate hidden concerns or confusion. These data help tailor communication and support for every member of the team.

2. **Team as the Instrument for Change**:
   - **Map Alignment.** Map the team's certainty and agreement on each principle with the Stacey Matrix to spotlight strengths and gaps.
   - **Foster Interactive Engagement**: Boost engagement with interactive activities such as polls, challenges, and AI-driven scenarios during team sessions.

3. **Organization as the Instrument for Change**:
   - **Prioritize with Cynefin.** Use the Cynefin Framework to prioritize which actions need quick execution and which require deeper analysis or experimentation.
   - **Assign Weighted Priorities.** Assign priority scores to each change principle most relevant to your organization, allowing resources to flow where they can have the highest impact.

By harnessing individual understanding, collaborative team dynamics, and targeted organizational frameworks, this integrated approach enables leaders to translate strategic insights into actionable outcomes and build a cohesive, engaged workforce committed to tackling challenges head-on.

6.5.2 The Five Change Principles

To help you reflect on this chapter, we've compiled a list of self-assessment questions and tools mentioned in this chapter for the five change principles in Table 6.6.

TABLE 6.6

Self-Assessment Questions and a Highlight of Just a Few of the Many Tools for Action Planning

Principles of Change	Self-Assessment Questions	A Highlight of Tools Introduced in This Book to Address These Self-Assessment Questions
Frame the Evidence for Change	What assumptions shape our case for change? Are there data gaps undermining the "why"? Are our decision boundaries and non-negotiables clear?	• **AI-Assisted Brainstorming.** Generates clarifying questions and prompts to deepen team discussion and surface assumptions. • **Vroom-Yetton-Jago Decision-Making Model.** Clarifies who decides and how, establishing leadership boundaries.

TABLE 6.6 *(Continued)*

Self-Assessment Questions and a Highlight of Just a Few of the Many Tools for Action Planning

Principles of Change	Self-Assessment Questions	A Highlight of Tools Introduced in This Book to Address These Self-Assessment Questions
Assess with Engagement	Where do we align or diverge on the "what" and the "how"? Whose voices are missing from our assessment?	• **Stacey Matrix.** Maps each principle for readiness and maturity. • **Gamification/Team Challenges.** Engages the team in collaborative problem-solving and adaptive learning.
Embrace Systems Thinking	What interdependencies and ripple effects could help or hurt us? What bottlenecks or feedback loops are driving issues? What small, fast moves could stabilize chaos?	• **Causal Loop Diagrams and Rich Picture Mapping.** Visualize feedback loops and interdependencies to uncover drivers, leverage points, and unintended consequences. • **Cynefin Framework.** Translates assessment into actionable priorities based on context and available resources across the organization.
Target Results *and* Outcomes	How do we prioritize our actions and sequence our plan for maximum impact? How will we measure and track progress toward desired outcomes or the need to pivot?	• **AI-Assisted Action Plan Drafting.** Synthesizes input into a phased plan. • **Cynefin-Guided Prioritization with Priority Scores.** Quantifies urgency and importance for sequencing actions.
Sustain What Works	What mechanisms will we use to reinforce and sustain successful change over time? How do we ensure ongoing communication and adaptability as we implement change?	• **Regular Review and Update Cycle.** Encourages teams to revisit, reassess, and update scores and actions in response to new challenges and resources. • **Team Reflexivity.** Promotes continual group reflection and adaptive action.

Now that you have reviewed the Three Instruments for Change and the Five Core Change Principles, it's time to focus on your key areas for action. Consider one of Mitch's most powerful reminders: *To be a leader is to teach. If you're not teaching, you're not leading.* After you have selected one action that matters to you, teach it to someone else. Explain why it's important and how it could help them lead change. Then, have a follow-up conversation with them regarding any opportunities they may envision to lead change in new, creative, and successful ways. With this simple strategy, you're not just teaching—you're leading change!

NOTES

1 Vignesh, M. (2020). Decision making using Vroom-Yetton-Jago model with a practical application. *International Journal for Research in Applied Science and Engineering Technology, 8*(10), 330–337.
2 Davis, P. J. (2006). Critical incident technique: A learning intervention for organizational problem solving. *Development and Learning in Organizations: An International Journal, 20*(2), 13–16.
3 Stacey, R. D. (2011). *Strategic management and organizational dynamics: The challenge of complexity to ways of thinking about organizations* (6th ed.). Pearson.
4 Snowden, D. (2007). *Cynefin Framework.*
5 Nachbagauer, A. (2021). Managing complexity in projects: Extending the Cynefin framework. *Project Leadership and Society, 2,* 100017.

References

Aithal, P. S., Kumar, P. M., & Shailashree, V. (2016). Factors & elemental analysis of six thinking hats technique using ABCD framework. *International Journal of Advanced Trends in Engineering and Technology (IJATET)*, *1*(1), 85–95.

Ajzen, I. (2020). The theory of planned behavior: Frequently asked questions. *Human Behavior and Emerging Technologies*, *2*(4), 314–324.

Amabile, T., & Kramer, S. (2011). *The progress principle: Using small wins to ignite joy, engagement, and creativity at work*. Harvard Business Review Press.

American Psychological Association. (2023). *APA dictionary of psychology*. https://dictionary.apa.org/

Badzik, V. (2021). Why strategic initiatives fail—Lessons from a practitioner. In *The public productivity and performance handbook* (pp. 106–115). Routledge.

Bambi, S., Foà, C., De Felippis, C., Lucchini, A., Guazzini, A., & Rasero, L. (2018). Workplace incivility, lateral violence and bullying among nurses: A review about their prevalence and related factors. *Acta Medica*, *89*(Supplement 6), 51–79. https://doi.org/10.23750/abm.v89i6-S.7461

Barnett, M. (2024, July 11). Failure to launch: Why 60%-90% of business strategies fail before they start. *Forbes*.

Beckhard, R. (1989). *Organizational transitions: Managing complex change*. Addison-Wesley.

Bento, F., Tagliabue, M., & Lorenzo, F. (2020, July 24). Organizational siloes: A scoping review informed by a behavioral perspective on systems and networks. *Societies*, *10*(56). https://doi.org/10.3390/soc10030056

Bolman, L. G., & Deal, T. E. (1999, January 1). Four steps to keeping change efforts heading in the right direction. *Journal for Quality and Participation*, 6–11.

Bott, G., & Tourish, D. (2016). The critical incident technique reappraised: Using critical incidents to illuminate organizational practices and build theory. *Qualitative Research in Organizations and Management: An International Journal*, *11*(4), 276–300.

Brassey, J., Herbig, B., Jeffery, B., & Ungerman, D. (2023). *Reframing employee health: Moving beyond burnout to holistic health*. McKinsey Health Institute.

Bridges, W. (2009). *Managing transitions: Making the most of change*. Da Capo Press.

Bridges, W., & Bridges, S. (2019). *Transitions: Making sense of life's changes*. Balance.

Cavanaugh, K. J., Logan, J. M., Zajac, S. A., & Holladay, C. L. (2021). Core conditions of team effectiveness: Development of a survey measuring Hackman's framework. *Journal of Interprofessional Care*, *35*(6), 914–919.

Cooper, W. O., Spain, D. A., Guillamondegui, O., Kelz, R. R., Domenico, H. J., Hopkins, J., Sullivan, P., Moore, I. N., Pichert, J. W., Catron, T. F., Webb, L. E., Dmochowski, R. R., & Hickson, G. B. (2019, June). Association of coworker reports about unprofessional behavior by surgeons with surgical complications in their patients. *JAMA Surgery*, *154*(9), 828–834.

Davis, A. P., Dent, E. B., & Wharff, D. M. (2015). A conceptual model of systems thinking leadership in community colleges. *Systemic Practice and Action Research*, *28*, 333–353.

Davis, P. J. (2006). Critical incident technique: A learning intervention for organizational problem solving. *Development and Learning in Organizations: An International Journal, 20*(2), 13–16.

Drexler, A. B., Sibbet, D., & Forrester, R. H. (1988). The team performance model. In R. W. Brendan & K. Jamison (Eds.), *Team building: Blueprints for productivity and satisfaction* (pp. 45–61). NTL Institute for Applied Behavioral Science.

Errida, A., & Lotfi, B. (2021). The determinants of organizational change management success: Literature review and case study. *International Journal of Engineering Business Management, 13*(21). https://doi.org/10.1177/18479790211016273

Faraj, S., & Yan, A. (2009). Boundary work in knowledge teams. *Journal of Applied Psychology, 94*(3), 604–617.

Feitosa, J., Grossman, R., Kramer, W. S., & Salas, E. (2020). Measuring team trust: A critical and meta-analytical review. *Journal of Organizational Behavior, 41*(4), 325–348. https://doi.org/10.1002/job.2436

Finkelstein, S., & Mooney, A. (2003). Not the usual suspects: How to use board process to make boards better. *Academy of Management Executive, 17*(2), 101–113.

Flanagan, J. C. (1954). The critical incident technique. *Psychological Bulletin, 51*(4), 327.

Frei, F., & Morriss, A. (2000, May–June). Begin with trust. *Harvard Business Review,* 112–121.

Gabelica, C., Van Den Bossche, P., De Maeyer, S., Segers, M., & Gijselaers, W. (2014). The effect of team feedback and guided reflexivity on team performance change. *Learning and Instruction, 34*, 86–96.

Gallo, A. (2025, Summer). How to navigate conflict with a coworker. *HBR Special Issue,* 10–15.

Garcia, J. (2022, March 29). *Common pitfalls in transformations: A conversation with Jon Garcia.* McKinsey & Company. https://www.mckinsey.com/capabilities/transformation/our-insights/common-pitfalls-in-transformations-a-conversation-with-jon-garcia

Goodman, E., & Loh, L. (2011). Organizational change: A critical challenge for team effectiveness. *Business Information Review, 28*(4), 242–250.

Grosser, T., Kidwell, V., & Labianca, G. J. (2012). Hearing it through the grapevine: Positive and negative workplace gossip. *Organizational Dynamics, 41*, 52–61.

Hackman, J. R. (1998). Why teams don't work. In *Theory and research on small groups* (pp. 245–267). Springer US.

Hackman, J. R. (2002). *Leading teams: Setting the stage for great performances.* Harvard Business School Publishing Corporation.

Hart, J. (2016). The science of well-being reveals health benefits: Greater Good Science Center, University of California, Berkeley. *Alternative and Complementary Therapies, 22*(6), 266–268.

Higgins, M. C., Weiner, J., & Young, L. (2012). Implementation teams: A new lever for organizational change. *Journal of Organizational Behavior, 33*(3), 366–388.

Howard, C., Logue, K., Quimby, M., & Schoeneberg, J. (2009). Framing change. *OD Practitioner, 41*(1).

Jacobs, R. (1997). *Real time strategic change: How to involve an entire organization in fast and far-reaching change.* Berrett-Koehler Publishers.

Jen Su, A. (2025, Summer). Get over your fear of conflict. *Harvard Business Review Special Issue, 28*–29.

Jones, J., Firth, J., Hannibal, C., & Ogunseyin, M. (2018). Factors contributing to organizational change success or failure: A qualitative meta-analysis of 200 reflective case studies. In R. Hamlin, A. Ellinger, & J. Jones (Eds.), *Evidence-based initiatives for organizational change and development* (pp. 155–178). IGI Global.

Kegan, R., & Lahey, L. L. (2001). *The real reason people won't change* (p. 75). Harvard Business Review.

Keller, S., & Meaney, M. (2003). *Tapping the power of hidden influencers.* McKinsey Quarterly. https://www.mckinsey.com/featured-insights/leadership/tapping-the-power-of-hidden-influencers

Keller, S., & Meaney, M. (2017). *Leading organizations: Ten timeless truths.* Bloomsbury Publishing.

Kivunja, C. (2015). Using De Bono's six thinking hats model to teach critical thinking and problem-solving skills essential for success in the 21st century economy. *Creative Education, 6*(3), 380–391.

Kneisel, E. (2020). Team reflections, team mental models and team performance over time. *Team Performance Management: An International Journal, 26*(1/2), 143–168.

Kouzes, J. M., & Posner, B. Z. (2023). *The leadership challenge* (7th ed.). Jossey-Bass.

Kusy, M. (2017). *Why I don't work here anymore: A leader's guide to offset the financial and emotional costs of toxic employees.* Routledge/CRC Press.

Kusy, M., & Essex, L. (2005). *Breaking the code of silence: Prominent leaders reveal how they rebounded from seven critical mistakes.* Lanham, MD: Taylor Trade Publishing/Rowman & Littlefield Publishing Group.

Kusy, M., & Holloway, E. (2009). *Toxic workplace! Managing toxic personalities and their systems of power.* Jossey-Bass.

Kusy, M., & Holloway, E. (2010). Detox your workplace: A culture of respect can add to our company's bottom line. *Marketing Health Services, 30*(3). https://aura.antioch.edu/facarticles/54

Kusy, M., & Holloway, M. (2014, March–April). A field guide to real-time culture change: Just "rolling out" a training program won't cut it. *Medical Practice Management,* 294–303.

Lencioni, P. M. (2010). *The five dysfunctions of a team: A leadership fable.* John Wiley & Sons.

Lipmanowicz, H., Singhal, A., McCandless, K., & Wang, H. (2015). Liberating structures: Engaging everyone to build a good life together. In *Communication and "the good life"* (pp. 233–246). Seattle, WA: Liberating Structures Press.

Littlefield, C. (2022, October 25). A better way to recognize your employees. *Harvard Business Review.* Harvard Business School Publishing. https://hbr.org/2022/10/a-better-way-to-recognize-your-employees

MacLellan, L. (2018, November 27). The surprising fragility of a powerful perk: Company culture. *Quartz at Work.*

Mauer, C. (2024, August 8). *Incivility's cost to employers: $2 billion per day.* www.shrm.org.

McVanel, S., & Zalter-Minden, B. (2015). *Forever recognize others' greatness: Solution-focused strategies for satisfied staff, high-performing teams, and healthy bottom lines.* BPS Books.

Mostashari, F., & Moore, G. (2025). Crossing the chasm: How to expand adoption of value-based care. *NEJM Catalyst Innovations in Care Delivery, 6*(4), CAT-24.

Nachbagauer, A. (2021). Managing complexity in projects: Extending the Cynefin framework. *Project Leadership and Society, 2,* 100017.

Pfefer, J., & Sutton, R. (2006). *Hard facts, dangerous half-truths, and total nonsense: Profiting from evidence-based management.* Harvard Business Review Press.

Porath, C., & Pearson, C. (2013). The price of incivility. *Harvard Business Review, 91*(1–2), 114–121.

Rogers, E. M., Singhal, A., & Quinlan, M. M. (2014). Diffusion of innovations. In *An integrated approach to communication theory and research* (pp. 432–448). Routledge.

Rosenstein, A. H., & O'Daniel, M. (2008). A survey of the impact of disruptive behaviors and communication defects on patient safety. *The Joint Commission Journal on Quality and Patient Safety, 34*(8), 464–471.

Schwartz, H. L., & Holloway, E. L. (2025). *Essentials of constructivist critical incident technique.* American Psychological Association.

Seppala, E., & Cameron, K. (2015). Proof that positive work cultures are more productive. *Harvard Business Review, 12*(1), 44–50.

Smith, R., King, D., Sidhu, R., & Skelsey, D. (Eds.). (2014). *The effective change manager's handbook.* Kogan Page Publishers.

Snowden, D. J., & Boone, M. E. (2007). A leader's framework for decision making. *Harvard Business Review, 85*(11), 68–76. Harvard Business School Publishing.

Spencer, J., & Watkins, M. (2019, November 26). *Why organizational change fails.* ERE Recruiting Innovation Summit.

Stacey, R. D. (2011). *Strategic management and organizational dynamics: The challenge of complexity to ways of thinking about organizations* (6th ed.). Pearson.

Sull, D., Sull, C., Cipolli, W., & Brighenti, C. (2022, March 16). Why every leader needs to worry about toxic culture. *MIT Sloan Management Review.*

Sutton, R. I. (2018). *The asshole survival guide: How to deal with people who treat you like dirt.* Harper Business.

Tannenbaum, S. I., & Cerasoli, C. P. (2013). Do team and individual debriefs enhance performance? A meta-analysis. *Human Factors, 55*(1), 231–245. https://doi.org/10.1177/0018720812448394.

Thompke, S. (2020, March–April). Building a culture of experimentation. *Harvard Business Review,* 40–48.

Thompson, R. (2025). *Enough! Eradicate Incivility & Bullying in Healthcare.*

Tollman, P., Keenan, P., Mingardon, S., Dosik, D., Rizvi, S., & Hurder, S. (2017). *Getting smart about change management.* BCG Perspectives.

Tuckman, B. W. (2001). Developmental sequence in small groups. *Group Facilitation,* (3), 66.

Vignesh, M. (2020). Decision making using Vroom-Yetton-Jago model with a practical application. *International Journal for Research in Applied Science and Engineering Technology, 8*(10), 330–337.

Vroom, V. H. (1973). A new look at managerial decision-making. *Organizational Dynamics, 1*(4), 66–80.

Vroom, V. H., & Jago, A. G. (1974). Decision making as a social process: Normative and descriptive models of leader behavior. *Decision Sciences, 5*(4).

Waschgler, K., Ruiz-Hernández, J. A., Llor-Esteban, B., & Jiménez-Barbero, J. A. (2013). Vertical and lateral workplace bullying in nursing: Development of the hospital aggressive behaviour scale. *Journal of Interpersonal Violence, 28*(12), 2389–2412.

Yang, M., Schloemer, H., Zhu, Z., Lin, Y., Chen, W., & Dong, N. (2020). Why and when team reflexivity contributes to team performance: A moderated mediation model. *Frontiers in Psychology, 10,* 3044.

Index

For Product Safety Concerns and Information please contact our EU
representative GPSR@taylorandfrancis.com
Taylor & Francis Verlag GmbH, Kaufingerstraße 24, 80331 München, Germany

9 781041 032335